POST-CHARISMATIC?

Post-charismatic?

Rob McAlpine

First published 2008
Published by David C. Cook
Kingsway Communications Ltd
26–28 Lottbridge Drove, Eastbourne BN23 6NT, UK

David C. Cook
4050 Lee Vance View, Colorado Springs, CO 80918, USA

David C. Cook Distribution Canada
55 Woodslee Avenue, Paris, Ontario, Canada N3L 3E5

David C. Cook and the graphic circle C logo
are registered trademarks of Cook Communications Ministries.

The website addresses recommended in this book are offered as
a resource to you. These websites are not intended in any way to be or imply
an endorsement on the part of the publisher.

Unless otherwise indicated, Scripture quotations are from the
Holy Bible: New International Version © 1973, 1978, 1984
by the International Bible Society.

ISBN 978 1 84291 350 5

Cover photo © Jelani Memory/iStockphoto.com
Cover design: PinnacleCreative.co.uk

Printed by Thomson Litho Ltd, East Kilbride, Scotland
1 2 3 4 5 6 7 8 9 10

Contents

Hat-tips

A project like this doesn't get written overnight, and there are a number of people who have contributed to it in many ways, both directly and indirectly. I would like to acknowledge their contributions, with a hat-tip of gratitude to:

- The many post-charismatics I know personally; they have shared their stories with me, been the impetus behind beginning a project of this length in the first place, and continue to encourage me by their ongoing pursuit of God in spite of the things they have experienced at the hands of others.
- Those whom I know only through email and blogs, who have also shared their stories with me, and encouraged me to see this project through.
- Jamie Arpin-Ricci (www.emergentvoyageurs.com), for his thoughtful editorial comments as the project neared completion.
- Brother Maynard (www.subversiveinfluence.com), for walking with me, section by section, providing timely feedback and critique along the way, and for prodding me to finish.
- My family, for putting up with the stacks of books, dozens of binders filled with printed notes, and general mayhem

that took over the living room for a whole year – in two
provinces.

- And Wendy, who not only has walked this post-charismatic
  journey with me, but has also been patient with my writing
  obsession, and provided much excellent feedback and critique as she endured many discussions on a topic that con-
  sumed so much of my thinking and time.

Prologue

'You know, we've probably lost about five hundred people in the past two years alone, from the very issues you're going to be writing on.'

I was having a late night coffee-and-nachos conversation with a pastor I'd met in Toronto a few years ago, and had begun to explain the idea behind writing a project on the growing number of post-charismatics that I knew personally, and was hearing more and more about. He listened as I explained some of the themes that were emerging as I delved into the reason why there seems to be a growing exodus of people from Pentecostal and charismatic groups, including the issues of hype, abuse of prophetic ministry, and various Latter Rain doctrines that had survived long after the Latter Rain movement was rejected as heretical (even though it had begun as a genuine revival).

As the conversation came to a close, he made the observation quoted above. I wasn't surprised to hear that people had been leaving, but even for a very large church, a five hundred person exodus in just two years is not something you can just ignore or explain away.

Another post-charismatic friend of mine, who had been in leadership for fifteen years in a large charismatic church, shared with me a story he had heard when he first became involved on the leadership team. Someone had visited their church in the 1970s and asked if they were involved in the Shepherding movement. The reply from a lay leader (at the time) was, 'Brother, we *are* the Shepherding movement!'

In the years since, as the Shepherding movement was discredited and its leadership disbanded, that particular church has buried any reference to the Shepherding movement. Certainly, by the time my friend became involved, there was no longer any mention made of the Shepherding movement; but some of the signature teachings, which laid the foundation for much of the spiritual abuse associated with the Shepherding movement, still continue today.

'Could you get me access to some of your church's teaching tapes or books?' I asked my friend. Not likely, was his response, since he'd stepped out of leadership and was no longer attending the church. 'They keep that part of their history pretty quiet, which would be fine, *if* they had also abandoned the "covering" and "being under authority" teachings of the Shepherding movement,' he said, 'but they haven't. And that's why people are leaving.'

A third conversation I found myself having during that season was with a Baptist pastor, a good friend who is trying to carefully and gracefully lead his congregation into a more charismatic practice, but, in his words, 'without the weirdness'.

'Are you planning to write on the Prosperity stuff?' was his question, as we sat in his 'office': a local Montana's Steakhouse restaurant. I replied that I would probably give it a brief mention, but that I thought there were other issues that needed more attention.

'Dude, you *have* to write about it,' he exclaimed. 'Most of the guys in my denomination think that "name it and claim it" is all there is to the charismatic movement. There are lots of conservative evangelicals who are more open to charismatic gifts these days, but if we could learn from the mistakes of the past, and maybe avoid them today. . .'

The Pentecostal, charismatic, and Third Wave movements of the past century have quickly become the fastest-growing segment of Christianity. A seminary professor once remarked to me that she felt the Pentecostal/charismatic theology of South American believers would likely become the dominant, and defining, theology of the twenty-first century, a concept that terrified her, as an ardent cessationist.

While the spread of Pentecostal and charismatic movements in other parts of the world developed separately, and at times pre-dated the North American movement, for the purposes of this writing, we will be looking primarily at the North American expressions of it. The issues of ecclesiology (which includes an understanding of what constitutes biblical leadership), the effects of postmodernism, and the sheer numbers of the emerging generations who are self-described post-charismatics are the motivating factor behind this writing, and while there may be overlap to non-North American expressions of the charismatic movement, I am writing mainly in response to the issues that I see here in the United States and Canada. To help provide a context outside of North America, Dave Roberts (former editor of the charismatic magazine *Renewal*) has contributed a UK dimension at certain points.

For those who will (rightly) view this project as primarily Western in focus, I can only say 'guilty as charged'; it is my hope that writers in other arenas of the charismatic movement worldwide will raise their voices to speak to the issues most affecting them.

Many Christians in the early twenty-first century, particularly those who consider themselves a part of the conversation surrounding the emerging/missional church, represent a quickly growing segment of Christianity that is questioning both theology and ecclesiology, and especially the latter. While the emerging generations make up the bulk of this group, to assume that it's a youthful development would be inaccurate. There are many people, of all ages, who are questioning church structure, the role of leadership, the foundations of theological thought, and many of them are also leaving established churches at an increasingly significant rate.

Within this group are many people who also refer to themselves as being 'post-charismatic'. In some ways they are very akin to those postmodern people I meet who are open to God but indifferent or hostile to church. These self-described post-charismatics are open to the working of the Holy Spirit, but due to excesses and abuses that they have seen or experienced, they are sceptical and even wary of ministries that are charismatic. Further, there are some who have come to a place where they overtly reject – or passively neglect – the more obvious supernatural workings of the Spirit.

Through my own blog (www.robbymac.org), my visits to similar sites, and ongoing interaction with many representatives of the emerging generations, it becomes clear that a significant portion of those who could be called part of the emerging/missional church were also formerly involved in churches that were Pentecostal, charismatic or Third Wave.

Emerging/missional church – this phrase does not refer to specific groups associated with the 'emerging movement', or conversation, such as www.emergentvillage.com. The phrase 'emerging/missional church', as I will use it here, is merely a form of shorthand to refer to the wide diversity of people who are reading books, surfing websites and blogs, conversing with each other, creating experimental church plants and communities, and generally exploring an expression of Christianity that is biblically orthodox, rooted in the pre-modern creeds of the early church, and yet conversant with a postmodern society. At the risk of oversimplification, being 'missional' simply means that we stop viewing ecclesiology and missiology as separate, and explore ways of being a missionary presence in our postmodern society.

Recapturing discernment

Jack Deere, a former professor at Dallas Theological Seminary, once wrote the following:

> If you were to lock a brand-new Christian in a room with a Bible and tell him to study what Scripture has to say about healing and miracles, he would never come out of the room a cessationist.[1]

I couldn't agree more.

On the other hand, I would like to suggest that this same person, after studying healing, miracles and the gifts of the Holy Spirit, would also never come out of the room expecting to drop to the floor wailing as if they were in excruciating abdominal pain whenever they heard the word 'intercession'.

The extremes of some charismatic teachings and practices are the culprit behind the choice that many people – particularly among the emerging generations – have made to adopt a much more passive (if not outright dismissive) approach to spiritual gifts, and a lowering of their expectations of how God works among his people.

Charismatic – I will be using this phrase to refer to the whole spectrum of Pentecostal, charismatic, and Third Wave (neo-Pentecostal) movements. While there are significant differences between these three waves, it would get quite tedious to have to list all three every time, so, from now on, I will use the term 'charismatic' to refer to the whole grouping, unless there is a need to differentiate.

Post-charismatic – this phrase should not be confused with being *non*-charismatic, and certainly not as being *anti*-charismatic. The process of separating what is truly of the Holy Spirit and what is needless – and often harmful – baggage is the whole idea behind developing a post-charismatic understanding of how a supernatural God works supernaturally amongst and through the mystical gathering called the body. In other words, post-charismatic but not post-Spirit.

My own journey has been entwined with charismatic brothers and sisters for many years. A significant number of them came from conservative evangelical backgrounds initially, but entered a different realm (and theology) of the Holy Spirit as they sought for a deeper walk with Jesus. Now, some years later, they are leaving the same charismatic fellowships that once represented a breath of fresh spiritual air for them.

I have also had many conversations with youth and young adults who have been raised in charismatic churches, who are questioning the same things. In many ways, they've seen and done it all, but now, like their conservative evangelical friends, they are growing disillusioned with some of the teachings, and the practices based on those teachings.

It would probably be more accurate to call these people not 'post-charismatic', but rather 'post-*hype*'. They are tired of hearing great stories about the good old days, jaded from hearing too many prophecies about the great move of God that seems to be always just around the corner, fed up with exaggerated or even fabricated stories of healings and miracles, and disillusioned with a view of spiritual formation that is lived through a weekly crisis moment at the front of the church.

In years past, most of them would not have voiced these questions out loud, out of concern for being labelled rebellious or lacking faith. Even recently, most of the concerns that have been voiced to me have been done in a context of two or three friends sharing a table at a coffeeshop or pub; they wouldn't be comfortable voicing their concerns in the church at large.

Broadly speaking, there are four major areas that come up repeatedly as reasons for post-charismatics pulling away from their charismatic roots. The four areas are:

1. Abuses and elitism in prophetic ministry, coupled with a 'carrot and stick' approach to holiness that many find legalistic, manipulative and repressive.
2. The excesses of Word of Faith teachings (Health and

Wealth, Prosperity doctrine) which clash with the emerging generations' concern for a biblical approach to justice and ministry with the poor.

3. Authoritarianism and hierarchical leadership structures that exist more to control people than to equip the saints for works of service.

4. An approach to spiritual formation (discipleship) that depends on crisis events – whether at 'the altar' in a church service, or in a large conference setting – but either neglects or deliberately belittles other means of spiritual maturation.

In order to adequately assess a post-charismatic response to these stated areas of disillusionment, we will look at the roots of the teachings that led or contributed to these areas, attempting to ascertain what was good and of God originally, and where things got off track and later led to the abuses that are rampant today.

To that end, we will be looking at the Latter Rain movement, which is the genesis of many of the teachings that resulted in item #1 above; the Word of Faith teachings (as set out originally by E.W. Kenyon and Kenneth E. Hagin) in response to #2; the Shepherding movement as the most recent exporter of the *covering* and *under authority* concepts that typify the abuses of authority in item #3; and for #4, taking a retrospective look at what discipleship means and how it could be approached in a way that is Spirit-led while not neglecting human responsibility.

Then, our gaze will shift to the future advancement of the kingdom, as we explore a reformed praxis (practice) of the gifts of the Spirit, to build up, encourage and strengthen the body of Christ.

There has always been an ongoing need for those in the Pentecostal, charismatic, and Third Wave streams to practise the biblical gift of discernment, but it appears in recent years that more and more people, describing themselves as post-charismatic, are actually exercising this gift.

J. Lee Grady, editor of *Charisma Magazine*, estimated that in 1990 there were as many as 92 million believers world-wide who identified themselves as post-charismatic. Some had moved into more conservative evangelical churches, and many had dropped out of church altogether. Grady describes post-charismatics in this way:

> Burned out on hype and pulpit showmanship, weary of learning 95 ways to use spiritual gifts when they recognize more basic needs, these believers are in search of a deeper spirituality that emphasizes the fruit of the Spirit as much or more than the gifts.[2]

Grady's words, written over a decade ago, ring true today for many post-charismatics. Unfortunately, many of them find it too difficult, or too emotionally exhausting, to sort through all the practices and teachings to discern the good from the bad. They simply withdraw and consider that chapter of their lives closed. A good friend of mine, recently leaving a charismatic fellowship, commented to me that he was planning to attend a more mainline, liturgical church – not because he really wanted to join the church, but because he'd heard that 'it's the church where wounded ex-charismatics tend to go'.

I will be tracing the origins of some of the theology of Pentecostalism, as well as those of the charismatic renewal of the 1960s and 1970s, and also those of the Third Wave (or neo-Pentecostals as others call them). Following that, I will be addressing some of the classic problems that I have observed, and have had many younger charismatics cite as reasons why they would rather be post-charismatic.

As much as postmodernism is a critique of modernism, and the emerging/missional church is a critique (but hopefully much more) of the modern church, I am hoping that a post-charismatic understanding of how the Holy Spirit works in individuals and communities of faith will serve as a critique of 'charismania' excesses and questionable teachings, and lead ultimately to a more mature and balanced understanding, expectation and functioning in the Spirit of Christ.

My motivation for doing this is best summed up by J. Lee Grady, who urges us:

> Rather than watch our wounded brothers and sisters turn their backs on the faith or reject genuine spiritual experiences, those of us who identify with the charismatic renewal should determine to help rid our movement of its extra baggage.[3]

PART ONE

HISTORY

Historical roots

The Pentecostal, charismatic and Third Wave movements comprised the fastest growing segment of Christianity in the twentieth century; some estimates place their combined numbers at above 600 million. Beyond their own denominational borders, the Pentecostal, charismatic and Third Wave movements have had a profound impact on mainline and evangelical denominations as well.

In his excellent history of the Vineyard movement, *The Quest for the Radical Middle*, Bill Jackson refers to what church historians have called the 'routinisation of charisma'. What this means is simply that, while God may sovereignly begin a work of revival and renewal among his people, humanity has a tendency – within a generation or two – to institutionalise a great move of God, which then calcifies into forms without power. This has been a cycle in church history for centuries.

J. Lee Grady, editor of *Charisma Magazine*, laments the sobering reality that: 'Too many times in this century, movements that were born of the Spirit ended up as spiritual miscarriages. And in every case, men and women were responsible for derailing God's holy purpose.'[1]

In order to understand the increasing numbers of people who self-identify as post-charismatic, it is very important that we trace the journey that led to the rise of the Pentecostal/charismatic/Third Wave movements during the past century.

Similar to other significant moments in the history of the church, the Pentecostal movement did not suddenly spring out of nothingness at the Azusa Street Mission in 1906. Just as the Protestant Reformation had its roots in an ongoing cycle of reformation and revival long before Martin Luther nailed his 95 Theses on the doors at Wittenberg, so the Pentecostal – and later the charismatic and Third Wave – movement has theological roots that go much further back.

John Wesley and 'entire sanctification'

Perhaps the most significant roots of the Pentecostal story go back to the Great Awakening, and particularly some of the teachings of John Wesley. Of particular interest to our discussion of the growing number of post-charismatics is Wesley's teaching on 'entire sanctification', which is contained in his booklet *A Plain Account of Christian Perfection*, published in 1766.

An important part of the Wesleyan background is the decidedly Arminian understanding that Wesley – and later Pentecostals and some charismatics – had of salvation and the ongoing work of the Spirit in the lives of Christians.

> *Aside*: I will in no manner attempt to reconcile the Arminian/Calvinistic debate in this writing, and I recognise that there are many nuances and emphases in both theological camps that will not be adequately articulated here. I will be touching on issues surrounding these theological constructs only in so far as it sets the groundwork for looking at the post-charismatic question.

Wesley rejected the unconditional election motif that classic Calvinists insist on, believing that human will and responsibility was involved as well. Wesley also did not want to err to the opposite extreme of Pelagianism, which proposed that people could choose to follow Jesus solely based on their own decision without any reliance or necessity of the intervening grace of God.

To avoid the Pelagian accusation, Wesley appealed to the Arminian teaching on 'prevenient grace' – that there exists grace from God for all humanity to respond to Jesus, but free will is still involved in that they must choose to submit to Jesus as Lord. Many denominations have adopted this explanation, and others choose to live in the tension between predestination as developed by Calvinists and free will as advocated by Arminians.

The Arminian leanings of Wesley are important because one of the implications of free will included the possibility of 'losing salvation', which again clashed with the Calvinist doctrine of 'perseverance of the saints'. If salvation can be lost, then the question of how one can tell if one is still 'in' or not becomes extremely important.

Calvinism, or predestination, was articulated at length by France's John Calvin (1509–64) in his *Institutes of the Christian Religion*. Predestination is the idea that God determines who will – and who won't – become Christians; to Calvinists, free will (the power of contrary choice) is an illusion. The acronym TULIP is often used to identify the five main points of Calvinism:

- Total depravity (the imago Dei was completely obliterated when Adam and Eve sinned; humanity is incapable of seeking God).
- Unconditional election (God sovereignly chooses who will be saved, based solely on his grace).
- Limited atonement ('for God's good will and pleasure' – a

favourite Calvinist phrase – the blood of Jesus is only for those who are the elect; the non-elect have no option other than damnation).

- Irresistible grace (those who are predestined *must* respond – they can do nothing else).
- Perseverance of the saints (once saved, always saved).

Arminianism was developed from the writing of Jacobus Arminius (1559–1609). Known as 'the quiet Dutchman', Arminius' writings emphasise free will, and subsequent Arminian theologians developed a five-point synopsis similar to Calvinism's TULIP:

- Natural ability (the imago Dei is marred but not obliterated; however, humanity is dependent on the Holy Spirit for new birth).
- Election (based on God's foreknowledge of who would respond with free will to the gospel).
- Unlimited atonement (salvation is available to all, but effective only for those who respond).
- Prevenient grace (preparatory work of the Holy Spirit enabling humanity to respond to the gospel).
- Conditional perseverance (believers are empowered for victorious life, but are capable of turning from grace and losing salvation).

Part of the answer to this was Wesley's teaching on entire sanctification. For Wesley, this was a 'second work of grace', a crisis event following salvation, where the believer was enabled to overcome sin in this present life. Wesley maintained that absolute perfection was impossible this side of heaven, but his

second work of grace teaching meant that the believer was motivated by love for God and others, and any sinful actions or
words that happened after this point would be minor mistakes
and small slips. 'Wesley did not believe that every Christian
achieves this state (of perfection) during the course of this life.
But he did believe it ought to be preached. . . for, he insisted,
when salvation and the Christian life stand still, they erode.'[2]

For many Methodists (those who followed John Wesley's
teachings), this second crisis experience of entire sanctification
(or 'Christian perfection' as some called it) became the crucial
evidence that they were definitely headed for heaven. There was
a lot of emphasis in early Methodism on 'tarrying' or waiting on
God, coupled with a time of soul-searching and repenting of all
known sin, before this second crisis moment would come. John
Fletcher, one of Wesley's co-workers, was the first to identify this
second blessing as the 'baptism of the Holy Spirit', which was
thought to bring inner cleansing and the ability to live in 'Christian perfection'.

'Many Methodist holiness leaders already taught that on the
day of Pentecost, the 120 were entirely sanctified in the Wesleyan sense.'[3] This made it quite easy to equate the Wesleyan
doctrine of Christian perfection with the baptism of the Holy
Spirit.

The Holiness and Keswick Higher Life movements

This gave rise to what has been called the 'Holiness' tradition in
the mid- to late 1800s. Basically stated, the Holiness movement
stressed the second blessing – or baptism of the Spirit as it had
become popularly called – was towards a holy, separated life, and

also that the path to receiving this second blessing was to purify one's self of 'worldliness'. Not surprisingly, there were differing views on what 'worldliness' looked like, but there was a general trend towards extreme conservatism and not a little legalism. 'They were overwhelmingly Arminian in their basic theology and strongly perfectionistic in their spirituality and lifestyle.'[4]

In Great Britain, a movement called the 'Keswick Higher Life' conference came to prominence in 1870, attracting many people from across a variety of denominations to their camp meetings. They tempered the Wesleyan teaching on entire sanctification in two ways:

1. The emphasis on the baptism of the Spirit shifted from achieving entire sanctification, and became more nuanced towards being empowered for Christian service.
2. Unlike their American Methodist cousins, they didn't accept that sin could be eradicated by this baptism of the Spirit, but instead 'they taught that sin was counteracted by the experience. . . allowing for a joyful and victorious Christian life'.[5]

Many of the participants in both the British and American Keswick meetings believed that unity of the church would come through the holiness movement, rather than the ecumenical efforts of the existing denominations. However, there also arose a group that was identified as 'a "come-outer" movement led by radicals who abandoned any prospects of renewing the existing churches'.[6]

Even with the activities of these splinter groups within, the Higher Life movement, as part of the larger Holiness tradition, saw thousands of people claim to experience the second work of grace – the baptism of the Holy Spirit – during that last quarter of the nineteenth century. But for many, the question remained: how can I know for sure that I've received this baptism?

Famous evangelists like Charles Finney (1792–1876) and Dwight L. Moody (1837–99, founder of Moody Bible Institute) contributed to the common understanding of the baptism of the Holy Spirit as a second work of grace, empowering one for service. Finney at one point questioned the salvation of a colleague because Finney wasn't convinced his colleague had experienced the second blessing. 'If he had ever been converted to Christ, he had failed to receive that divine anointing of the Holy Ghost that would make him a power in the pulpit . . . He had fallen short of receiving the baptism of the Holy Ghost, which is indispensable to ministerial success. . .'[7]

D. L. Moody's experience came in 1871 after two Free Methodist women confronted him after he had preached his sermon, and told him that he needed the power of the Spirit. Moody initially declined to let them pray for him, but later relented. While in New York shortly afterwards, Moody 'felt such an overwhelming sense of God's nearness that he rushed to a friend's house and begged for a room where he could lock himself in . . . and as he put it, "I had such an experience of His love that I had to ask Him to stay His hand."'[8]

Moody's biggest influence on the American Keswick movement was that his view of Holy Spirit baptism was primarily concerned with power for service, and not freedom from sin. This became the predominant understanding of those touched by the American Keswick movement.

Still, despite the many people on two continents (and those who travelled from afar to attend the Keswick conferences) being significantly impacted, with many claiming to have received the baptism of the Spirit, there was still the unanswered question of knowing whether or not they'd continued to walk in the Spirit's baptism; their Arminian understanding taught them that they could lose their salvation, so the need to feel assurance ran high.

The National Holiness Association arose in the late nineteenth century in America as a protest movement against the perceived stagnation of the churches there. The second blessing teaching was promoted here as well, and numerous well-known evangelicals were a part of this movement, including A. J. Gordon, Andrew Murray, A. B. Simpson (the founder of the Christian and Missionary Alliance), and R. A. Torrey, who was the president of Moody Bible Institute at the time.

Torrey's view of the second blessing is evidenced in his writing, 'A man may be regenerated by the Holy Spirit and still not be baptized with the Holy Spirit.'[9]

The National Holiness Association was unfortunately characterised by an extreme version of legalism. Dr Sam Storms recounts that they 'defined holiness as abstinence. On their list of taboos: the theatre, ball games, playing cards, dancing, lipstick, tobacco, alcohol, all forms of female make-up, the curling or colouring of one's hair, neckties for men, Coca Cola, chewing gum, rings, bracelets, or any form of worldly "ornamentation", etc.'[10]

While not very attractive, this insistence on holiness is in keeping with a view of sanctification that includes purifying oneself in order to receive the baptism of the Holy Spirit, coupled with the lingering expectation in some circles that this baptism was to usher in Christian perfection – or at least allow one to progress quickly along the path to greater sanctification.

During these years, there were various splinter groups that advocated the recovery of the charismatic gifts of tongues, prophecy, healing, etc. Most of these groups were on the fringe, and some, despite having evidence in their early days of a genuine move of the Spirit, degenerated into various elitist teachings and abuses that caused them to be shunned by the more mainstream expressions of the Holiness movement. Even so, the possibility of the charismatic gifts being associated with the baptism of the Holy Spirit had been introduced.

The Pentecostal movement

Disclaimer. There are many well-known people in the Pentecostal movement whom you won't read about here. People like John G. Lake, Smith Wigglesworth, Kathryn Kuhlman, David DuPlessis (nicknamed 'Mr Pentecost'), and many others make for fascinating and challenging reading, but my intent in this section is to trace the historical roots as they pertain to the developing theology and praxis of the movement, not to write an exhaustive historical account.

In the years bridging the nineteenth and twentieth centuries, one of the more imaginative thinkers of the day, Benjamin Irwin, developed a series of baptisms that one might expect from the Holy Spirit. This was not unlike John Fletcher's (John Wesley's associate) teaching regarding multiple fillings of the Spirit, but with a new twist. The believer, according to Irwin, was 'the potential recipient of multiple infusions of power, the baptism of the Holy Spirit and fire being but the first. Later blessings he characterized by various explosives: dynamite, lyddite, and oxidite.'[11] Irwin's moral failings led to the demise of the denomination he started, but among those who sat under his teachings was one Charles Fox Parham.

Parham's single greatest contribution to what would later be known as the Pentecostal movement was his teaching that the evidence of the baptism of the Holy Spirit was the gift of tongues, although his initial emphasis was that these would be known languages – *xenoglossolalia*, as was the case in Acts 2 – and would result in a great missionary movement around the world.

On New Year's Day 1901, one of Parham's students, Agnes Ozman, spoke in tongues (presumed to be Chinese), and was unable to speak or write English for three days afterwards. While Ozman was not the first person to speak in tongues in America – D. L. Moody saw tongues in evidence at some of his meetings, and they were reported during the Welsh Revival a few years later – 'what made Parham's group unique was their insistence that tongues were the necessary evidence of Spirit-baptism'.[12]

William J. Seymour, a black Holiness preacher, had been influenced by Parham's teachings from the school hallway where he was forced, as a non-white, to remain while Parham was teaching. Seymour took the teaching of tongues as the initial evidence of the Spirit's baptism with him when he accepted a pastorate in Los Angeles, although he himself had not yet experienced it. After some people began to speak in tongues at a Bible study Seymour was leading, space was rented at 312 Azusa Street in Los Angeles, and the movement called Pentecostalism was off and running. Nightly revival meetings were held for three years (1906–1909), and were attended by people from all walks of life, and many different geographical locations.

Opposition was strong from some quarters – even R. A. Torrey, who had taught that the baptism of the Spirit was a second blessing experience, declared that Pentecostalism was 'emphatically not of God',[13] while G. Campbell Morgan famously denounced the Pentecostal revival as 'the last vomit of Satan'.[14] This lent additional fodder to the come-outers, who saw this rejection as another evidence of the true work of God being shunned by a spiritually bankrupt institutional church – a charge repeated throughout the centuries in the cycle of revival, routinisation and renewal. This come-outer mentality will play into other areas that we will consider later.

The initial belief that tongues would be known languages for the purpose of evangelising the nations quickly gave way as eager missionaries discovered to their puzzlement that 'the nations' didn't understand what they were saying at all. Alfred G. Garr, who had received his baptism experience at Azusa Street in the early days of the revival, arrived in Calcutta in early 1907, 'only to find that he could not speak in what he thought was Bengali after all.'[15] Garr was one of the first to teach that the gift of tongues was the initial evidence of the Spirit's baptism, but he focused more on the 'tongues of men and angels' approach. His views caught on quickly among those who had genuinely experienced a baptism of the Spirit, but also had discovered that the language they had received was unknown.

It is useful to note that around this same time, near the end of the nineteenth century, non-charismatic theologians were developing an interpretive grid called Dispensationalism, which reinforced and further developed the cessationist views of charismatic gifts and the role of the Holy Spirit in the life of the church.

Cessationism – the theological view, popularised by Benjamin Warfield in the late 1890s, that the more obviously supernatural, or 'sign' gifts (tongues and their interpretation, prophecy, healing, words of knowledge and wisdom, etc.) ceased to exist after the first century. Cessationists taught that these gifts were given to authenticate the apostles' ministry in spreading the gospel, but once the canon of the Bible was declared closed, the gifts were withdrawn by God. This teaching is based largely on a strained eisegesis of 1 Corinthians 13:8–10. ('Exegesis' is the interpretation of a biblical text; 'eisegesis', according to the Merriam Webster Dictionary, is 'the interpretation of a text – as of the Bible – by reading one's own ideas into it'.) To be blunt, cessationism is not a biblically defensible doctrine, but since Pentecostals and charismatics do not hold to this view, we will not be covering cessationism in detail.

In 1910, Charles Harrison Mason published his 'finished work' theology of gradual, progressive sanctification, which was instrumental to the formation of the Assemblies of God denomination in 1914. Today, this denomination is one of the largest Pentecostal denominations in the world.

An early controversy within the Pentecostal movement arose out of a group who claimed the doctrine of the Trinity was unbiblical. These 'Jesus-only' proponents insisted that the proper baptismal invocation was in the name of Jesus, and that the Trinitarian formula was misguided at best, and heretical at worst. Some groups required the re-baptism of anyone who had been baptised in the Trinitarian manner.

The Assemblies of God took a public stand against the Jesus-only teaching in 1916, which resulted in over 100 congregations leaving. The United Pentecostal denomination is one of the largest Jesus-only, or 'Oneness', groups in America, and north of the border the Apostolic Churches of Canada (started by Frank Small in Winnipeg during the 1920s) were their northern counterparts. Small was a major proponent of the Oneness doctrine in Canada, and Zion Apostolic Church, which he was instrumental in starting, is still active today, although the entire denomination has reverted to Trinitarian belief in recent years.

During the late 1940s and onward, a movement arose from North Battleford, Saskatchewan, in Canada that became known as the Latter Rain movement. While the phrase 'latter rain' was a common one among Pentecostals, referring to the outpouring of the Holy Spirit in the twentieth century, the movement that called itself by the same name developed many of its own unique teachings and practices.

William Branham, one of the major figures in the Latter Rain movement, was adamantly Oneness in his theology, and insisted on re-baptising any Trinitarian converts to his New Order of the Latter Rain. We will examine some of Branham's more controversial teachings – such as his 'Serpent Seed' and 'Manifested Sons of God' doctrines – as part of the Latter Rain discussion later.

The Assemblies of God and the Pentecostal Assemblies of Canada, among other prominent Pentecostal denominations, condemned the Latter Rain movement as heretical in 1949. However, a number of Latter Rain teachings survived and re-surfaced in the charismatic renewal and later in the Third Wave movements, so we will look at the Latter Rain's teachings and continuing influence in greater detail later.

But for many Pentecostal/Holiness believers, the gift of tongues as the initial evidence of the Spirit's baptism became a vital link in their spiritual journey – now they at last had tangible evidence that they had indeed received the second work of grace that would result in increased holiness and/or power for service. Referring to the tangible benefits of the gift of tongues as the initial evidence of the Spirit's baptism, A. A. Boddy wrote in 1910 of the 'wondrous joy that the Spirit has thus sealed the believer unto the day of redemption'.[16]

Again, I am not attempting to interact with all the theological nuances of these developments; they are simply important to understand in the trajectory that has led to the post-charismatics.

The charismatic renewal

It was in 1960 that the movement dubbed the charismatic renewal first became widely known, as a result of the much-publicised story of an Episcopal priest named Dennis Bennett. The difference from the existing Pentecostal movement – now established well enough that they were even accepted in the National Association of Evangelicals – was revealed in their emphasis on the 'renewing' of mainline denominations: Episcopal, Lutheran, Anglican, Catholic, etc.

While the early Pentecostals found themselves ostracised from existing denominations – and encouraged to leave by the come-outers – the charismatic renewal developed predominantly within the mainline denominations. After some initial resistance, most of these denominations settled into allowing the charismatic expressions within to co-exist with the more traditional congregations.

Dennis Bennett, while not the first person in a mainline denomination to speak in tongues, became famous/notorious because he ventured to speak about it openly from the pulpit of his church in Van Nuys, California. Although Bennett had received the baptism of the Holy Spirit and the gift of tongues in 1959, he kept it quiet initially, until rumours started to circulate and he knew he had to publicly address the situation.

'This he decided to do on Passion Sunday, April 3 1960. At all three morning services, Bennett explained in a quiet, unemotional way how he had been led to receive the power and the fullness of the Holy Spirit, and how this had included the "gift of unknown tongues". After the second service, an associate priest resigned, and a church officer called for Bennett's resignation. Bennett announced his resignation at the third service.'[17]

Things might have faded quickly afterwards for Bennett, but an associate of his contacted the national magazines *Newsweek* and *Time*, and they ran stories on Bennett's charismatic experience and the resulting turmoil in Van Nuys that resulted in his resignation. Bennett ended up in a small, struggling parish in Washington State, which experienced explosive growth in numbers and a significant move of the Holy Spirit, with the support and blessing of the local bishop.

The charismatic renewal spread quickly. 'Within a decade, this movement had spread to all the 150 major Protestant families of the world, reaching a total of 55,000,000 people by 1990.'[18] They were initially referred to as 'neo-pentecostal', but 'the word "charismatic" came to be used to refer to folks from old-line denominations who were receiving the freedom of the Holy Spirit while continuing in their respective traditions'.[19]

At the same time, 'the Second Vatican Council, which

concluded in 1965, created an atmosphere of openness to the charismatic work of the Holy Spirit',[20] and it was only two years later that charismatic experiences began to take place at Duquesne University in Pittsburgh. 'In the more than 30 years since its inception, the Catholic charismatic movement has touched the lives of our 70,000,000 Catholics in over 120 nations of the world.'[21]

A key component for the charismatic renewal, which gave it a growing relationship with the Pentecostal denominations – over time – was a common understanding of the baptism of the Holy Spirit accompanied by the initial evidence of speaking in tongues.

An Arminian understanding of salvation and sanctification, while not as universal as the doctrine of tongues as the initial evidence of the baptism of the Holy Spirit, also created a level of commonality among these groups and the Pentecostal movement. While some of the come-outers were quite wary of other denominations, which they saw as Babylon resurrected (part of the Latter Rain's continuing legacy), many bridges were built around common experiences of the Spirit.

In many ways, rather than much new theological development, this new movement represented an adoption of Pentecostal theology of the baptism of the Holy Spirit with the initial evidence of speaking in tongues. Much of the existing liturgy, for example in the Anglican *Book of Common Prayer*, was easily compatible with this new experience of the Holy Spirit.

The 'Jesus Movement' of the late 1960s and early 1970s was another manifestation of the charismatic renewal, as literally thousands of hippies and other counter-cultural youth and young adults suddenly turned to Jesus. The current Christian recording industry began out of the evangelistic efforts of early 'Jesus Music' groups, which were at first very controversial for their use of rock music (however tame they sound by today's standards). Thousands of new believers, not always welcome at established churches, often ended up starting their own; in some cases, these fledgling groups eventually became cultic and damaging. Discipleship for these anti-establishment former hippies became a serious issue in the early 1970s.

Ministry focusing on 'inner healing', or the 'healing of memories', began in this period, with John and Paula Sandford's Elijah House concept. Their books, such as *The Transformation of the Inner Man*, *Healing the Wounded Spirit*, and *The Elijah Task*, put a stronger emphasis on the Holy Spirit's role in counselling, and on the gifts of prophecy and words of knowledge and wisdom.

The Shepherding movement (also called the Authority and Submission movement in some circles, such as Assemblies of God) arose in the 1970s, partly in response to the need for young believers to be discipled. However, the movement created a serious crisis point for Pentecostals and charismatics alike, due to the extreme nature of some of their teachings on submission to spiritual leaders.

At the time, many charismatic leaders denounced the Shepherding movement as authoritarian and abusive, and most of its main proponents abandoned their teachings in the 1980s, and several publicly repented in 1989. Because of the Shepherding movement's influence behind the concepts of 'covering' and being 'under authority', which have survived despite the disbanding and renunciation of the late 1980s, we will look at this movement separately and in greater detail later.

It was also during these years that the Word of Faith movement began to pick up steam – it had been around for some time already, but with the advent of Christian broadcasting, suddenly millions of people had access to what would become some of the most embarrassing and outlandish events on television.

Some of the most disturbing aspects of televised charismatic personalities steamrollered into the public eye in the late 1980s, of which the most cynically received event was probably Oral Roberts' infamous prophetic word that God would 'take me home' if he failed to raise $8,000,000 for his Faith Centre in Oklahoma. Oral managed to see all the money come in before the deadline (pardon the pun), but his Faith Centre closed permanently only two years later.

Jim and Tammy Faye Bakker's sudden fall from fame occurred in 1987, when Jim was accused of having a sexual relationship with a church secretary, and later sent to jail for defrauding his viewers via his PTL (Praise the Lord, later People That Care) television show and theme park. Tammy Faye admitted to a drug problem and divorced her husband. Jim came out of prison and wrote a book refuting all his Prosperity (Health and Wealth) teachings, entitled *I Was Wrong*.

Probably the most devastating moment for many Pentecostal believers was the fall of Jimmy Swaggart, also in 1987. Swaggart was known for his fiery sermons and angry attacks on Christian rock music in the mid-1980s, but when he was caught with a prostitute, he resigned from the pastorate in a tearful apology. When he was discovered with a second prostitute not long afterwards, his influence went sharply down, although he continues to minister today.

The cynicism felt by many of the emerging generations

towards the extravagant lifestyles of televangelists – particularly in light of the increased concern in the emerging generations with social justice and ministry among the poor – was compounded greatly by these events.

The Third Wave

The term 'Third Wave' was coined by C. Peter Wagner in the early 1980s to describe a growing number of 'evangelical Christians who, while applauding and supporting the work of the Holy Spirit in the first two waves (classic Pentecostalism and the charismatic renewal), have chosen not to identify with either'.[22] Some have referred to the Third Wave as being synonymous with the Vineyard movement begun by the late John Wimber, but that assumption is inaccurate. While it is true that Vineyard would fit the classic definition of a Third Wave church, the Third Wave encompasses more than just the Vineyard.

The reasons for not completely identifying with the first two waves are largely theological in nature; one Pentecostal writer says of the Third Wave that they 'disdain labels such as "Pentecostal" or "charismatic"'[23] – disdain is probably a harsher word than is warranted.

'The "third wave", therefore, is the embracing by evangelicals of the gifts of the Spirit while at the same time rejecting several of the classical Pentecostal and charismatic distinctives such as:

1. the insistence that the baptism in the Holy Spirit is a distinct experience separate from conversion;
2. the insistence that speaking in tongues is the initial physical evidence of baptism in the Spirit;

3. the insistence that since "healing is in the atonement" all believers may justifiably "claim" complete physical health in this present age.

'The "third wave" has also distanced itself from the errors of the Word of Faith movement as well as other forms of the so-called "Health and Wealth" or "Prosperity" gospel.'[24]

During the Jesus People movement of the late 1960s and early 1970s, Calvary Chapel rose to prominence as literally thousands of hippies were baptised in the Pacific Ocean near Costa Mesa, California. Calvary Chapel's pastor, Chuck Smith, became one of the key leaders in a counter-cultural revival.

Another key figure in the Jesus People movement, during the heyday of Calvary Chapel's involvement, was the controversial figure of Lonnie Frisbee. Lonnie was a converted hippy, passionate preacher and tireless evangelist. He had a significant impact on Calvary Chapel, but found himself increasingly being set aside due to his unorthodox appearance and behaviour.

Lonnie would surface again in the early days of the Vineyard movement, although until recently, Vineyard writings never acknowledged him by name, opting instead to refer to him as a 'young evangelist' or 'young preacher'. The famous 'Mother's Day Incident' in 1980 at John Wimber's Vineyard Christian Fellowship (Anaheim, California), which really launched the Vineyard into its signs and wonders emphasis, came from Lonnie preaching and inviting the Holy Spirit to fall on the young people in the congregation.

However, Lonnie's ongoing struggles with homosexuality (he died from AIDS in 1993) caused both Calvary Chapel and the Vineyard to distance themselves from him, despite the benefits of his ministry there. At his funeral, he was charitably compared to Samson – an anointed person, but with crippling human frailty.

Another key doctrinal difference is that the overwhelming majority of evangelicals come from a more Reformed (Calvinistic) theological grid. What makes this significant is that Third Wave groups have typically not adopted the Holiness understanding of entire sanctification; they would generally assume that the filling of the Holy Spirit is a repeatable event to empower and gift believers for service (similar to Finney).

'Arminianism says "If we, then God. . .", while Reformed believers would say, "Because God has, we will. . ."[25] For the majority of those who consider themselves part of the Third Wave, there is a bemusement at the Pentecostal and charismatic insistence on tongues, as they are not aware of the implications of the history behind the Holiness emphasis on the baptism of the Holy Spirit as it builds on the Wesleyan concept of Christian perfection.

The Vineyard movement contributed its fair share of controversy over the years, beginning with John Wimber's writings on 'power evangelism', a belief system that sought to utilise the power of the Spirit – through prophecy, words of knowledge and particularly healing – as a door-opener for sharing the good news of Jesus Christ. The Vineyard expanded quickly, and many evangelicals – with their predominantly Calvinistic theology – were introduced to spiritual gifts in a manner that was more easily accepted into their existing theology and praxis than classic second blessing teachings.

One of the Vineyard's main emphases was on 'everybody gets to play' – an attempt to practise the priesthood of all believers in terms of spiritual gifts. At the same time, Vineyard at one point embraced the Kansas City Prophets, another controversial group, whose influences included some of the rejected Latter Rain doctrines. Because of the typical Third Wave history – not having been exposed to, or even heard about, the Latter Rain controversy of mid-century – the Vineyard adopted the Kansas City Prophets into their movement, and attempted to bring correction to some of their teachings. But eventually they distanced themselves from the Prophets, and with the departure of Metro Vineyard (now known as Metro Christian Fellowship) in 1996, the Kansas City Prophets' era in the Vineyard ended.

In the UK throughout the sixties and seventies there was a groundswell of fascination with new church structures, mingled with a growing frustration over traditional ones. John Stott and Martyn Lloyd-Jones famously polarised two different approaches: the former calling evangelicals to stay within the historical denominations and work for their renewal – not least the Church of England – and the latter, 'the Doctor', calling on evangelicals to come apart. Many of those who left embraced the new expressions of worship coming into Britain from down under and over the water (Australasia and North America), and a collection of songs made under the guidance of Jeanne Harper, called *Sounds of Living Water*, was particularly influential in spreading the thirst for spiritual refreshment.

Arthur Wallis was a Bible teacher whose books strengthened the biblical backbone of part of this rising movement of 'come out and be separate' evangelicals. *In the Day of Thy Power* was followed up by *Rain from Heaven* and, somewhat later, *The Radical Christian*. Those who gathered themselves around this teaching, especially Bryn Jones and Terry Virgo, began to talk of a 'restoration' of New Testament church principles and spiritual gifts to the church. Harvestime and the Dales Bible Week in the north of England, and the Downs Bible Week in the south, became major landmarks on the British spiritual landscape.

In his book *Restoring the Kingdom* sociologist Andrew Walker gives a fuller account of the British developments, including the formation of the New Frontiers network of churches under Terry Virgo, with their particular brand of Reformed theology and charismatic expression; as well as Ichthus, under the leadership of Roger and Faith Forster, and Pioneer, the looser confederation of churches and fellowships under Gerald Coates, both of which favoured a more Arminian view.

The Toronto Blessing began in 1994, and suddenly the Vineyard was once again in the middle of a controversial move of the Spirit. As other outpourings of the Spirit in history had already demonstrated – from Jonathan Edwards' concerns in the Great Awakening to Azusa Street – there was a mix of Spirit and flesh, and therefore a great need for careful discernment.

Significant outcomes included the number of churches from Great Britain that were affected; Holy Trinity Brompton, out of which the Alpha Course had been developed, became a prominent renewal church.

As the Blessing progressed, and thousands of people from around the world hopped on aeroplanes to make a pilgrimage to Toronto, concerns about some of the physical manifestations – and especially about attempts by some to give these strange manifestations prophetic significance – alarmed the Vineyard movement at large. As these concerns increased, some Latter Rain teachings (which we'll identify later on), so recently dealt with as a result of the Kansas City Prophets, began to surface again. In December 1995, the Toronto Airport Vineyard was asked to leave the Vineyard movement, and became Toronto Airport Christian Fellowship.

Similar events happened at the Brownsville Assembly of God church in Pensacola, Florida, beginning in 1995, but with a more Pentecostal flavour and theology attached to it. Many were comparing it to the Azusa Street beginnings of Pentecostalism.

The 'spiritual mapping' emphasis found its strength as the charismatic and Third Wave movements developed a stronger emphasis on world missions in the 1990s (the Pentecostals had been heavily involved in missions for many years already), and applied some of their understanding of spiritual warfare and deliverance ministry to their missiology. The basic premise was that, unless territorial spirits were exposed and removed, through what was called 'strategic level spiritual warfare', evangelism would be hampered. But once these controlling spirits had been dealt with, the gospel would be received on a much wider scale. While this became another source of controversy, both inside the charismatic movement and out, there were also reports of the effectiveness of dealing with territorial spirits in numerous cities.

Some charismatics are uneasy with the Third Wave because it 'denies that there is any experience of a baptism in the Holy Spirit following salvation, but that it all happens when we accept Jesus. It maintains that it is not necessary to speak in tongues in order to be baptized in the Spirit . . . This is mainly and usually because people have not themselves received the baptism in the Holy Spirit, and therefore sympathetic and well-meaning brothers and sisters are commenting on something they have not entered into.'[26]

As graciously as Dennis Bennett worded the foregoing quote, those in the Third Wave would continue to disagree with his idea regarding the baptism of the Holy Spirit as a second work of grace, accompanied by the initial evidence of speaking in tongues.

The arc of the work of the Spirit in North America and Britain in the twentieth century began with the creation of a new wing in the church – the Pentecostals who either chose or were forced to form their own denominational alliances – and then saw the mainline denominations touched by a similar move of the Spirit, and finally, conservative evangelicals (including many former cessationists) expanding their theological world-view to include all the gifts of the Spirit.

Post-charismatics

As mentioned earlier, J. Lee Grady wrote that in 1990 there were estimated to be 92 million people who considered themselves 'post-charismatic' – meaning that they had left the charismatic movement and returned to their original denominations, joined a new denomination (often liturgical), or stopped going to church altogether.

The main areas that need to be discussed before we look at a post-charismatic theology of the Holy Spirit's work, in and through the body of Christ, are so entwined that it is problematic to try and separate them into different sections. However, in order to make sense of how they have conspired to create such a level of disillusionment, I am forced to make some arbitrary divisions; the cross-pollination will be addressed as effectively as I can attempt.

As I see it, based on the materials available to me at the time of this writing (see Bibliography for a working list of material), the main areas that are turning people into post-charismatics, and therefore need to be deconstructed before we attempt to reconstruct a post-charismatic praxis, would include:

1. An in-depth examination of the teachings of the Latter Rain movement, which would include their view of modern-day apostles and prophets, and particularly their view of requiring submission to said apostles and prophets, which in turn connects to:

2. The Shepherding movement, which is the progenitor of many of the current models of authoritarian teachings that continue to crop up in charismatic circles (e.g. concepts such as 'who is your covering?' or 'who are you submitted to?').

3. The growing disgust for anything even remotely related to televangelism and the Prosperity (Health and Wealth) teachings, as social justice and ministry to the poor have become areas of major importance to the emerging generations in particular.

4. A more balanced view of discipleship – spiritual formation, maturing in the faith, becoming more Christ-like, etc. This includes a better understanding of the role of suffering, and the growth that comes from dying to self as we take up our cross daily, as opposed to the weekly crisis prayer time which many charismatic churches seem to depend on (although without negating the reality that God works in legitimate crisis moments as well).

When I was a guest lecturer on *Postmodernism and the Emerging/*

Missional Church at Tyndale Seminary in Toronto, I framed the presentation around the idea of 'what questions are being asked by the emerging/missional church' – regardless of where one saw oneself on the modern-postmodern continuum. If the emerging/missional church was asking legitimate questions and raising legitimate concerns, then those questions and concerns needed to be honestly wrestled with.

My intent is neither to discredit nor excessively applaud the charismatic movement, but the questions surrounding why the number of post-charismatics is growing also cannot be ignored. My hope and desire is to sort through some of the teachings (and practices based on those teachings) and emerge on the other side with a praxis that is Spirit-empowered, but without the unnecessary baggage of 'charismania'.

I firmly believe that, as Dennis Bennett wrote years ago, 'The Church is not primarily a preaching or teaching institution. It must be charismatic. It must manifest the Gifts and Fruit of the Spirit, for they are the continuing signs that Jesus is alive and ready to bless people now.'[27] The packaging, the theology and the practices are in need of careful re-thinking and reconstructing, but ultimately, if our missional communities are not Spirit-empowered, safe places where people are encouraged to discover, develop and flourish in whatever gifts the Spirit has given them, we will become an inoffensive, but ineffective, caricature of what we could have been.

THE
LATTER RAIN
MOVEMENT

The evening session of the youth conference started off normally. The band had led the 1,500 conference attendees in
worship for about 45 minutes, followed by a brief video presentation on the plight of Third World children; the money given
in the subsequent offering was to go to these Third World children through the host church's missionaries.

We were really glad to be at this yearly youth conference
again; it was always great to have an opportunity where, as youth
leaders, we weren't responsible for running an event, and could
instead enjoy building relationships with the youth and receiving ministry alongside them. And over the years, we had come to
know other youth groups who came to this conference, and seeing them again, and hearing their stories of how God was working in their lives, was also encouraging.

When the guest speaker for the evening began to speak, we all
settled down to listen. He was warm and witty in his introduc-
tory comments, sharing personal anecdotes as he developed a
rapport with the audience. Several of our youth had their note-
books out – they took notes on everything, and their journals
were an intriguing combination of sermon notes, poetry and
written prayers. They were ready, pens in hand, to scribble down
tips and insights from the speaker.

Then, almost as if somebody had thrown a switch somewhere, the speaker's tone of voice, and physical demeanour,
completely changed. Gone was the relaxed, light-hearted, low-
key sharing; the speaker's stance became more combative, his
lower jaw jutted out, and his speaking became strident and
angry as he paced about the platform.

He was calling out the 'chosen generation' of youth who
would 'take the land that the previous generation failed to enter'.

We listened, somewhat taken aback, to a lengthy diatribe about how anyone over the age of 26 was a complete failure in the eyes of the Lord, because they had somehow, through unbelief and lack of holiness, failed to 'take the land'.

Then he launched into a rant about the lack of holiness in the lives of the youth present. Apparently, Jesus Christ *really wanted* to come back, but he couldn't because the youth were living compromised lives of worldliness. 'You are *holding back* the Second Coming of Jesus,' he yelled, shaking an accusatory finger at the audience, 'and what you need to do is learn to ask Jesus, every 30 minutes, to show you all the ways you've offended him. Then you'll start to learn about holiness, and God will finally be able to use you, and Jesus will see his will being done on earth, and you'll be worthy to take the land that the previous generation failed to.'

We sat stunned on the floor; the pens that were poised for taking notes had frozen in mid-air or had been put away. In the passionate, highly charged delivery of this message, something disturbing was taking place. I listened carefully, trying to decide what it was. Holiness – well, as any student of the word of God and apprentice of Jesus, I was all for holy living. The emerging generation stepping into what God was doing – hey, I was a youth pastor; my whole focus was on seeing youth giving their lives totally to Jesus. And seriously, who *wouldn't* want to see the next generation even more passionate about Jesus than the current one? Still, something just didn't sit right with the content of this speaker's message (his manipulative methodology is a whole other topic).

Without realising it at the time, we were hearing classic Latter Rain teachings.

The beginnings

In the history of the Pentecostal, charismatic and Third Wave movements, the Latter Rain would normally be a small footnote. While it lasted as long as the Azusa Street revival of 1906 (three years), it was situated in a tiny, remote town in the northern prairies of Canada. However, as many made the pilgrimage to this small centre, the influence of the Latter Rain has proved to be far more reaching than its early beginnings would have otherwise indicated.

Many popular catch-phrases that are still heard around charismatic circles had their origins in the Latter Rain movement. Most people are unaware of the doctrinal and practical baggage that is associated with these phrases.

- As in the natural, so in the spiritual. Or, the natural speaks of the supernatural
- Joel's Army, Man-child Company, Moses-Elijah Company, or Overcomers
- Joshua and Caleb Generation – they will possess the land that the previous generation failed to

On the surface, these phrases appear reasonably benign, and to those who don't embrace the theological and eschatological package that usually accompanies them, these phrases are just part of the jargon that every group develops over time. Not everyone who uses these phrases is automatically Latter Rain in their theology.

As stated above, the Latter Rain movement occupied a brief time span – 1947–1949 – and the origins of the movement were in the far north of Saskatchewan, Canada, in the town of North

Battleford. There are parallels to the Azusa Street revival in 1906, and the more recent Toronto Blessing in 1994, as pilgrims from all over the world made the trip to North Battleford to observe and participate in the outpouring of the Spirit there.

From all accounts, there was a genuine move of the Holy Spirit that occurred during those years. The infamy associated with the moniker 'Latter Rain' (or 'New Order of the Latter Rain') came later, as numerous troubling teachings came to prominence which ranged from questionable to outright heretical.

Considering the brevity of the actual revival movement in North Battleford, it is fascinating to observe how some of the more controversial teachings that came out of it – despite repeated denunciations by other denominations and leaders – have survived and continue to spread decades later.

There is no shortage of websites on the Internet denouncing the Latter Rain and attempting – with varying success and credibility – to link the Latter Rain's teachings and leaders to current revival and renewal movements. In the course of researching primary sources, including many transcribed sermons and writings of key Latter Rain leaders, I have discovered that these heresy-hunting websites are *sometimes* not far off the mark in reporting their concerns, but their questionable research methods and often thinly veiled antagonism towards their subject matter makes much of their contribution highly suspect.

Heresy hunters: While all Christians are called to follow the example of the Berean believers who 'searched the Scriptures to see if these things were so' (Acts 17:11), and to exercise common biblical sense and discernment, there are ministries – usually self-appointed – that exist solely to denounce other believers whom they disagree with. These groups tend to be unaccountable and react quite abusively to anyone who questions their methods or conclusions.

The danger of these groups is that their research is often slanted, and their 'findings' are usually written in volatile, abusive language. In their zeal to prove their accusations against anyone who disagrees with them, erroneous reporting and, at times, obvious falsehoods are rampant. They tend to depend on, and over-use, the 'guilt by association' tactic, by which almost every ministry on the planet could be held in suspicion – 'six degrees of Googled separation', as one person called it.

Generally, it is best to visit links on these sites that describe ministries that you are already familiar with, and see if they are correctly represented; if not, then it's likely (even probable) that their 'research' into other people and ministries could be equally spurious. Often, they end up quoting each other's errors, but after much repetition, people can't remember who said what, and the error is simply accepted as 'fact'.

Just because some of these sites may agree with your own opinion on certain movements doesn't make them a credible source. Primary sources are still the best.

It is precisely because of the pervasiveness and tenacity of the Latter Rain teachings that I want to spend some extra time expanding the timeline and examining the roots of the teachings more fully.

Two of the most prominent names that are associated with the Latter Rain movement are William Branham and George Warnock. While neither was present at the beginning of the Latter Rain revival, both became linked and were often identified as the main voices of the movement.

William Branham is more properly connected to the healing evangelists of the 1950s, and had already begun his itinerant ministry before the Latter Rain began. As word spread of the outpouring of the Spirit in North Battleford, Saskatchewan, Branham made a trip to be a part of it, and spread the word in his continuing widespread ministry.

Branham's theology was not altogether typical of the Latter Rain – his 'Jesus only' doctrines were a departure from the Trinitarian view of the majority of the Latter Rain, and one of his most well-known doctrinal departures, the Serpent Seed (more later), was not widely accepted in the Latter Rain. Also, in contrast to the Wesleyan theology of the various Pentecostal denominations, many of the Latter Rain leaders were more Reformed in their doctrine.

George Warnock became widely regarded as one of the chief writers in the Latter Rain movement, publishing his most influential work, *Feast of Tabernacles* – considered to be the 'manual' of the Latter Rain movement – shortly after the Latter Rain revival ended its three-year heyday. Warnock and Branham were contemporaries, but Warnock was more directly involved long-term with the Latter Rain, while Branham continued his itinerant ministry, mostly in the United States, until his untimely death in a car accident.

Where George Warnock and William Branham's teachings intersected was their anti-denominational views, the teaching on the 'Seven Church Ages', and the most controversial doctrine to arise from the Latter Rain movement, the 'Manifested Sons of God'.

Timeline

Key figures in the original outpouring at North Battleford included George and Ern Hawtin, P. G. Hunt, Herrick Holt and Milford Kirkpatrick. The common ground this group of friends and co-workers had was a small school that they had started in North Battleford to train people for missions. Originally, George Hawtin had begun a school called Bethel Bible Institute in Star City SK, but had moved it in 1937 to Saskatoon to affiliate the school with the Pentecostal Assemblies of Canada (PAOC), which was finalised in 1945, ten years after the school's beginning.

However, 'disputes between Hawtin and PAOC officials led to Hawtin's resignation under pressure in 1947; another Bethel teacher, P. G. Hunt, resigned in sympathy.'[1] Together with Holt, Kirkpatrick, and Hawtin's brother Ern, they began a new school called Sharon Orphanage and Schools in nearby North Battleford.

'The Latter Rain Movement emerged at Sharon Orphanage and Schools in North Battleford, Saskatchewan, Canada, when about 70 students had gathered to fast, pray, and study the Word of God in November of 1947.'[2] As described by Ern Hawtin, 'some students were under the power of God on the floor, others were kneeling in adoration and worship before the Lord . . . Soon a visible manifestation of gifts was received when candidates were prayed over, and many as a result began to be healed, as gifts of healing were released.'[3]

As word of this outpouring began to spread, within a very short time people began to flock to North Battleford, much like the early days of the Azusa Street revival. Many people favourably compared the early days of the Latter Rain to the events in Los Angeles 40 years earlier. This was significant for many Pentecostals, as 'the movement was characterized by many reports of healings and other miraculous phenomena, in contrast to the preceding decade, which was described by Pentecostals as a time of spiritual dryness and lack of God's presence'.[4]

'Thousands from both Canada and the U.S. attended the Sharon Camp Meeting in North Battleford on July 7–18, 1948, while reports of healings and the power of God were plentiful.'[5] Invitations to speak came in from as far as Vancouver, and visitors from other cities who were affected by the meetings carried the message and power back to their home churches. As time went on, new leaders emerged who became more identified with the Latter Rain movement than the original five leaders in North Battleford.

It is worth noting again that there were reports of genuine healings during this time, and the attitudes of many of the participants appear to have been characterised by humility and a sense of 'brokenness', which are noteworthy and positive attitudes. Stanley Frodsham wrote of his dismay of the association of 'this new revival which God is so graciously sending, where so many souls are being saved, where so many lives are being transformed, where God is so graciously restoring the gifts of the Spirit, with the fanatical movement of the past 40 years'.[6] (Meaning the Pentecostals who had come before them.)

However, controversy was not far behind, as numerous teachings and practices became associated with the Latter Rain, which led to its eventual denunciation by the Assemblies of God, the Pentecostal Assemblies of Canada and other charismatic denominations in 1949.

Some of the more problematic teachings/practices that led to this decision, as articulated by Bill Jackson in *Quest for the Radical Middle: A History of the Vineyard*, included:

- *Restorationism* – they argued that God had been progressively 'restoring' to the church NT truths that had been lost for centuries. . .
- *Five-fold ministry* – the emergence of the five-fold ministry of Eph. 4:11, in particular the offices of apostle and prophet
- *Laying on of hands*. . . for the purpose of imparting spiritual gifts was an important part of their practice
- *Prophecy* – the prophetic gift was strongly emphasized, but often abused when employed to give directional (controlling) guidance to people
- *Recovery of true worship* – the restoration of David's Tabernacle as a model for true worship was stressed
- *Immortalization of the saints* – some in the movement taught that those who fully embraced the restoration would be blessed with immortality before the second coming of Christ. Although only a small minority taught this view,

the entire movement soon became identified with it in the minds of its critics

- *Unity of the church* – the church will attain an unprecedented unity in the faith before the return of Christ
- *The Manifested Sons of God* – some associated with the movement embraced the idea that the church on earth is the ongoing incarnation of Jesus Himself. . .[7]

After the decision of 1949 to denounce the Latter Rain, you would expect that the movement would fade into obscurity, but this was not the case. Many churches left their respective denominations – the 'come-outers' found more ammunition for their views – and as time went on, the preaching of William Branham and the writings of George Warnock took on an increasingly come-outer paradigm, with Branham repeatedly telling audiences that all denominations were satanic in origin, and that only those who accepted his teachings were the true church.

The charismatic renewal of the 1960s and 70s saw elements of Latter Rain teachings resurface in some sectors, and the Third Wave experienced similar inroads through the 'Kansas City Prophets' in the early 1990s. The recurring nature of some of the more controversial teachings, as expounded by Branham and built upon by Warnock, require further investigation in order to understand their contribution to the out-flux of post-charismatics today.

Another key figure in the Latter Rain was Franklin Hall, whose book *Atomic Power with God through Prayer and Fasting* highlighted the practice of fasting and prayer as a key to spiritual power. Like William Branham, Hall was fascinated by the zodiac, and also spoke of the need for the 'Manifesting of the Sons of God'. His book on fasting and prayer also contains many similar ideas to the later Word of Faith (Health and Wealth) ministries, and so we shall look at Franklin Hall's influence in that section rather than this.

At the same time, we should make a cautionary note that many of those accused of holding Latter Rain doctrines in the present, actually fall into two categories: (1) those who knowingly have embraced and are promoting these teachings, and (2) those who have absorbed elements of the teachings but would not actually follow them to their logical and historically attested conclusions. Differentiating between the two is very important, so that genuine teachers and leaders are not arbitrarily denounced as false teachers. Indeed, many people who have been affected by lingering Latter Rain concepts would be aghast when apprised of the whole picture of Latter Rain teaching.

Either way, it is important to again note the widespread influence of the Latter Rain's key figures in other controversies and movements.

William Branham

William M. Branham (1909–1965) was born in the hills of Kentucky, grew up in poverty and never received much in the way of formal education. His plain-spoken Southern demeanour was engaging, and his commitment to personal holiness, a simple lifestyle, and his 'come-outer' message resonated with a generation of believers who were disillusioned with large but seemingly compromised and lifeless churches and denominations.

Branham claimed to have had numerous angelic visitations since he was three years old, and also spoke of an angel that accompanied him onstage at his meetings, even telling him what to preach on as he went. Branham believed that the zodiac and the pyramids were on a par with Scripture, and after his untimely death in 1965, his tombstone was constructed in the shape of a pyramid, with the names of the angelic Messengers of the Church Ages engraved on it. Branham's name appears as the angelic Messenger of Revelation 3:14 to the last Church Age (more on this later).

Branham's teaching is not synonymous with Latter Rain in every detail. Some of his more fantastic teachings were not indicative of the movement in general, although much of Warnock's writing builds upon some of the foundations laid by Branham. And to be fair, some of the most damning quotes used to demonise Branham are taken out of context and trumpeted as 'proof' of his status as a false prophet.

Branham's followers have painstakingly transcribed his many sermons into text documents, which are readily available on the Internet. Unlike most written works referred to in this writing, which go by page number, the sermon texts are divided up by paragraphs – the Branhamites exegete his sermons much as evangelicals exegete Scripture. (Some Branhamites are also credited with distorting or exaggerating some of Branham's teachings, and so find themselves denounced by other Branhamites.) The paragraph numbers will be used instead of page numbers for our purposes as well.

Aside from many reports of Branham's extraordinary prophetic gifts and the healings that happened in his meetings, from reading his many sermons, I have come to recognise that Branham:

- had a profound commitment to personal holiness
- was humble and self-effacing to the point of telling his congregation that they shouldn't have named the church 'Branham Tabernacle', because he didn't want the glory for the ministry to go to anyone but Jesus
- pointed out repeatedly that membership in a church did not equate with genuine salvation
- had little time for the pomp and prestige of rich churches
- in a time when the civil rights movement was just getting underway, was very vocal about the equality of all races before God (although at the same time, he was strongly against interracial marriage)
- sought deeply to stay true to the things in the Bible that he had become convinced of; while we will not agree with many of his interpretations, he was a good example of standing firm despite all opposition

An example of an inappropriate use of a quote from Branham, which is used by many heresy-hunters as 'proof', is Branham's prediction of the End Times beginning in 1977. Obviously, the whole church did not go into apostasy at that time, as Branham predicted, which seems to lend credence to the arguments of the heresy hunters. However, to be fair, the quote needs a closer look. Branham says:

> Now, remember, 'predict', especially you listening at the tape. I don't say it will be, but predict that it will end by 1977, that the church will go completely into apostasy, and she'll be ousted out of the mouth of God.[8]

Yes, Branham used the word 'predict' but also pointedly reminded the congregation and the later tape audience, that 'I don't say it will be, but predict. . .'. It sounds as if Branham doesn't mean 'predict' in the same way we would – remember, he was an uneducated man who often used something less than the Queen's English – perhaps he was contrasting 'will be' (a certainty) with 'predict' (a possibility). It is a quick and easy cheap shot to denounce him as a false prophet based on his use of the word 'predict', but not necessarily fair or accurate.

Do not assume that my intent is to defend Branham, as many of the teachings we will examine now are very disturbing to me. But we need to rise to a higher standard than misrepresenting people in order to discredit them with the label 'false prophet/teacher'.

Teachings peculiar to Branham

As stated above, not all of Branham's teachings reflect the mainstream of the Latter Rain. For example, Branham's insistence on the gift of tongues – which is not surprising in charismatic circles generally – was 'defended' in some very imaginative ways:

> Jesus died, speaking in tongues. They said He spoke, and He spoke in another language. Sure, He did. 'He spoke in Hebrew.' He did not. That's not Hebrew writing. He spoke in a heavenly language.[9]
>
> (St. Columba) would have nothing less . . . with speaking in tongues, the baptism in the Name of the Lord Jesus, carrying out the very things they started.[10]
>
> Each one of them that come out, come out with a Pentecostal blessing. That's exactly right. Even Martin Luther spoke in tongues.[11]

Virgin Mary, being the mother of Jesus Christ . . . was among them hundred and twenty, had the baptism of the Holy Ghost, speaking in tongues and acting like a drunk woman out there, under the Spirit of God. And if the Virgin Mary had to do that in order to get into glory, how are you going to get in it anything less than that?[12]

Branham was adamantly Jesus-Only in his theology, completely rejecting the doctrine of the Trinity. He insisted on re-baptising any converts to his way of teaching. In his later years, this teaching became more and more a central part of his sermons – no matter what his subject matter was, somehow his denunciation of the Trinitarian baptismal formula would come up.

Tell him his baptism in Father, Son, and Holy Ghost is of the Devil and of the Catholic Church, watch what happens to him.[13]

Now, what name did they use after they quit using Jesus' Name? Father, Son, Holy Ghost. And there ain't no such a thing. It's a dead theology.[14]

You show me one place where one person was baptized in the name of the Father, Son, Holy Ghost, I'll raise my hands and say I'm a false prophet . . . Paul commanded them to be baptized over . . . And they had to do it before they received the Holy Ghost.[15]

So, if we are teaching baptism in the name of Father, Son, and Holy Ghost, it's false prophecy.[16]

Branham also repeatedly denounced women with 'bobbed (short) hair', who wore shorts or trousers (since these were men's clothes) and wore make-up. While this is not an uncommon viewpoint even today in some fundamentalist evangelical and Pentecostal circles, Branham's strident denunciations, coupled with his equally strong denunciation of the Roman Catholic

Church as the whore of Babylon, are very extreme in their delivery.

> Now, remember, this is on tape too. A powerful woman, great woman, she'll either be President, or it'll be a woman representing the Catholic church (which I think it is) will take over here some-day and she'll rule this country. This nation is a woman's nation. Flag was made by a woman, it's thirteen. She started out, thirteen stars, thirteen stripes, thirteen colonies. Everything's thirteen, thir-teen, thirteen, right on down. Thirteen stars on her silver dollar now. Everything's thirteen. It's number thirteen, and appears in the 13th chapter of Revelations: completely thirteen. Everything is 'woman, woman, woman, woman, woman', right on down. She's took over Hollywood. She's took over the nation. She's took over the offices. She's took over everything there is; equal rights with the man, votes with the man, cusses like a man, drinks like man, any-thing else. And the . . . just bait for the Catholic Church, for the worship of a woman.[17]
>
> Also has been an evil thing done in this country; they have per-mitted women to vote. This is a woman's nation, and she will pol-lute this nation as Eve did Eden.[18]
>
> And by voting, they'll elect the wrong man some of these days. And you did at the last election. It was the woman's votes that elected Kennedy.[19]
>
> . . . by the woman's vote, the wrong man (Kennedy), which will finally be to full control of the Catholic Church in the United States; then the bomb comes that explodes her.[20]

However, Branham's most controversial teaching was on the 'Serpent Seed', which stated that the original sin in Genesis 3 had nothing to do with the fruit of the Tree of the Knowledge of Good and Evil, but instead revolved around Eve having sex with

Satan. Branham developed a very detailed understanding that there are two lineages at work in the world: God's and Satan's. God's descendants come through Seth (including King David and Jesus), and Satan's descendants come through Cain's lineage (including Judas Iscariot and the Anti-Christ). This may explain some of Branham's apparent antagonism towards women in general.

> Now, here I've never had a preacher to agree with this yet. . . You know eating an apple, that wasn't what they did, made them realize they were naked. Certainly it wasn't. It had to come through sexually. It had to be, 'cause they realized they were naked when they taken this forbidden fruit. Ain't a woman a fruit tree? Aren't you the fruit of your mother? That was the fruit that was forbidden to be taken.[21]

> I believe, and can support it by the Bible, that it is the serpent that did it. The serpent is that missing person (link) between the chimpanzee and the man . . . he was the smartest thing there was, and the more like the human being than anything else that was on the field; closest to a human being. He was not a reptile.[22]

> He (the serpent) begin making love to Eve. And he lived with her as a husband. And she saw it was pleasant, so she went and told her husband; but she was already pregnant by Satan. And she brought forth her first son, whose name was Cain, the son of Satan.[23]

> She said, 'the Serpent beguiled me.' Do you know what 'beguile' means? Means 'defiled'. The devil never gave her an apple.[24]

> And then when Cain saw his holy-roller brother had been accepted before God, and signs and wonders was being taken place down there, he got jealous of him . . . He killed his brother. He was a murderer. Could you call God a murderer? Adam was God's son, and that jealousy and envy and everything could not come out of

that pure stream. It had to come through another place. And it came through Satan, who was a murderer to begin with.[25]

They (Cain's descendants) were smart, educated, intelligent people. Is that right? They were builders, inventors, scientists: Not through the seed of the righteous, but through the seed of Satan, the serpent . . . And they were scoffers at the seed of the woman: Noah, the righteous.[26]

What was the seed of the serpent? Adultery. You follow it? Adultery with Eve.[27]

Esau never harmed nobody, and Esau was of the devil. But Jacob, out of the same womb, was of God: the seed of the devil, the seed of the woman.[28]

The serpent was twice as smart. His seed has always been twice as smart . . . Your pastor that gone down and got a lot of intellectual knowledge, and he stands up . . . Where does the seed of the serpent staying at? In the smart intelligent places like that: smart, shrewd scholars, that's where he is at.[29]

Branham's influence on the Latter Rain

While Branham's Serpent Seed teaching was not widely accepted, some of his venomous attacks on the Roman Catholic Church were. Even to this day, you will encounter charismatics who revile Catholics on principle. And Branham's disdain for pastors and church leaders with religious education has too often been gladly perpetuated by charismatics everywhere.

Some of the areas where Branham's teachings have affected the Latter Rain, and continue to affect charismatic churches to this day, include his view of the corruptibility of denominational structures. Today, the emerging church has proponents within it that go so far as to state that hierarchical church structures are anti-biblical, and often cite the idea that the Reformation didn't go far enough, because instead of one Pope, now we have many.

Branham, of course, was far more extreme in his diatribes against denominations, but for those who don't investigate his teachings thoroughly, his ideas can initially seem compatible with today's house/simple church proponents. However, on further investigation, Branham's approach goes quite a bit further.

> They (Methodists) organized it, made an organization out of it, and God said, 'I hate the thing'. . .[30]

> Look what Billy Graham's had across the country. Oh, sure, a big regime, hired evangelists, paid song leaders.[31]

> As soon as a church goes into a denomination, it's dead. It never rises again . . . Martin Luther was all right, but when he organized, what did he do? Methodist was all right, when he organized, what did he do? Pentecost was all right, but when you organized it, what did you do? You hybrid it and bred it into the Nicolaitane Catholic church. Exactly what you done. Took up her form of baptism, took up her ways and actions, and the Bible said, 'You are a daughter to a whore, a harlot: a daughter of harlot.[32]

> If any man will hear My voice and open the door. . . Not 'if any church, if any organization' – No, sir. He don't deal with them; they're dead and gone to begin with. He hates it. He always hated it. He said He hated it. He hates it yet tonight . . . the messengers to the church and the message to every church age condemned denominationism.[33]

> And there is never one time that God ever organized His church. The mother of organized churches is the Roman Catholic hierarchy . . . And as soon as the revival breaks in any Protestant group, they go right back and do the same thing. And the Bible said she was a whore.[34]

> We do not believe in denominations, because we find it in the

Bible that denominations was never ordained of God. It was ordained of the devil. And proved it by the Bible.[35]

Branham's diatribes against denominationalism were second only to his attacks on Trinitarian baptism. When he came to one of his favourite topics – the Seven Church Ages – the themes of anti-Catholicism, baptism in the name of Jesus only, and his strong distaste for denominations came up in every sermon, almost in cyclical fashion.

Over the course of eight nights, as Branham preached an introduction to the book of Revelation, followed by one night each on the Seven Church Ages, these themes came up constantly.

Branham's teaching on the Seven Church Ages forms the backdrop against which George Warnock developed and wrote his seminal work, *The Feast of Tabernacles*, considered the manual or textbook on the Latter Rain's most well-known aberrant teaching, the 'Manifested Sons of God' (MSOG). Branham includes the MSOG teaching at various times, but it is Warnock who more fully develops it.

The Seven Church Ages is a teaching that Branham modelled on the letters to the seven churches in Revelation 1–3. He taught that each church represented a different church age, and that the angel of each church was an anointed apostolic messenger to that church age, each messenger having a unique message from God for that church age, which had to be obeyed.

The Seven Church Ages were divided as follows:

1. 53–70 AD – Ephesus; messenger was St Paul; fairly short age due to church's unbelief

2. 70–312 AD – Smyrna; messenger was Irenaeus, who believed God more than anyone else
3. 312–606 AD – Pergamos; messenger was Martin, while the Babylonian religion infiltrated the church through the Council of Nicea
4. 606–1520 AD – Thyatira; messenger was Columba, while the church blasphemed the name of God through the papacy
5. 1520–1750 AD – Sardis; messenger was Martin Luther, who as a tongues-speaker, restored the truth of justification by faith to the church
6. 1750–1906 AD – Philadelphia; messenger was John Wesley, who restored the truth of entire sanctification and brotherly love
7. 1906 AD to date – Laodicea; messenger is William Branham, who comes as a latter day Elijah to turn the hearts of the children (church) back to the (Pentecostal) fathers

In a vision that Branham spoke of during his sermon on the Church Age of Pergamos, he places himself in the role of the seventh and final angelic messenger to the Laodicean Church Age:

> (The angel) said, 'You can't see Him now,' but said, 'soon He will come. We're waiting for Him. But when He comes, He will come to you first. And you'll be judged according to the Gospel you preaching, and we will be your subjects. . .'
> I said, 'What about Saint Paul?'
> Said, 'He'll be responsible for his age.'
> 'Well,' I said, 'I preached the same Gospel he did.'
> And millions of voices raised, said 'We are resting upon that.' See? There you are, 'resting'.

So the angel of God, the messenger to the church is responsible if he preaches not the Word.[36]

Part of Branham's theology regarding the Laodicean Church Age includes the MSOG teaching. These Sons would be revealed during this last church age. To introduce this doctrine, Branham taught his 'three Bibles' view:

As I've often made this remark and said God made three Bibles. The first one, He put it in the sky, the zodiac . . . He made the next one in the pyramid, back in the days of Enoch, when they made the pyramids . . . And the stone on the capstone never was found . . . Why? The Capstone was rejected; Christ, the Headstone (see?) was rejected . . . Now, and in the Bible, we're living in the last days, the top of the pyramid, the crossed fishes of the cancer age in the zodiac, in the time of the coming of Leo the lion, in the capping Stone, and in the days of the manifestation of the sons of God in the Bible. See?[37]

In describing these Sons of God, Branham says:

You give me this spotless church tonight, this group of people, perfectly, perfectly in the promise of God with the Holy Ghost, walking in the Spirit, I'll challenge any disease, or any affliction . . . and all of the unbelievers that there is, to bring any sickness of affliction in this door, and they'll walk out perfectly whole. Yes, sir. God gave the promise; only sin of unbelief can keep it away.[38]

Before we hand the baton to George Warnock to develop the MSOG teaching more fully, we should note that Branham had an interesting way of dealing with the critics of his teachings, particularly those who opposed his Serpent Seed and MSOG theories.

Many current Pentecostals and charismatics would deny that the demonstration of the Spirit's presence in the use of spiritual gifts is given by God as a validation of theology. These charismatic gifts – *charismata* means 'grace gifts' or literally 'grace-lets' – are given solely based on God's grace towards us, not as rewards for spiritual maturity or to validate the messenger, only the Message.

Branham, however, takes the opposite approach:

> A lot of them say . . . 'I believe Brother Branham's a prophet, but let me tell you something. As long as the Spirit is on him, and he's discerning, he's the Lord's servant. But his teaching is rotten. It's no good.' Whoever heard of such tommyrot? It's either of God or it isn't of God. That's right. It's either all God or none God. That's the way it is.[39]

This level of presumptive unaccountability is also a precursor to some of the abuses in authoritarian control that we will see occur through the Shepherding movement. Branham's teachings have influenced the Word of Faith movement, the Shepherding movement, and the current prophetic movement. For an uneducated Kentuckian, his influence has been far-reaching indeed.

George Warnock

George Warnock wrote many articles and books, several of which would be considered classics for those in the Latter Rain movement. His most influential works were probably *The Feast of Tabernacles*, which outlined his most controversial teaching: 'The Manifested Sons of God' (MSOG), and *From Tent to Temple*, which dealt with the 'Tabernacle of David', another teaching that has survived to this day through the charismatic movement.

For the purposes of tracing the theological development of the charismatic movement, we will focus on these two teachings that are the legacy of George Warnock and the Latter Rain.

The Feast of Tabernacles

George Warnock wrote his influential work on the Feast of Tabernacles in 1951, although the copy which I was able to read includes a new foreword from Warnock, dated 1980. He builds upon the same foundations that Branham taught regarding the Seven Church Ages, believing that we are in the Laodicean Age.

Warnock was much more eloquent than Branham, and also much more linear in his presentation of his doctrines of the MSOG. Like Branham, Warnock was dismissive of denominations and higher theological education:

> When Jesus declared so emphatically 'I am the Truth', He there and then completely demolished the idea that Truth has anything in common with creeds and doctrines and theories about God and spiritual things . . . (truth) will find little acceptance at the hands of the learned or the ecclesiastical.[40]

At the same time, Warnock invests a great deal of time and energy in the early part of his book in setting a historical and biblical background for his teaching on the MSOG, in order to validate his teachings as being well-reasoned and biblically logical.

Warnock's main appeal in defence of the MSOG doctrine is to the Feast of Tabernacles in the Old Testament, although his hermeneutical approach was almost completely allegorical, as we shall see. 'The thesis of Warnock's book was that although the Feast of Passover was fulfilled in the death of Christ and although the Feast of Pentecost had had its fulfilment in the outpouring of the Holy Spirit on the Day of Pentecost, the third of Israel's great feasts, the Feast of Tabernacles, is yet to be fulfilled.'[41] Many of Warnock's insights into the fulfilment of this Feast came through direct prophetic revelations.

It is from Warnock that the phrase 'the natural speaks of the supernatural' gained prominence, as it formed part of his rationale for using Old Testament feast typology to explain the meaning of Tabernacles. Warnock also claimed that applying Old Testament scriptures in unorthodox ways to justify his teachings was just following the example of the New Testament apostles.

It is important, therefore, that we should always observe that which is first, and natural, and from the natural learn to discern in what way it typifies the spiritual.[42]

Then we care not in the least if orthodox theology forbids us to take Old Testament type and prophecy and apply them to the Church. The Apostles have already done so under the anointing of the Holy Spirit, and that is sufficient for men who believe in the verbal inspiration of the Holy Scriptures.[43]

And if you want to know what Paul meant by 'rightly dividing the Word of truth', all one has to do is to examine his own epistles and see how he applied the Old Testament. Over and over and over again he takes an Old Testament scripture completely out of its 'context' as men would say, and applies it to some glorious Church truth which he is expounding.[44]

By claiming the 'right' to apply OT scriptures in whatever manner was consistent with his own prophetic insights, Warnock seems to have considered his writings on a par with Scripture. Of those who questioned his teachings, Warnock writes: 'These things may sound fantastic to many Christians; but if so it is only because God's people in this modern age are so earthly-minded that they cannot appreciate nor understand the realities of the Spirit.'[45]

Like Branham, Warnock viewed denominations as deceived and carnal, but he blamed this on lack of unity between denominations and the sin of unbelief. Those who refused to accept his teachings were likened to the children of Israel who refused to enter Canaan and wandered 40 years in the wilderness due to their unbelief. Warnock applies this metaphor directly to the Pentecostal movement.

> The early generation of Spirit-filled people at the turn of the century took their journey from the blighting wilderness of denominationalism and encamped at their Kadesh-Barnea on the very doorstep of Canaan – but they too failed to enter in because of unbelief.[46]

As Warnock progresses in his development of the MSOG and the Feast of Tabernacles, this motif of 'not possessing the land' – or turning away because of unbelief – comes up repeatedly as a warning to embrace the Latter Rain teachings. Warnock also agrees with Branham that God is progressively restoring 'lost truths' to the church.

> And so from Reformation days and until now, God has graciously been restoring lost Truth; and the Reformation is by no means finished yet.[47]

Warnock takes John Wesley's theology of entire sanctification to a completely new level. Where Wesley prayed for a second work of grace, the baptism of the Holy Spirit, to enable him to live a life freed from sin's dominion – but still allowing for occasional slips and minor mistakes – Warnock taught that all sin could be eradicated in this life.

> God is hastening the day and hour of Christian perfection . . . God will hear that prayer of sincerity and reveal the channel and means by which perfection shall be attained. *But prayer and repentance in themselves are not the means by which the saints are to be perfected.*[48] (*emphasis added*)
>
> When we attain to this victory, there will be no need to formulate weak excuses why the victorious Christian can again fall into sin and suffer defeat – for this place in Christ knows no defeat . . . The promise, therefore, is held out to us at the ends of the ages, *as to no other people in any past dispensation.*[49] (*emphasis added*)

Warnock also added a second component to entire sanctification: that unlimited spiritual power would be given to the 'overcomers' who turned their backs on dead denominations and embraced what God was doing through the Latter Rain movement.

> What then? Are there no limitations to the measure of power which the saints may appropriate? Yes, indeed, but they are limitations that they themselves erect in unbelief.[50]
>
> When the power and glory of the Feast of Tabernacles begins to dawn upon the Church, God's people are going to be clothed upon with such power and authority that the very nations themselves will have to bow in submission.[51]
>
> But those who will reach out and appropriate this new life, and are initiated into this 'secret' of which we have been speaking –

theirs shall be the joy and delight of exploring the heavenlies long before they get there.[52]

Warnock stresses that the need for this band of overcomers who will be initiated into this secret is not just for the sake of the rest of the denominations left on earth during the Great Tribulation (punishment for not entering the land with the MSOG); the necessity of these overcomers (MSOG) is also to usher in the Second Coming of Jesus, who cannot return until the MSOG deal with Satan, the flesh and the denominational Babylon.

> And what is more, Christ is going to remain right where He is at God's right hand until there shall arise a group of overcomers who shall conquer over all God's enemies . . . There must arise a group of overcomers who shall conquer and become absolutely victorious over all the opposing forces of the world, the flesh, and the Devil – before this dispensation draws to a close.[53]
>
> God has placed His only Begotten at His own right hand in the heavenlies, until all his enemies have been placed under His feet . . . There He shall remain, in obedience to the Word of the Father, until there ariseth a people who shall go in and possess their heritage in the Spirit, and conquer over all opposing forces of World, Flesh, and Devil.[54]

The task of getting the bride ready for Jesus is an enormous one, according to Warnock, as there is a need for complete unity in the body of Christ before this can happen. Within our current denominational divisions, there is little hope, but the restoration of the offices of apostle and prophet – which had been 'lost' or 'stolen' by previous generations due to their unbelief – would give a divinely appointed governmental structure for this unity to take place. Of course, this would require people to recognise the true apostles and submit to their authority.

> Will they bring this unity to pass? To doubt it is to doubt God's Word. It is not a case of rejecting man, because of his faults and failures, but to reject the God-ordained ministry is to reject God who gave him. Many would much rather prefer to perfect themselves through prayer, fasting, reading the Word, and so forth. These have their place . . . but in themselves they will not produce this perfection. God has ordained ministries in the Body by which this perfection shall come to pass. To refuse the ministries, then is to say to Christ: 'I don't need your Ascension Gifts. I prefer to be perfected some other way.'[55]

As *The Feast of Tabernacles* moves towards its final chapters, Warnock begins to delineate more of the details of how the MSOG will bring about this unity and achieve sinless perfection and immeasurable spiritual power and authority.

Warnock interprets the Revelation 12 passage a little differently from most theologians (but remember, Warnock discounts all theologians because they don't recognise his prophetic revelation). Most interpreters see this passage as a description of Jesus being the male offspring who would 'rule the nations with an iron rod' (a reference to Psalm 2), but Warnock contends that this refers to a group of Christians in the last days who would be the MSOG that Romans 8:19 refers to: 'For the earnest expectation of the creature waiteth for the manifestation of the sons of God' (KJV).

For Warnock, the woman in Revelation 12 refers to the church, which will be enduring the Tribulation. The male son – called the 'Man-child' in most Latter Rain circles, but also referred to as the 'Moses-Elijah Company', as well as 'Joel's Army' – is seen as a company of overcoming Sons of God, who will achieve sinless perfection, have authority over nations, overthrow Satan and his demonic hordes in the heavens, give comfort to the persecuted church during the Tribulation, and bring about the perfecting of the bride that Jesus is returning for.

> By this time this man-child company, this group of overcomers brought forth by the travail of the Church, is in a place of power and authority in the 'heavenliest', and the church that brought forth the man-child through much pain and spiritual travail, is left in the earth.[56]
>
> It is this wrestling with the spiritual hosts of wickedness in 'the heavenlies' that shall cause . . . Satan and his hosts to relinquish their kingdom into the hands of the Sons of God . . . And then into the very heavenlies shall they ascend, first of all in the Spirit, to take possession of the kingdom left vacant by the casting out of Satan, and his evil hosts. Then shall they be in a position to administer peace and life and blessing to a Church and a world that are in bondage and under oppression.[57]
>
> But the Dragon, having lost his kingdom, roams through the earth in great wrath, tormenting men, and attempting to persecute the Church which was responsible for bringing forth the overcoming man-child.[58]
>
> The Great Tribulation itself is going to be cut short because of the Sons of God . . . so the Sons of God, through the exercise of their royal priesthood, shall actually shorten the Great Tribulation. Jesus has declared that they would.[59]

The final section of Warnock's development of the MSOG as the fulfilment of the Feast of Tabernacles has to do with the

entire body of Christ, out of which the MSOG are only a part –
albeit an elite part.

Warnock proposed that since Jesus is considered the Head,
and Christians are the body of Christ, then it only stands to reason that we complete Christ, and that without the body, the
Head is only half a body (this teaching is sometimes referred to
as the 'Corporate Christ' doctrine).

> Christ the Head, therefore, is not complete without Christ the
> Body . . . And the ages to come are going to reveal, what is now
> revealed by the Spirit to those whose understandings have been
> quickened, that Christ is the Body – the whole Body, and not just
> the Head.[60]
>
> The Son of Man in heaven is not complete without the fullness
> of the Son of Man on earth, even the Body.[61]

While most Christians would agree that we are the body of
Christ in that we carry out his mission in the world, Warnock
takes it one step further, to suggest that we *are* Christ in a very
real sense, and not merely in a representational sense. This is
seen as a privilege for only a select few to understand and accept,
which may mean that they are the potential MSOG.

> But a great secret in God's counsels was this: Christ was to appear
> twice, first in Incarnation, and secondly at the ends of the ages . . .
> Christ's first appearing was in the Head only, in one Man. Hence
> Elijah appeared in one man, even John the Baptist – for his spirit
> and power rested upon him. Now Christ will appear in His Church
> the Body. Hence the Moses-Elijah company, the fullness of Christ
> in many.[62]
>
> There shall come a day . . . when every eye shall see Him; when
> the same Jesus that was taken up into heaven, shall come in like

manner as they saw Him go. But first there is the Appearing of Christ in the midst of His people by the Spirit, to establish the Kingdom of God within, and that is the hope of the Church.[63]

Warnock concludes the writing of *The Feast of Tabernacles* with great promises for those who will accept his teachings, warnings to those who oppose or question his teachings, and exhortations to Christians to seek to become one of the MSOG, although aside from warnings about denominations and 'worldliness' in general, there is not much provided beyond the tantalising prospect of being one of these all-powerful overcomers.

To those who embrace the MSOG teachings found in *The Feast of Tabernacles*, Warnock lists the benefits in a long passage which simultaneously belittles his critics:

- A realm of the Spirit to such an extent that you live there constantly.
- The 'mind of Christ' in any degree of fullness so that you can actually think His thoughts, and say His words, and perform His works, and live His very own life.
- Enjoy real Divine health or Divine life to such an extent that your days will be lengthened excessively, without pain or feebleness or the abatement of your natural faculties.
- To be so positively free from the sin nature that 'sin hath no more dominion' over you.
- To go out to the nations speaking their language, with their accent, and understanding exactly what you say, and what they say.
- Be caught away in the Spirit like Philip or Elijah in this day of modern travel.
- Ascend up in the Spirit into 'the heavenlies' and literally

topple Satan from his throne, and enter into the realm of power and authority 'in the heavenlies in Christ Jesus'.[64]

To those who question or reject Warnock's teachings, he warns them: 'When the people of God ridicule these great truths concerning the rebuilding of God's holy Temple, and the perfection of the saints into one, vital, united Body – such ridicule is not against the saints, but it is against God Himself.'[65]

These teachings of the Latter Rain continue to surface again and again in the charismatic movement. Whether called Kingdom Now, Dominion Theology, Joel's Army, the Man-child or Moses-Elijah Company, the Joshua and Caleb Generation, or the original moniker of the MSOG, this is a teaching that just will not fade into obscurity. In a manner which sounds remarkably like many charismatic conferences today, Warnock sums up his admonitions to the readers of *The Feast of Tabernacles* with a rallying call:

> The whole question resolves itself into this: Are we going to remain in the condition of those who have been saved and baptized with the Holy Spirit? Or are we going to arise from the dusty sands of this great and terrible wilderness and follow our Joshua across the Jordan into real, triumphant, overcoming power in the Spirit of God?
>
> Thank God there ariseth a new generation that has caught the vision. A few Calebs and Joshuas have survived the blight and the dearth of the wilderness, and are leading the saints in the power of the Spirit into realms of glorious victory.[66]

The Tabernacle of David

The other influential teaching that Warnock contributed was the 'Tabernacle of David', in his book *From Tent to Temple*.

Central to Warnock's teaching, which was very much a part of the Latter Rain in general, was the idea that true, biblical worship needed to follow the pattern of Davidic worship as found in the Tabernacle of David.

The Old Testament scripture that is often heard is Psalm 22:3: 'Yet you are enthroned as the Holy One; you are the praise of Israel.' If this doesn't sound familiar, it's because that was the NIV rendering.

The preferred rendering – really, the necessary rendering in order to use this verse as a foundation for the Tabernacle of David – is the King James or New American Standard, which translates part of this verse as 'thou that inhabitest the praises of Israel' or 'You who are enthroned upon the praises of Israel'; this is one of the foundational verses for Davidic worship – that God is actively seeking a place where his glory can dwell permanently, as it did in the Tabernacle of David.

It is important to recognise that this phrase is found in the middle of the famous 'my God, my God, why have you forsaken me?' passage, which Jesus quoted from the cross. The context of the verse is not a prescriptive passage on how worship should be done in order to experience God's presence; it's a prophetic lament at God's seeming distance from David, and later, Jesus Christ.

The tabernacle that Moses had made, as per God's instructions, was seen as being surpassed in importance by David's tabernacle: 'It was a center of worship which stood in sharp contrast to the solemn worship of Moses' tabernacle. Instead of the sacrifices of animals, the sacrifices offered at David's tabernacle were the sacrifices of praise, joy and thanksgiving.'[67]

Warnock writes: 'We do not know how long the cloud of

glory rested on the Tabernacle. But we have good reason to believe that it gradually faded away. . .'[68] In common Latter Rain manner, the assumption is that the current church (in all of its denominational forms) had grown cold and lifeless, and that in order for God to return with his manifest presence, the church had to purify itself and make itself ready to be a people worthy of receiving that presence.

> There is a Hannah in the world today. She cries out in the distress of her spirit for a son . . . a 'manchild' . . . a people who will come forth in the full image and likeness of Christ out of a dying religious order, and who will be God's oracle to a confused Church. . .'[69]

Bill Jackson sums up this expectation by noting, 'He (God) is looking for a resting-place and He will one day find it in a people that finally get serious about the things of God.'[70]

Holiness was a key, alongside praise, to see the church become the kind of gathering that God would be pleased to inhabit. This emphasis on holiness (and who wouldn't be desirous of seeing more holiness in the church?) often ended up in a restrictive legalism, but in the beginning stages of the Latter Rain, it was a genuine passion for serving God in the hearts of broken and repentant people.

The assumption of the Tabernacle of David teaching is that there was a set pattern of worship that had to be followed, or the presence of God would not come and dwell. The pattern included: Levites (worship leaders) who were set apart, highly skilled, and who alone could carry the ark of God's presence, joyful praise and celebration, and finances released to pay the Levites for their non-stop praise.

While many Tabernacle of David proponents argue that the

Davidic worship of praise replaced the sacrifices of the Jewish faith – saying that the 'sacrifice of praise' was the new sacrifice – the Bible does not support this idea. Some proponents suggest that the sacrifices prescribed in the Pentateuch stopped once the ark of God's presence was brought into David's tabernacle – and that any true revival in the Old Testament record included a rejection of the Mosaic system and return to the Davidic.

The wording 'sacrifice of praise' is problematic in that most translations render it as 'giving thanks'; the idea of the sacrifice of praise being a model for New Testament worship only works if you prefer one (English) translation over another. In fact, the 'sacrifice of praise' in the Psalms (and Jeremiah) is dependent on the King James Version of the Bible. Where the phrase shows up in the New Testament is Hebrews 13:15, where it is found in the context of confessing Jesus' name, doing good and sharing with others.

As was seen in their reactions to others who questioned the doctrines in the Latter Rain, Warnock warned his critics that they were comparable to Uzzah, whom God struck dead for steadying the ark of the covenant when it was in danger of falling off the cart.

> The 'new cart' is man's device to keep the move of the Spirit steady – free from error, free from false doctrines – and to keep the ark of His presence and glory from going on the rocks . . . It is really man's attempt to keep things under control, to keep the revival from falling apart, to keep the doctrines pure, to keep the people from getting scattered, but in the long run it hinders what God is doing, and brings it to a halt.[71]

The true mark of spiritual leadership in the Davidic tabernacle was determined by 'the anointing' of the leader, which Warnock placed at odds with those concerned with doctrine: 'For we need no other credentials for ministry in the House of God, apart from the Anointing.'[72] Warnock used 'anointing' as his justification of taking Old Testament passages out of context in order to support his teachings, citing the example of the apostle Paul. Warnock's assumption was that under the 'anointing', his words were as authoritative as those of the New Testament writers.

Warnock outlines the need for the church to recognise the authority of the new apostles and prophets, so that their directives can be implemented. As with the writing of the Feast of Tabernacles, Warnock's conclusion is that the Davidic worship – which will provide a place for God to inhabit the praises of his people – will lead to the 'corporate Christ' being manifested: 'And as we submit to the law of the seed, and the law of the egg, and the law of the cocoon, we shall see – and those about shall see – the living Christ walking once again in the midst of men, in the corporate Body of Christ in the earth.'[73]

Warnock's writings, particularly *The Feast of Tabernacles*, have been and continue to be very influential in numerous charismatic circles; the Tabernacle of David teaching is part of the approach to Scripture that surfaced repeatedly in the charismatic renewal of the 1960s and 1970s, and continues to inform many expressions of Spirit-filled churches to this day.

The prophetic movement

There are a lot of personalities and ministries which could be discussed at this point. Many would immediately think of Rick

Joyner's Morningstar Ministries; others would think of the Kansas City Prophets (Bob Jones, Paul Cain, John Paul Jackson) or perhaps Mike Bickle (the pastor of the church where the prophets were situated in Kansas City) and Michael Sullivant.

But once you start trying to chase down all the recognised prophetic voices today, where do you stop? People like Graham Cooke, John Sandford, Andrew Strom, Todd Bentley, Wes and Stacey Campbell, Cindy Jacobs – the list would be both exhaustive and exhausting.

Numerous heresy-hunting books and websites label anyone who believes in prophetic ministry as being automatically Latter Rain. Oft-times, this is merely a cheap, easy way of discrediting people or organisations. Guilt by association is the main tactic that they employ, and generally, it's a sleazy methodology.

For example, Paul Cain (one of the Kansas City Prophets) is often castigated for saying that William Branham was a great prophet. This is offered as proof that Paul Cain is also a false prophet. However, Paul has made it very clear that he wasn't referring to Branham's teachings or doctrine, only recognising a genuine prophetic gift. That doesn't mean Paul Cain is off the hook, however, if he is actually teaching the same things that Branham and the Latter Rain teaches. But the guilt by association tactic is as prone to abuse as anything else, and we should never base our conclusions solely on who people currently or formerly were associated with.

We have spent a disproportionate amount of time on the teachings of the Latter Rain, compared to the historical overviews that other sections will employ. But the teachings of the Latter Rain have so influenced the charismatic renewal (in some areas, not all), the Word of Faith movement and the prophetic movement, and provided some of the eschatological foundation for the Shepherding movement, that I felt it necessary to invest time in exploring the Latter Rain's more controversial teachings.

It is up to all of us, as discerning people, to evaluate what we're being taught by others. The Berean Christians that everyone points to (Acts 17:11) did two things (often we only focus on one of them):

1. They listened with great eagerness. This means that they were open to the possibility of expanding their theological understanding, and had a teachable spirit. We would do well to stay teachable, and not confuse discernment with a critical, nit-picking attitude.
2. They searched the Scriptures, to be sure that what Paul was teaching lined up with Scripture. They had teachable attitudes, but that didn't mean that they were gullible and naively swallowed whatever they heard. They were willing to expand their understanding, but not to go beyond the boundaries of Scripture.

In the prophetic movement, like any movement, there is a range of theological positions on various non-essentials, as well as a range of maturity. Just because someone says in a sermon 'God is raising up the emerging generations' doesn't mean that they are preaching MSOG – although you might want to ask them to clarify what they meant. Ask, don't attack.

There is an old saying: 'bring it into the light.' The reason for spending so much time on the teachings of the Latter Rain is simply to give a grid for recognising where some current charismatic teachings and practices, which have been accepted as normative, actually come from.

The Kansas City Prophets (KCP) are probably the most well-known centre of controversy when it comes to modern examples of Latter Rain teaching – at least, so their critics would like us to believe. To be accurate, the phrase 'Kansas City Prophets' was not a title they gave themselves; it was bestowed on them by others, and they were stuck with it. But because of their notoriety, and continued influence, we will briefly look at them.

As Latter Rain teachings became known by other labels – Dominion, Restoration, Kingdom Now, etc. – all of these terms were in the accusations against the KCP. As is often the case, there was a genuine spiritual gifting in operation, but that doesn't automatically translate into dependable teaching and doctrine. A common mistake that many people make – charismatic and non-charismatic alike – is to assume that if God blesses the ministry of a person, group, or church, it's tantamount to putting a stamp of approval on their theology.

The Old Testament has stories of Balaam's donkey talking to him (and Balaam seeming to not be taken aback by this), Balaam himself unable to prophesy curses as he had been hired to do because God spoke blessing through him, and even King Saul prophesying, but in Saul's case it was a sign of judgment against him. Just because spiritual gifts are in evidence, we should not assume that God is therefore endorsing all of the beliefs of the person, group or church.

Some of the prophecies that became regular fare through the KCP had to do with the 'nameless and faceless army' that God was going to raise up. This became a staple in prophetic conferences, and was widely repeated through many charismatic churches and denominations.

Bill Jackson notes: 'It is interesting that even as the vision was shared that God wasn't going to use superstars any more, the entire restorationist premise was built on God raising up end-time apostles and prophets.'[74]

One of the repeated prophecies that made the rounds had to do with the 'emerging generations', which were referred to as the Joshua and Caleb generation, among other names. The premise was that the previous generation of believers (the Baby Boomers) had failed to enter the land, so God was going to use their children (Generation X) instead. This, of course, is exactly the same idea that the Latter Rain had proposed back in the late 1940s.

Many people believe that the term 'generation' in the Bible usually refers to a span of 40 years. This is significant because the Latter Rain considered itself the 'anointed generation', and made much of the fact that their movement was coming 40 years after the Pentecostal movement first began. Branham and others had labelled the Pentecostals the failed generation, giving rise to elitism among the 'next generation' in the late 1940s and 1950s. The groundswell of the prophecies of the 'nameless and faceless' generation started roughly 40 years after the Latter Rain, in the late 1980s and early 1990s.

The KCP – Paul Cain, Bob Jones, and John Paul Jackson – as well as the pastor of the Kansas City Fellowship (KCF), Mike Bickle, became the centre of more controversy when Ernie Gruen, another charismatic pastor in Kansas City, published his 233-page report, *Documentation of the Aberrant Practices and Teachings of Kansas City Fellowship (Grace Ministries)*. In this report, Gruen and his staff documented many of KCF's teachings, and the verdict from Gruen et al. was 'heresy from false prophets'.

Numerous Christian leaders were involved trying to sort things out, when John Wimber of the Association of Vineyard Churches stepped in and offered to bring KCF into the Vineyard family in 1990, and provide some instruction and account-ability for the church and the prophets. Gruen withdrew many of his charges later that year, and was subsequently removed from ministry due to an immoral relationship. To his credit, Mike Bickle was aware of Gruen's immorality, but never used this knowledge to defend KCF from Gruen's charges.

The Vineyard publicly dealt with several issues arising out of KCF's ministry, most notably 'allowing prophetic people to teach who were not gifted in teaching, and the attempts by some of the prophets to establish doctrine based on prophecy'.[75] This was also a practice in the Latter Rain movement, which does not mean that the KCP came straight from the Latter Rain, but that their views had been influenced by it.

The Vineyard, as a movement, had been influenced by the KCP for a couple of years prior to them joining the Vineyard officially in May 1990, but it was almost exactly a year later that they began to distance themselves from the prophetic move-ment, while still adopting a greater value for prophetic ministry in general. The Vineyard's methodology had always been to equip the saints to do the ministry, and the 'end times army' motif ran against that. 'Ministry was in the hands of the new breed and dread champions. John (Wimber) had always taught us that everyone gets to play – we just have to play nice and share our toys. Dread champions we were not.'[76]

Tom Stipe is a former Vineyard pastor who left the movement

at the same time as the Vineyard was beginning to distance itself from the KCP, although his comments in the introduction to Hank Hannegraaf's 'Counterfeit Revival' suggest otherwise.

Stipe had some specific allegations that are hard to prove – you just have to take his word for it. However, some of the things he listed sounded very familiar:

- People moving to new places/churches at prophetic direction that turned out to be wrong – they blamed God
- Teenagers who were promised stardom (mostly musicians who would 'go to the nations') but then nothing happened
- People in local churches who had been promised special ministry becoming angry that their pastors didn't recognise and release them into their 'new anointing'
- Pastors and leaders seemingly afraid to lead strongly, if by doing so they weren't doing what the prophets had instructed

By 1995, the Vineyard had come to a much stronger conclusion regarding the KCP – while recognising and embracing prophetic ministry in general, there was a consensus that the pendulum had swung too far in one direction, and needed to come back into balance. 'At the Pastors Conference in the Vineyard's new facility in Anaheim Hills in 1995, Wimber told the movement that he regretted leading the Vineyard into the prophetic era, saying that it did, indeed, get us off track.'[77]

Mike Bickle voluntarily removed his church from the Vineyard movement in 1996, citing a need to be faithful to the prophetic themes that had characterised his church in its earlier days, and which he felt were being stifled in the Vineyard.

Of the three most well-known prophets, Bob Jones was

removed from ministry for sexual sin in 1991. Bob has since returned to ministry, although the Vineyard does not permit him to minister in their churches. John Paul Jackson started Streams Ministries in New Hampshire, where he continues to teach on the dread champions that will be raised up, and offers dream interpretations for visitors to his website. Paul Cain was recently exposed by prophetic colleagues Rick Joyner (Morningstar Ministries) and Jack Deere for an unrepentant addiction to alcoholism and homosexuality. Paul has since confessed publicly and is in a process of restoration that at the time of writing is still unconcluded.

Some would like to point their fingers at Jones' and Cain's sin, and use that as proof that they were false prophets, or that all prophetic ministry is therefore bogus, but this would be an unfair conclusion which would contradict Scripture. King David's adultery would therefore be in the same category, as would Samson's many dalliances, and Gideon – the great warrior who defeated an army of thousands with only three hundred men – who made a golden ephod that caused the people of Israel to 'prostitute themselves by worshipping, and it became a snare to Gideon and his family' (Judges 8:27).

Just as we can't claim God is validating our theology when we see the Holy Spirit clearly at work, neither can we reject the Spirit's genuine work because of flawed vessels.

Bill Jackson, in *The Quest for the Radical Middle*, offers the following as a way of sorting through prophetic ministry, which would also serve as a good filter for Latter Rain emphases:

> We should embrace the gifts and outpouring of the Holy Spirit but refrain from any kind of apocalyptic exegesis and fervor. . .

We need not to get so caught up in a particular interpretation that we lose sight of the fact that we could be wrong.

We should never try to establish doctrine from prophecy. Doctrine is derived from the exegesis of Scripture. . .

We should beware of any kind of elitist attitude in connection with prophetic ministry. . .

We need to affirm that our pastoral call is to equip the saints for the work of ministry. . . not needing to wait either for the anointed apostle or prophets or for the coming revival. . .

We need to be careful about our motives in pursuing prophecy . . . we are to encourage prophecy in the local church, let us beware of fostering a climate that is no different than why people pursue astrologers. . .[78]

Post-charismatic

While many people who call themselves post-charismatic are not aware of all the teachings of the Latter Rain movement, they are often reacting to excesses and abuses that have resulted from being in church settings where the Latter Rain has informed both belief and practice.

Prophetic abuses

I have a friend who is clearly of East Indian descent. His great-grandparents emigrated to Canada in the late 1800s, making him a fourth generation Canadian. However, it became a standing joke with those of us who knew him about the kind of prophecies that were regularly spoken over him by visiting ministers.

The prophetic words usually sounded something like this:

'God is going to send you to the city of your grandfathers, to the land of your ancestors, and you will speak before kings and the nation. . . etc.'

My friend would turn to us and, with a raised eyebrow and a quizzical look, wonder aloud, 'Vancouver?'

Unfortunately, these well-intentioned people were prophesying mostly out of their own assumptions about my friend's obvious ethnicity. No harm done, but not exactly prophetic, either.

Reckless use of this kind of 'directional' word can be potentially devastating. People have actually moved their whole families to new cities as a result of such prophecies, only to encounter much hardship and disillusionment as they discover that the prophetic word was bogus. Generally, a prophetic word that contains directional content should serve as a *confirmation* of what God has already been speaking to the person. My East Indian friend was mature enough to recognise this, but there have been some serious problems created for people, especially youth and young believers, with this (frankly) presumptuous use of prophetic ministry.

Many post-charismatic people are simply worn out with grandiose prophecies, especially when the prophecy doesn't come to pass, and they get blamed for the prophecy not happening; the usual accusation is that they didn't have enough faith, or had somehow not fulfilled some mysterious conditions that were required.

For a while, in Canada at least, it seemed that everyone was being called to record CDs and/or discover new musical rhythms that would change the world, or that they would stand before kings and nations and call them to repent, or in some way to have a very successful high-profile ministry. As one friend recently joked, 'Oh yeah, and it's *to the nations*' – a phrase that seemed to be used almost constantly.

Post-charismatics are asking the question, 'Doesn't anyone feel called to deny themselves and take up their cross any more?' They are reading Jesus' words about being great in the kingdom meaning that we are to be servants of all, and that God opposes the proud, which seem to conflict with the attitudes of those who have believed prophetic words about their impending greatness.

Another abuse of the prophetic is when those who have placed themselves in authority use prophetic words to control the direction of the church, home group, or even the individual lives of people in the congregation. We will cover this more in the Shepherding movement section, but it deserves mention here as well, since it abuses prophecy in order to control people.

One of the reasons that the Latter Rain was rejected back in 1949 was its abuse of directive prophecy, and unfortunately, we are seeing the same thing happen today. Many pastors and laypeople alike are suspicious of self-proclaimed 'intercessors' and 'prayer warriors' who seem to excel in legalistic judgments against everyone, and who question the spiritual depth of anyone who doesn't agree with them. This has produced a reaction in post-charismatics that results in missing out on the genuine benefits of intercessory prayer, and also causes them to wonder why everything they thought they were hearing from God was somehow wrong.

Post-charismatics are asking, 'Can't I hear the voice of God for myself?' Their concern is echoed by many who remain in the movement. The high-profile charismatic teacher John Bevere felt so strongly that he penned a book-length warning on abusive prophecy entitled *Thus Saith the Lord?*.

Elitism

In recent years, as many people within the prophetic movement have prophesied about the 'Joshua and Caleb Generation' who would take the land that their parents didn't due to their unbelief or worldliness, another generation has been encouraged to think that they are the chosen ones.

The Jesus movement thought the same about itself, but now they are being labeled as the 'failed generation' (as Baby Boomers). While the Bible teaches us to honour older Christians, these prophecies tend to produce an elitist and unteachable attitude in those who believe they are part of the chosen generation. After all, if you're part of the chosen generation, what could you possibly learn or receive from an unbelieving generation of older failures?

Post-charismatics are asking, 'Why do some people have to be disqualified (Boomers) in order to validate others (emerging generations)?'

Another painful observation that I have heard repeatedly is that, in a movement that speaks of a 'nameless and faceless' army being raised up, there is actually quite a small number of 'anointed' people doing all the ministry, while the rest of the 'army' merely attends conferences.

One teenager I met felt really 'called' to the emerging generations, but when I suggested that he get involved in his local church's youth ministry, he was very resistant, not wanting to be hindered by the weekly commitment of being a youth leader – but he had a great desire to be on stage! It would be easy to view him as egotistical and opportunistic, but he was really just responding to what was being modelled for him.

In a time where many in the emerging church (charismatic and non) are envisioning a plurality of leaders and less hierarchy, the emphasis on modern apostles and prophets (as the foundation that the church is built on) seems to grate harshly. It is true that the church is built on the foundation of the apostles and prophets (Ephesians 2:20), but in context, this verse is not talking about modern apostles being part of the foundation – it was referring to the original apostles.

While there is a legitimate functioning of apostolic ministry in the twenty-first century, it should not result in an attitude or culture of elitism that makes another layer in an ecclesiastical hierarchy. Many post-charismatics have grown tired of a mindset that fails to equip the body of Christ to do the works of the kingdom (the purpose of the five-fold ministries), and instead builds a perceived elitism among the 'have's' who are in power.

Post-charismatics are asking, 'Is it my turn to minister yet? Will it ever be?'

Striving

Whether it's the teaching of the Tabernacle of David, which stipulates that if we don't get our worship just right – the kind of worship that God is seeking in order to inhabit – we will miss the move of God; or the overall thrust of *The Feast of Tabernacles* – that only the 'overcomers' will usher in the Second Coming of Jesus, who is stuck in heaven until then – the bottom line is that these teachings place an inordinate amount of stress on believers.

Jesus accused the Pharisees of the same thing: 'They tie up

heavy loads and put them on men's shoulders, but they themselves are not willing to lift a finger to move them' (Matthew
23:4). Post-charismatic people are those who are tired of being
promised great wonders *if* they can just get their act straight, get
their worship just right, fast and pray enough, and be holy
enough. If the prophecies don't come to pass, they are blamed
for not fulfilling the conditions somehow, which only serves to
(a) make them discouraged so they give up, thinking God has set
them aside in favour of the truly anointed, or (b) they strive even
harder, becoming more legalistic and harsh with others whom
they feel aren't trying hard enough.

Post-charismatics are not so much asking questions this time,
as they are turning their backs on genuine prophetic ministry,
unable to differentiate between what is a genuine understanding
of prophecy and what has been coloured by the confusing doctrines of the Latter Rain movement.

If there is anything praiseworthy coming out of the Latter
Rain movement, it was their genuine emphasis on personal holiness. While this may have been partly motivated by the belief
that they would be better equipped to usher in Jesus' second
coming by being part of the Joshua and Caleb generation, they
were also reacting against a perception of spiritual coldness and
moral laxness among their Pentecostal churches.

> The question posed by the Latter Rain had to do with the role of
> human obedience in helping or hindering the sovereign plan of
> God. On what basis or for what motive do we serve Him? How
> does revival come?[79]

The other area that was abused, and yet is a biblical gift of the
Spirit that is given for the edification of the body, is the place

and practice of prophecy. To downplay or neglect prophecy is firmly consistent with the old adage of 'throwing the baby out with the bathwater'.

In order for post-charismatic believers to truly function as the body of Christ, indwelt and empowered by the Holy Spirit, the issues of holiness and the gift of prophecy need to be thought through with great care. There needs to be a biblical basis, an expectation that there is a non-legalistic way of pursuing holiness, and a non-hyped, non-manipulative way for prophetic gifts to function, as 'all of these must be done for the strengthening of the church' (1 Corinthians 14:26b).

After looking more closely at the Shepherding and Word of Faith movements, and developing a post-charismatic concept of spiritual formation, we will revisit these areas and attempt to create a more balanced understanding and praxis that is Spirit-led and less weighed-down by the baggage that has caused so many to walk away.

PROSPERITY AND HEALING

Word of Faith

Shortly after we were married, Wendy and I took a group of teenagers to a Christian music festival west of Toronto, where we spent the next five days enjoying leaky tents, mostly cooked campfire food, and a lot of great Christian bands.

During the festival, we met many friends whom we hadn't seen in a while, and it was a great time of catching up with them, as well as building deeper relationships with the teenagers who had accompanied us.

One day in particular was grey and overcast, and as we sat on the grass about 20 yards from the main stage, we were remarking about the threatening sky; thunderstorms in southern Ontario, after all, can be quite intense.

A friend from summer camp, Carolyn, looked up at the heavy clouds and wished aloud, 'Man, I sure hope it doesn't rain.'

A woman seated a few yards away turned to us, quite agitated. 'Don't talk like that!' she rebuked Carolyn. 'Don't you know your words have power, and the demons can make it rain because of your bad confession?'

We had never heard anyone speak this way in person; televangelists, sure, but we weren't expecting this at a Christian rock festival. 'Oh, and I suppose you think God wants us all rich and healthy, too, right?' asked Carolyn.

'Of course!' the woman cried. 'As your faith is, so be it unto you!' And with that, she abruptly turned on her heel and stormed away. We all looked at each other, eyebrows raised, and then collectively shrugged and went back to waiting for the next concert to begin.

'I still hope it doesn't rain,' said Carolyn, with an impish grin. (It didn't.)

For years, many conservative evangelicals would refer to the 'health and wealth' or 'positive confession' teachings as a warning against the entire charismatic movement, believing that this doctrine – actually known as 'Word of Faith' – was normative for the mainstream of the charismatic movement.

What may come as a surprise to many conservative evangelicals (since Pentecostal, charismatic and Third Wave also fit under the heading of 'evangelical'), is that some of the strongest criticisms of the Word of Faith movement have come from within the charismatic realm itself.

> Years before the Jim Bakker/PTL scandal, many believers in America were so repulsed by money-grubbing TV preachers that they returned to their denominational churches in disgust.[1]

While many conservative evangelicals have avoided the charismatic movement because of their disdain for Word of Faith teachings and the extremes of televangelism, post-charismatics also cite the Word of Faith movement as one of the reasons that they wish to distance themselves from being called 'charismatic'.

There are several accusations made against the Word of Faith movement's original writers that need to be addressed before digging deeper into the teachings themselves.

Evangelical authors have written numerous books denouncing the Word of Faith teaching; the most well known would include John MacArthur's *Charismatic Chaos*, Hank Hannegraaf's *Christianity in Crisis*, and D.R. McConnell's *A Different Gospel*. We will not be examining the claims of these books, but they are listed here to indicate the fascination with and opposition to the Word of Faith movement.

McConnell's book created quite a stir when it was first published in 1988, because it accused Kenneth E. Hagin, the acknowledged 'father' of the Word of Faith movement, of plagiarising the earlier works of E.W. Kenyon. McConnell included a side-by-side chart of Kenyon's and Hagin's writing, and the evidence is damning, despite Hagin's protestations that he had developed his teaching before he had even heard of Kenyon. Hagin does concede, however, that he may have come across some of Kenyon's sermons or writings but had not recalled this fact when he wrote his own material. 'Reading or hearing something once was all that was necessary for him to recall it verbatim.'[2]

Joe McIntyre, president of the Healing Rooms ministry and Kenyon's Gospel Publishing Society, is currently the publisher of Kenyon's writings and has authored a book entitled *E.W. Kenyon and His Message of Faith: The True Story*. McIntyre concedes that the similarities between Hagin's and Kenyon's work are too obvious to ignore, but contends that (a) Kenneth Hagin (called 'Dad' Hagin by many in the movement) has a photographic memory, which could account for his inadvertent verbatim wording, and (b) that E.W. Kenyon would have been thrilled with the work that Hagin has done in promoting the Word of Faith teachings, so it's not really an issue between Kenyon and Hagin. Either way, according to McIntyre, 'from his vantage point in heaven, Kenyon is probably delighted that Kenneth E. Hagin has been so successful in getting the message of faith, so dear to Kenyon's heart, out to so many in the world in this generation.'[3]

Whatever the reason behind the similarities between Kenyon's and Hagin's writings, what remains is that McIntyre – as the inheritor and promoter of Kenyon's written legacy – confirms that their message is one and the same. Without resorting to accusations of plagiarism, we need to focus on the content of their joint message.

The New Thought connection

The other common accusation and assumption made about E.W. Kenyon is his connection to what was called 'New Thought' at university. As the *Dictionary of Pentecostal and Charismatic Movements* puts it:

> Conceptually, the views espoused by E.W. Kenyon can be traced to his exposure to metaphysical ideas derived from attendance at Emerson College of Oratory in Boston, a spawning ground for New Thought philosophical ideas. The major tenets of the New Thought movement are health or healing, abundance or prosperity, wealth, and happiness.[4]

McIntyre takes exception to McConnell's suggestion that Kenyon was influenced by this New Thought movement: 'Kenyon wasn't actually in Boston during the time McConnell believes he was . . . As to Kenyon's being influenced at Emerson College, when Kenyon went there for the one year he attended, he was not walking with the Lord and was not seeking any kind of religious training.'[5]

While McIntyre may be able to prove, historically, that Kenyon was not at Emerson College when the main proponent of New Thought (Ralph Waldo Trine) was there, the argument that therefore Kenyon wasn't influenced still seems weak. Even if Kenyon was not following the Lord, it doesn't mean that he would therefore be impervious to any embryonic New Thought concepts that he was exposed to.

Again, as with the evidence of plagiarism, the similarities between New Thought and Word of Faith are striking. While this in and of itself doesn't necessarily prove a common root, it cannot be ignored either. While it is a common heresy hunter tactic to discredit a teaching by 'proving' (or at least insinuating) a connection to occultic or unbiblical roots, what is really important is the content of the teaching itself.

Regardless of whether one believes McConnell or McIntyre on the issue of New Thought roots in the writings of E.W. Kenyon, the point remains: how does the teaching itself stand up?

E.W. Kenyon

Essex William (E.W.) Kenyon (1867–1948) hailed from upstate New York, and much of his early ministry years were spent in the New England area. After numerous pastoral positions, he started the Dudley Bible Institute – which soon moved to Spencer Massachusetts and was renamed Bethel Bible Institute – where he served as president for 25 years. The school relocated again some years later, and became Providence Bible Institute.

When Kenyon later relocated to Los Angeles, he pioneered in the area of radio broadcasting there and later in Seattle.

Kenyon later devoted himself more fully to itinerant ministry and writing ... Although he was not Pentecostal, his work *The*

Wonderful Name of Jesus (1927) was widely read among Oneness Pentecostals. His writings have had a broad acceptance in the Deeper Life and charismatic movements.[6]

For someone who was not Pentecostal himself (all of his churches were actually Baptist), Kenyon has had a profound impact on the charismatic movement. One of those influenced heavily by Kenyon was W. J. 'Ern' Baxter, who would later become William Branham's manager, a participant in the Latter Rain movement, and would become best known in recent years as a member of the 'Fort Lauderdale Five' who started the Shepherding movement.

Others who have been influenced by Kenyon's writings include Kenneth Copeland, Don Gossett, Charles Capps, and of course, Kenneth E. Hagin and Kenneth Hagin Jr.

Kenneth E. Hagin

Kenneth Hagin is widely considered to be the father of the Word of Faith movement, by friends and critics alike. Certainly, through his Rhema Bible Training Center in Tulsa, Oklahoma, his daily radio programme 'Faith Seminar of the Air', over 50 million copies of his 125 books, monthly tapes, and his half-million-subscriber *The Word of Faith* magazine, Hagin is one of the most influential and well-known proponents of Word of Faith teaching.

Hagin was born with a heart condition that he was not expected to survive, although he was 15 before his health failed to the point of making him an invalid. During his sixteenth year, 'during a ten minute period, his vital signs failed three times. On each occasion, he witnessed the horrors of hell. This led to his conversion on April 22, 1937.'[7] By the time Hagin was 17, he had been healed of his heart condition, and began a ministry mostly among Baptist congregations. After experiencing a baptism in the Holy Spirit at age 20, Hagin began to minister among Pentecostals, and pastored numerous Pentecostal churches.

Hagin began an itinerant ministry twelve years later, in 1949, serving as a Bible teacher and evangelist. 'During the following 14 years he had a series of eight visions of Jesus Christ, who in the third vision granted him the gift of discerning of spirits, enabling him to pray more effectively for the healing of the sick.'[8]

Richard Riss charitably says of him, 'Kenneth Hagin emphasizes the message of uncompromising faith in God's desire to bless, in every area of life, all who do not doubt him . . . his message emphasizes the need to pray only according to God's principles as found in the Judeo-Christian Scriptures.'[9]

Word of Faith teaching

Legal or covenant foundation

The main thrust of the Word of Faith teaching, or 'Positive Confession' as it is sometimes referred to, is that our words have the power to determine the quality of life that we live. A positive confession – speaking only words of health, prosperity and success – will result in our lives being characterised by health, prosperity and success. Contrarily, a negative confession – which is interpreted to be lack of faith or the presence of doubt – will negate all the good things that God has guaranteed those who will only believe him at his word, and may bring the opposite upon the undiscerning believer who makes the negative confession. 'As your faith is, so be it unto you' is a common catchphrase to sum this up.

Kenyon regularly employed legal wording in describing this emphasis: 'Christianity is a legal document . . . You have as much right to demand healing as you have to demand the cashing of a cheque at a bank where you have a deposit.'[10] This kind of approach is foundational to understanding the Word of Faith mindset. The assumption is that God has promised healing, prosperity and success, and that the only thing that believers need to do is just claim the promises that God has already made. Hagin writes, 'That's how it is with our rights and privileges in Christ. Healing belongs to us. God has provided it for us. But we have to possess it.'[11] And the key to possessing healing (and prosperity) is the spoken word of positive confession.

Echoing this 'legal' viewpoint is Kenneth Copeland, another prominent figure in the Word of Faith movement. Copeland uses the term 'covenant' rather than Kenyon's reference to a 'legal document', but his meaning is the same: 'Discipline everything you do, everything you say, and everything you think to agree with what God does, what God says, and what God thinks! God will be obligated to meet your needs because of His Word.'[12]

These words sound strong – demand, possess, obligate – but to the Word of Faith movement, they would only be arrogant and presumptuous *if God has not already promised these things.* From their theological vantage point, the Word of Faith movement is merely choosing to be obedient and believe all that God has promised in Scripture, and the rest of the evangelical/charismatic church is divorcing the truth of Scripture from the daily lives of believers.

> The Church took spiritual blessing and left the prosperity and healing portions of the promise. It is true that spiritual redemption is a greater blessing than prosperity or healing, but God never asked you to choose . . . He held out the new birth, prosperity and healing. The Church took the new birth and disregarded prosperity and healing.[13]

In the Word of Faith understanding, salvation includes healing and prosperity; a favourite verse that is quoted is Isaiah 53:5: 'But he was pierced for our transgressions, he was crushed for our iniquities; the punishment that brought us peace was upon him, and by his wounds we are healed.' This is perhaps the best known verse to support the idea that 'healing is in the atonement'. Consider Hagin's words:

> The sinner does not need to beg God to save him. The work's already been accomplished. All he needs to do is accept it and thank God for it – then it becomes his.
> The believer doesn't need to ask God to heal him because Jesus has already borne our sickness. All the believer needs to do is know that healing belongs to him.[14]

Word of Faith adherents are honestly and deeply concerned about the fact that other Christians don't accept their teaching – indeed, to them, the rest of charismatic Christendom is failing to truly believe God. Kenyon writes: 'How glad the Father would be, if we would arise and take our Legal Rights . . . A literal translation would read: "If ye shall demand anything in my name, that will I do". . . . In the face of this mighty Fact, poverty and weakness of spirit are criminal.'[15]

This approach to interpreting God's written word becomes the lens through which Word of Faith proponents view all of Scripture. This approach puts us in the position of being able to hold God to account for promises in his word, which he may not have actually made. 'The self-defined phrase "confessing the Word of God" takes precedence over hermeneutical principles and rules for biblical interpretation. This approach not only does violence to the text but forces the NT linguistic data into artificial categories that the biblical authors themselves could not affirm.'[16]

Use of rhema

A key approach to the Scriptures that shows the hermeneutical principles that Word of Faith operates under, is their concept of the Greek words *rhema* and *logos*. Simply put, they define *logos* to be the written word of God and *rhema* as the 'living word' or the 'now' word of God. 'The major premise of *rhema* doctrine is that whatever is spoken by faith becomes immediately inspired and therefore dynamic in the particular situation or event to which it is addressed.'[17]

Many Christians are familiar with the concept of a '*rhema* word' from Scripture, even if they have not used that term to describe it. From across the denominational spectrum, stories are told of reading a well-known passage of Scripture, when suddenly, a certain verse or phrase seems to jump off the page, and the reader knows beyond a doubt that the Holy Spirit is speaking through that verse or phrase. It is a 'now' (*rhema*) word that is found in the 'written' (*logos*) word of God. (We will look at how even this understanding is an inappropriate understanding of *rhema* shortly.)

The Word of Faith teachers take this idea much further than having a verse stand out during a Christian's Bible reading. Word of Faith applies the *rhema* principle to the words spoken by Christians. It goes beyond rhema as a 'now word' and becomes a way of speaking into existence the desires and thoughts of the individual Christian.

> The positive confession emphasis has a tendency to include state-ments which make it appear that man is sovereign and God is the servant . . . This puts man in the position of using God rather than man surrendering himself to be used of God.[18]

Word of Faith teachers stress that the positive confession that a believer makes must be based on the word of God. Some try to distance themselves from the idea that people are determining what they are confessing, based on their own greed or wants. Indeed, Kenneth Copeland makes a point of urging generosity in the heart of those making a positive confession for prosperity: 'Now you can see that the basic reason for the operation of faith is to meet the needs of mankind. You may not need much money to be happy and successful in your own life, but people are starving and dying throughout the world. Someone must provide for them.'[19]

However, even with this appeal to caring for the needs of others, the overall tenor of the prosperity aspect of Word of Faith is based on the assumption that it is God's will that all believers live in total health and material prosperity: 'God has established His covenant – for salvation, for healing, for deliverance, for prosperity – and these provisions of the covenant are set out in God's Word.'[20]

A favourite verse to prove the use of *rhema* is Romans 10:8: 'But what does it say? "The word is near you; it is in your mouth and in your heart," that is, the word of faith we are proclaiming. . .' For Word of Faith proponents, this proclamation of the 'word of faith' is the active participation of the believer in speaking forth the promises found in God's word. This particular verse has become a signature catch-phrase to encourage positive confession.

It is interesting to read Romans 10:8 in its context, which aids greatly in understanding what Paul meant by the phrase 'the word of faith we are proclaiming':

> But what does it say? 'The word is near you; it is in your mouth and in your heart,' that is, the word of faith we are proclaiming: that if you confess with your mouth, 'Jesus is Lord,' and believe in your heart that God raised him from the dead, you will be saved. For it is with your heart that you believe and are justified, and it is with your mouth that you confess and are saved. (Romans 10:8–10)

In context, this verse is actually referring to salvation, not to the positive confession that would lead to prosperity, healing, and deliverance. Of course, Word of Faith teachers will quickly point out that the word for 'salvation' includes wholeness, healing and peace, as well as the normally understood saving function of faith. The emphasis in the Romans passage, however, is not on the power of the believer's confession to authoritatively claim prosperity, but rather Paul is proclaiming the message ('word') of faith that the Romans can be saved by faith in Jesus.

Finally, in the New Testament, the words *logos* and *rhema* are used almost interchangeably. Even the example of the 'now word' that was used earlier does not do justice to the biblical text.

> In the case of the Septuagint, both *rhema* and *logos* are used to translate the one Hebrew word *dabar*, which is used in various ways relative to communication . . . The Word of God, whether referred to as *logos* or *rhema*, is inspired, eternal, dynamic, and miraculous. Whether the Word is written or spoken does not alter its essential character.[21]

A verse that is employed frequently to demonstrate negative confession is Proverbs 6:2: 'If you have been trapped by what you said, ensnared by the words of your mouth. . .' This verse is used as a proof-text to defend the idea that negative words have power to bring destruction into a believer's life, or at the very least cause us to lose the promised blessings, so we need to be extremely cautious about our negative confession.

E. W. Kenyon writes: 'The enemy (Satan) will try to make you deny your confession. He will try to make you confess weakness and failure and want. . .'[22] And, 'We do not come with that quiet assurance that we would if some banker had given us his word in regard to our financial standing at the bank. This leads to weakness, to doubt and fear. It makes a vacillating type of faith.'[23]

Kenneth Hagin concurs: 'I began by telling them it is unscriptural to pray, "If it be Thy will" concerning anything which God's Word has already promised us. When you put an "if" in your prayer, you are praying with doubt.'[24]

Kenneth Copeland echoes the same theme: 'I have prayed with people and when I finished said, "It is done and it will come to pass." Then the other person who was supposed to be agreeing with me would say, "I certainly do hope so, Brother Copeland." At that point I am forced to say, "Well, it won't. I agreed; you hoped."'[25]

But if we return to the Proverbs 6:2 passage, we will see a different application arising from the plain meaning of the verse when read in context of Proverbs 6:1–3:

> My son, if you have put up security for your neighbour, if you have struck hands in pledge for another, if you have been trapped by what you said, ensnared by the words of your mouth, then do this my son, to free yourself, since you have fallen into your neighbour's hands: Go and humble yourself; press your plea with your neighbour!

In context, Proverbs 6:2 has nothing to do with a negative confession; the verse is a father giving advice to his son on how to extricate himself from a hasty pledge that he is unable to fulfil. The advice is for the son to humble himself and negotiate with the neighbour with whom the son has made the hasty vow.

This hermeneutical approach to Scripture – lifting verses or fragments of verses out of context – is grounds for holding the positive/negative confession teaching at a healthy distance. The immediate context of the verses suggests that the Word of Faith understanding is not based on sound biblical exegesis, and the broader witness of Scripture also does not back up the Word of Faith teachings.

> When the positive confession teaching indicates that to admit weakness is to accept defeat, to admit financial need is to accept poverty, and to admit sickness is to preclude healing, it is going beyond and is contrary to the harmony of Scripture[26]. . . When the

positive confession doctrine indicates a person can have whatever he says, it fails to emphasize adequately that God's will must be considered.[27]

The last area of concern with how the *rhema* doctrine is developed is the idea that our words can have the same creative power as God's. Kenyon states:

> We can bind Demons, bind disease, and habits, and bind men so that they cannot go on in the will of Satan; or use fearsome power to deliver souls over to Satan for the destruction of the body[28]. . . . We see Peter striking a man and woman dead for lying. Awful power this is; power to heal and power to slay. They were walking in the omnipotence of the authority given them by Jesus.[29]

A quick reaction to what Kenyon has stated would be that Peter no more than foretold the deaths of Ananias and Sapphira – the Scripture does not support the idea that Peter was the one who actually struck the two of them dead. While Christians can certainly walk in the authority that Jesus has given them, to describe it as 'omnipotence' is treading on thin ice – omnipotence is one of the 'incommunicable' attributes of God; he shares it with no one.

Hagin has advanced a similar idea – that we are able to 'bind' people to God's purposes:

> I raised my Bible in one hand, lifted my other hand to Heaven, and said, 'In the Name of the Lord Jesus Christ, I break the power of the devil over my brother Dub's life and claim Dub's deliverance. That means deliverance from the devil and full salvation in Jesus' Name. Amen.'
>
> And this is a critical point on salvation, on faith, and on receiving whatever you need from God: As long as Satan can hold you in

the arena of reason, he will whip you every time – in every battle, every conflict.[30]

The power of the creative word builds on another of Kenyon's ideas, although it is developed more fully by later Word of Faith teachers, and (surprisingly) was akin to some of the teaching of John G. Lake a few decades earlier.

Kenyon wrote: 'John 10:10: "I came that they may have life, and may have it abundantly." What is Life? Life is the Nature of God. You may have the Father's Nature abundantly.'[31] Christians would normally understand that we are partakers of the divine nature (2 Peter 1:3–4), but this is usually understood in terms of the imputed righteousness of Jesus and empowerment for living a holy life. To equate the 'abundant life' of John 10:10 with possessing God's nature is a stretch, to say the least. And as unworthy servants who have the undeserved privilege of partaking in the divine nature, humility would be a more appropriate and fitting response.

John G. Lake was more succinct: 'Man is not a separate creation detached from God; he is part of God Himself . . . God intends us to be gods. The inner man is the real governor, the true man that Jesus said was a god.'[32] (Lake's ideas were influenced by Phineas P. Quimby, a progenitor of New Thought in the mid-1800s, whose writings were also an influence on E.W. Kenyon, as well as William Branham.)

Later Word of Faith proponents also referred to Christians being 'little gods', which landed several in hot water at one point. However, the idea has not been totally abandoned. 'Earl Paulk of Atlanta wrote recently, "Just as dogs have puppies, and cats have kittens, so God has little gods. Until we comprehend that we are little gods and we begin to act like little gods, we cannot manifest the Kingdom of God.'"[33]

Kenneth Hagin's terminology is not as controversial, but his understanding is very much in keeping with Paulk's: 'Notice that through Jesus, we have been made righteous. We believers (we who have been born again) don't have to try to become righteous – because we are righteous.'[34] In the general understanding that we are positionally righteous before God because of the finished work of Christ on the cross, we will agree with this statement. However, in the Word of Faith understanding, it goes beyond positional righteousness and becomes part and parcel of possessing the nature of God himself, as 'little gods' with the power of the creative spoken word.

Most Christians, including post-charismatics, would agree with the position taken by the Assemblies of God: 'When believers recognize the sovereignty of God and properly become concerned with the will of God, they will not talk in terms of compelling God or using God's power. They will speak of becoming obedient servants.'[35]

Healing

Very early on, Kenyon set the course for believing that healing is a God-ordained right for all believers: 'We have come to believe that it is just as wrong for a believer to bear his sickness when Jesus bore it, as it is for him to bear his sins when Christ bore them.'[36] This concept of healing being synonymous with salvation is repeated today in Word of Faith circles.

Hagin writes: 'I can't push a button or pull a lever, so to speak, and make the gifts start working. They operate as the SPIRIT wills. Yet we are instructed not to wait for Him, since He has already done something about our healing at the Cross[37]. . . Likewise, it is not a matter of God healing an individual; it is a matter of the person accepting the gift of healing God has already provided.'[38]

Kenneth Copeland puts it this way: 'When the Word says you are healed, you are healed! It doesn't matter what your body says about it. If you will believe this and operate accordingly, then the covenant you have with God – His Word – will become the absolute truth in your situation, and your physical body will come into agreement with the Word[39]. . . God has established His covenant – for salvation, for healing, for deliverance, for prosperity – and these provisions of the covenant are set out in God's Word.'[40]

Word of Faith believes that physical healing and wholeness is bound up in our salvation. Healing is part of the 'legal document' that Kenyon speaks of, or the covenant of Copeland's writings – this approach is what led to the unflattering but generally accurate phrase 'name it and claim it' that critics have labelled the Word of Faith movement with.

> In the mind of the Father, you are healed. Jesus knows that He bore your diseases. How it must hurt Him to hear you talk about bearing them yourself. Learn to say: 'I am healed because He did that work and satisfied the Supreme Court of the Universe.'[41]

To not appropriate the healing that is promised in salvation is, at best, foolishness, and at worst, the sin of unbelief. If you talk with Word of Faith people, they are genuinely puzzled, and at times frustrated, with other Christians who believe that suffering might be a part of God's plan/will for a believer.

The Word of Faith movement has been described as having an 'over-realised eschatology'. Poverty, disease and sin will be eradicated from the earth at the return of Jesus to usher in the kingdom in its fullness, but, to quote Aragorn in his rousing speech in the film version of J.R.R. Tolkien's *The Return of the King*, 'This is not that day!'

Kenyon's passionate declaration fits this over-realised eschatology: 'The hour will come when you will awaken to the fact that he (Satan) cannot put disease upon you, that he cannot give you pain and anguish in your body. The hour will come when you will know that want and poverty are things of the past as far as you are concerned.'[42]

Prosperity

While many charismatics and post-charismatics have a general acceptance and understanding of divine healing, although differing from the emphasis of the Word of Faith movement, the issue of 'it is God's will that you be rich' as a part of positive confession provokes an even stronger reaction than the idea of 'claiming' healing.

The prosperity side of Word of Faith is based on their understanding that prosperity, like healing, is an implied part of our salvation. Many Word of Faith teachers see financial prosperity as a part of God's original plan at the creation of the world. Gloria Copeland, Kenneth's wife, puts it this way:

> God's will for Adam was abundance and plenty. Poverty and lack came only after Adam changed gods and began to operate under Satan's dominion . . . Since His will does not change, God's will for

His people today is abundance (James 1:17) . . . From the beginning of time, He has provided financial prosperity for His people through obedience to His Word.[43]

This view of prosperity as a part of God's will is found in Kenyon's writings, although not as prominently as his admonitions to claim healing: 'This Redemption is real. Satan is defeated, disease is outlawed, and want is banished.'[44]

A popular verse that is used to refer to prosperity (aside from Old Testament passages about the covenant with Abraham) is 3 John 2: 'Beloved, I wish above all things that thou mayest prosper and be in health, even as thy soul prospereth' (KJV).

The word translated 'prosper' in this verse is the Greek word *euodoo*, which can be translated to mean:

1. To grant a prosperous and expeditious journey
2. To grant a successful issue, to cause to prosper
3. To prosper, be successful

Word of Faith contends that this is a clear statement that financial prosperity is to be the norm for Christians everywhere.

John was a wise old man, strong in the Lord, and he said, 'I wish above all things that you prosper and be in health.' Through our traditional ideas, we have been led to believe that prosperity is bad or ungodly. However, John writes that we should prosper and be healthy.[45]

It is interesting to note that the meaning attached to 3 John 2 by Word of Faith teachers is dependent on the King James Version's rendering. If we were to look at the same verse in a different version, we find a different note being sounded: 'Dear friend, I pray that you may enjoy good health and that all may go well with you, even as your soul is getting along well.'

If we refer to the three possible definitions for the word 'prosper' (Greek *euodoo*), the plain sense of the New International Version's translation makes better contextual sense than the Word of Faith's interpretation. John is writing a personal greeting to Gaius (the recipient of the original letter), and this phrase should not be taken, as Word of Faith suggests, as anything other than a good friend's well-wishing. It is the pre-amble to the meat of the letter; this brief verse is not written to establish doctrine or suggest the normative practice of the church.

The Word of Faith movement has difficulty accepting the notion that adverse circumstances could be a part of God's plan. Hagin notes: 'People will say about someone, "Well, God used that tragedy to bring him to salvation." But that kind of thinking is not in line with the Bible.'[46] The emphasis is on God's love and covenant promise to bless – physically, spiritually, and financially – those who have the understanding of, and faith to believe, his covenant. Poverty, or even humble circumstances, is seen as unbiblical.

> You won't find a Jew who believes in poverty because poverty is not in the Old Covenant. It is in religion, not in the Bible. It was put into Christianity as a religion during the Dark Ages when the Word was taken from the people and put away in monasteries. Poverty oaths were fed into Christianity when the religious hierarchy took over. The men operating it were not born-again men.[47]

Knowing the covenant is the key to getting what you are promised (prosperity): 'He cannot establish His covenant in your life without prospering you. The man who holds to poverty rejects the establishment of the covenant . . . The covenant cannot be established in your life unless you believe God's Word concerning prosperity. Let there be no doubt about God's will. God's will is to establish His covenant in the earth. Prosperity is a major requirement in the establishment of God's will.'[48]

Unbelief, then, or lack of understanding concerning this covenant, leads to tragic results, according to Word of Faith understanding:

> Moses went forth in the name of the covenant, performed miracles by the power of God in the face of Pharaoh, and led God's people out of bondage. They could have gone free 400 years before, but they didn't know their covenant![49]

> This view advocates that God wants believers to wear the best clothing, drive the best cars, and have the best of everything. Believers need not suffer financial setbacks. All they need to do is to tell Satan to take his hands off their money. The believer can have whatever he says whether the need is spiritual, physical, or financial.[50]

Kenyon echoes this same sentiment: 'There is no excuse for the spiritual weakness and poverty of the Family of God when the wealth of Grace and Love of our great Father with His power and wisdom are all at our disposal.'[51] Copeland agrees: 'You can have what you say! Remember, we said earlier that all the material substance you will ever need is already in the earth. Everything you need is already here. The confession of your mouth will cause you to possess it. God will see to that[52]. . . You must realize that it is God's will for you to prosper (see 3 John 2). This is available to you, and frankly, it would be stupid of you not to partake of it!'[53]

Franklin Hall

Almost as a parenthetical observation, brief mention should be made at this point of Franklin Hall, who was involved in the Latter Rain movement, and wrote the book *Atomic Power with God through Prayer and Fasting*. Like William Branham, Franklin Hall was involved primarily in the Latter Rain and Restorationist churches; although he was not a part of the Word of Faith movement itself, some of his (and Branham's) ideas dove-tailed with the Word of Faith approach. This explains why Word of Faith concepts keep surfacing in charismatic groups that are not directly connected to Word of Faith's most recognisable spokespersons.

Like Branham, Franklin Hall was fascinated with the Zodiac, and likened Scorpio (a scorpion) to the sex drive that is also connected to life and death in God's economy. He also shared the Latter Rain's view that the church had quickly 'lost' many vital teachings after the days of the apostles:

> They (the early Christians) not only failed to have power to do the impossible, but after the days of the apostles the church became powerless, and eventually began to say that the days of healing were over; that the miracles were not for them anymore; the Holy Spirit, after the Bible pattern, was forsaken, and the power of the apostolic age was lost.[54]

The extreme judgment against all denominations – another common Latter Rain theme – is also continued in Hall's writings, as is his belief that the Manifested Sons of God will set things right.

The cripples, the sick, the suffering, the insane asylums filled with the distressed, and hospitals running over with sick and wounded, the groanings of suffering humanity everywhere, all is because the Sons of God do not have the vision, and know not how to manifest. The Laodicean, denominational, bound Church has so much riches, comfortable pews, stained-glass windows. But the CHRIST is left outside.[55]

Remember Hagin? 'As long as Satan can hold you in the arena of reason, he will whip you every time.'[56] Franklin Hall states:

While reason is nervous, excited, and troubled; faith is patient, relaxed, and calm. It is necessary to be founded on the Word of God and believe the Word of God to retain our healing ... We would be healed, but if our faith was not definitely established in the WORD OF GOD, there would be a possibility of the return of the ailment.[57]

Finally, Franklin Hall proposes the same sense that healing and prosperity are linked to salvation that Kenyon, Hagin, Copeland, etc. also share: 'If Jesus did not redeem the whole man, including his physical body and his material welfare, then Christ did not redeem any part of a man! It is a disgrace and a shame that Christians can have every kind of sickness that a sinner can have, and die a Devil's painful death in the same manner as a person without God can die and still claim salvation!'[58]

Hall's influence in the charismatic renewal of the 1960s, through his writings and those who had absorbed them earlier, sheds some light on why Word of Faith teachings continue to proliferate among churches that are not generally associated with the rest of the Word of Faith movement.

Post-charismatic

A good friend of mine, who was also one of the pastors of the church we were attending at the time, was diagnosed with cancer late one autumn. Over the next winter and spring, he battled the disease, making some progress, and then suffered a setback, followed by more progress and then another setback.

During this season, hundreds, if not thousands, of people were praying for his healing. He was well known around the city, and numerous churches sent their entire staff and eldership teams to anoint him for healing. Some church pastors came to him, as he lay in his hospital bed, to repent to him for their attitudes towards him in previous years, and they would pray for each other.

The summer was looking better, and hope for healing continued to ride high, but as August drew to a close, another setback reared up, and within six weeks he was gone.

It was, understandably, a devastating time for everyone who knew him, not least his wife and children. The grieving process had barely begun, when one of his teenagers was approached by a group of students from one of the Christian high schools.

They were brief, but devastating, in their remarks. Your father, they stated unequivocally, died because your church had not embraced the Word of Faith understanding, and had failed to claim his healing. If your father had been at their church, they said, he would still be alive today. The grieving family was out of line, in their opinion, to ask the Spirit to be their Comforter, as the Spirit was offended that all of us had failed to claim the healing that could have been.

Needless to say, their words brought no comfort or encouragement to a grieving teenager.

Many people outside of the charismatic movement have avoided it based on the perception that the Word of Faith teachings are typical of all charismatics. Examples such as the one just mentioned only serve to reinforce such a stereotype. Post-charismatics also point to the excessive lifestyles of televangelists, the performance-orientation resulting from being accused of 'lacking faith' if healing and/or prosperity were not being experienced in their own lives, and the negligence towards caring for the poor and seeking justice for the oppressed, as reasons behind their decision to distance themselves from their charismatic backgrounds.

The emerging generations have been raised in a much more globally aware society than the generation before. By 'globally aware', I mean also that they are more aware of their responsibility in the world for the state of the world. For a generation raised after Live Aid in 1985, there is a strong sense of taking responsibility for the suffering in other nations.

Organisations such as World Vision, the Voice of the Martyrs, Make Poverty History, Live-8, and others have served to heighten the average Christian's awareness of global opportunities to alleviate suffering and carry out Jesus' commands to care for the poor.

When the apostle Paul went to Jerusalem to meet with the other apostles, and set forth the message that he had been preaching among the Gentiles (as recounted in Galatians 2:1–10), James, Peter and John approved of Paul's presentation of the gospel, and agreed that Paul and his companions should continue as they had been among the Gentiles, and 'all they asked was that we should continue to remember the poor, the very thing I was eager to do' (Galatians 2:10).

Many post-charismatics are asking the legitimate question, 'What are we doing for the poor?' and not finding any satisfactory answers. The Word of Faith response, of course, would place the blame on the poor themselves, because it was their lack of faith that accounted for their condition, and only by claiming their inheritance in the covenant could they extricate themselves from their current economic situation.

It should also be noted that, among non-charismatics, the emerging generations are asking similar questions, and likewise are not impressed with the answers they are getting. Disdain for the so-called 'social gospel' – caring for people's physical needs but not sharing the good news of the gospel – has been the legitimising excuse for many non-charismatics for their lack of attention to the needs of the poor and oppressed. This is sometimes an outgrowth of their pre-tribulational, pre-millennial eschatology (a topic too large to consider here). Suffice it to say that it's not just Word of Faith proponents who are neglecting a biblical understanding of ministry among the poor and oppressed.

Post-charismatics will read verses like Isaiah 58:6–7 and resonate with what the Spirit of God is saying prophetically through Isaiah: 'Is not this the kind of fasting I have chosen: to loose the chains of injustice and untie the cords of the yoke, to set the oppressed free and break every yoke? Is it not to share your food with the hungry and to provide the poor wanderer with shelter – when you see the naked, to clothe him, and not to turn away from your own flesh and blood?'

Many post-charismatics are looking at New Testament passages such as James 2, which clearly advocates a 'faith and works' dynamic in the lives of individual believers, and finding themselves feeling as though they have just discovered a missing jewel in their Christian experience. 'Suppose a brother or sister is without clothes and daily food. If one of you says to him, "Go, I wish you well; keep warm and well fed," but does nothing about his physical needs, what good is it?' (James 2:15–16)

Many are also tired of the constant need to be checking their 'positive confession' (and avoiding the 'confession cops', as one friend put it), to ensure that they aren't negating their confession by admitting weakness, doubt, pain or lack of finances. The Assemblies of God published a document on their denominational website, *The Believer and Positive Confession (1980 General Council of the Assemblies of God)*, which includes the following thoughts that put many of the claims of maintaining a 'positive confession' into biblical perspective.

- Paul admitted weakness and then stated that when he was weak, he was strong because God's strength is made perfect in weakness (2 Corinthians 12:9–10).[59]
- It was after the disciples recognized they did not have enough to feed the multitudes and admitted it that Christ marvellously provided a more than adequate supply (Luke 9:12–13). It was after the disciples admitted they had caught no fish that Jesus directed them to a most successful endeavour (John 21:3–6).[60]
- Paul even went so far as to glory in his infirmities instead of denying them (2 Corinthians 12:5–10).[61]
- Paul had been shown he would suffer (Acts 9:16). Later he rejoiced in his sufferings for the Colossians.[62]

While many post-charismatics (and non-charismatics) also point to the outlandish and manipulative promises made by tel-evangelists as part of their desire to distance themselves from the charismatic movement, it would be (in a sense) too easy to pick on the extremes of this part of the Word of Faith movement.

We have already noted Oral Roberts' infamous claim in 1988 that God had told him he would 'take him home' if his followers didn't come up with $8 million. The Christian and secular media jumped on this story and it became a widely rebroadcasted window into the televangelism of the 1980s. This kind of manipulation earned charismatics the contempt of many, as evidenced by U2's Bono commenting during the Joshua Tree tour, 'I can't tell the difference between ABC News, Hill Street Blues, and a preacher of the Old Time Gospel Hour, stealing money from the sick and the old. Well, the God I believe in isn't short of cash, mister.'

And yet, by the deadline, Oral had the $8 million, although the non-Christian businessman who supplied the outstanding amount suggested that Oral use the money to get some counselling.

Post-charismatics find themselves agreeing with many non-charismatics who point out that the Word of Faith teachings neglect the very real existence of suffering, and the reality of the fallen world that we live in, where sometimes bad things happen to good (even faith-full) people.

> God promises to supply the needs of believers, and He knows how to deliver the godly out of temptation; but reigning in life as Christ did may also include suffering. The committed believer will accept this. He will not be disillusioned if life is not a continual series of pleasant experiences.[63]

One of the most famous missionary stories that came out of the twentieth century was that of Jim Elliott and his five companions, who were murdered by the Auca Indians they were hoping to share the gospel with. Jim's widow, Elisabeth Elliott, returned later to the same area, and eventually many of the tribe were converted to Christianity, including some of the men who had killed her husband and his friends. *Through Gates of Splendour* was written by Elisabeth to chronicle the events that led to the conversion of so many Auca Indians. It goes without saying that Word of Faith teachers would not use this story as an example of the spread of the gospel, as it contradicts their assertion that God does not use misfortune to bring people to himself.

After Judas' suicide, all but one of the original twelve disciples died martyrs' deaths, as did Paul. Only John lived to an old age – in exile on the penal island of Patmos. Paul's 'résumé', found in 2 Corinthians 11:23–28, included beatings, imprisonment, shipwrecks, knowing thirst and hunger, and going without food many times. His life was certainly not characterised by ongoing prosperity and triumph – from a human standpoint. And at the end of this 'résumé of pain', Paul concludes with, 'If I must boast, I will boast of the things that show my weakness' (2 Corinthians 11:30).

This recognition that the Word of Faith doctrine doesn't square with the rest of Scripture – outside of the out-of-context proof-texts that Word of Faith is based on – was recognised by one of Word of Faith's primary spokespersons, Jim Bakker, after his prison term for defrauding thousands of Christians of millions of dollars. J. Lee Grady, in *What Happened to the Fire?*, quotes Bakker as saying, 'There is no way, if you take the whole counsel of God's Word, that you can equate riches or material things as a sign of God's blessing . . . I have asked God to forgive me and I ask all who have sat under my ministry to forgive me for preaching a gospel emphasizing earthly prosperity.'[64]

The position paper of the Assemblies of God also contains a serious question about whether or not the prosperity message was somehow peculiar to an already-affluent North American culture: 'Does the teaching have meaning only for those living in an affluent society? Or does it also work among the refugees of the world? What application does the teaching have for believers imprisoned for their faith by atheistic governments? Are those believers substandard who suffer martyrdom or grave physical injury at the hands of cruel, ruthless dictators? The truth of God's Word has a universal application.'[65]

Grady cites this as a corroborative example: 'In 1993 healing evangelist Benny Hinn stunned some of his followers when he announced that he was washing his hands of the so-called "prosperity gospel" . . . God would not permit him, he said, to stand before the poverty-stricken people of Manila and promise them that if they gave in the offering, God would bless them with more money. If the prosperity message should not be preached in the Philippines, Hinn decided, it should not be preached in America. "It is not a message from God," he said.'[66] Sadly, even a cursory look at Hinn's website suggests that he does not retain the same conviction today.

It is this perception that the Word of Faith teachings only work in already-affluent societies that has many charismatics and post-charismatics distancing themselves. The many verses in both the Old and New Testaments that speak of God's people being commissioned to maintain and pursue justice are overwhelming, when considered alongside the reality that the Word of Faith subculture is largely a Western, affluent one.

Finally, the performance-orientation of the Word of Faith movement is wearying for many, and to those who have already dealt with issues of striving and works-based sanctification, it is anathema. The idea that our reality is shaped by our positive or negative confession puts all the responsibility on human effort, and precludes God's grace (unmerited favour) being active in the individual believer's daily walk. 'The disciples of Kenyon speak of prosperity as a "divine right" and have formulated laws of prosperity to be rehearsed daily by persons seeking health and wealth.'[67]

This wariness of performance-orientation is compounded by Franklin Hall's understanding of fasting as a way of getting God to perform his part of the covenant: 'Jesus fasted in order to secure His perfect faith from His humanity side . . . Jesus received the Holy Spirit, but this did not seem sufficient. It requires fasting and prayer to operate the Holy Ghost.'[68]

To post-charismatics, this just sounds like more works-based performance. And the unspoken (and sometimes spoken) other side of the coin is that if prosperity, health and victory are not apparent in a believer's life, the problem is the believer's faulty faith. This judgmental accusation usually serves to destroy whatever faith the person might have had. 'All of God's blessings and provisions are conditional. He gave us His Word to let us know what conditions must be met in order for us to receive these blessings.'[69]

The truth of God's word is that he does provide for our needs, and instructs us to pray for our daily bread – as well as our other needs – but this is based on a deepening relationship with Jesus, not a contractual obligation that God is held to if we can just muster up the right kind of faith. And there are many stories of God's miraculous healing power being released in people's lives, as well as miracles of financial provision, but nowhere does Scripture teach us that these things are our 'rights'; they are, as everything else we receive from God, gifts of grace that flow out of his will.

COVERING AND AUTHORITY

When Wendy and I first met Jeremy, he and his wife were the kind of Christians that you enjoyed hanging out with so much that you almost want to invent more reasons to spend time with them. They were friendly, hospitable, and you always came away feeling encouraged, and just a little closer to Jesus for having spent time with them.

Jeremy was a gifted worship leader, and there were few things he enjoyed more than worshipping, whether all by himself, in a house group or leading a congregation into the presence of God. For Jeremy, leading worship was just another way of expressing his love for Jesus, and his attitude of being a servant.

We lost touch for a number of years, after Jeremy and his family got involved in a new church. They seemed happy at first, and would remark on the great things that God had promised for this church. We assumed, as anyone who knew Jeremy would, that he would be leading worship at this new church in a reasonably short time.

When we ran into them again, some years later, Jeremy had just been 'released' to be a worship leader at the church a few weeks earlier, after being there for more than eight years. We were incredulous. Apparently, Jeremy had to first prove his trustworthiness, but his desire to lead worship was labelled 'worldly ambition', so he was placed 'under the covering' of an overseer who would test and try him until he was convinced Jeremy was properly 'submitted'.

Finally, after more than eight years, Jeremy had finally been released as a worship leader. His wife had given up on the church some years earlier, finding the services far too painful to be a part of. Jeremy shared with us, 'He (the overseer) said, "I feel that I can now release you to lead worship, because you've proven that you're submitted to my authority.'"

As I looked at him, a shell of who he had been – the vibrancy and cheerfulness that both he and his wife had been known for now gone – I really did not know what to say. Finally, I simply asked, 'And what did you say to him when he released you?'

He looked down at the ground, his whole demeanour suggesting weariness and resignation. 'I thanked him,' he finally said. Crossing his arms over his chest, he slowly shook his head in disbelief, not looking us in the eye. Softly but angrily, he continued through clenched teeth, 'Can you believe that? I actually *thanked him.*'

Among post-charismatics, there appears to be no teaching or practice that elicits stronger negative reactions than the concepts of 'being under a covering', or 'being under authority'. While the Word of Faith represents only a very small part of the charismatic movement overall, the teaching regarding 'covering' has apparently been much more widespread, and has caused much more damage.

Coupled with the teaching of 'touch not the Lord's anointed' (don't question your leaders' teaching or conduct), the covering doctrine has resulted in many charismatics abandoning the movement.

The Shepherding movement is probably the most widely known recent example of the widespread dissemination of the covering and authority doctrines, although the movement can hardly be credited with creating these teachings. The Shepherding movement only stands as testimony to the most recent version of an ages-old problem. However, any mention of the Shepherding movement continues to elicit strong reactions, which have not dulled with the official dissolution of the movement.

Many who have been in or observed the Shepherding movement would find themselves in agreement with the following summation:

> Quite a number of pastors have been guilty of demanding unquestioning submission and obedience from members – many claiming that as the Lord's 'anointed' they were only answerable to God, and no one else had the right or the authority to question them, their teachings, their behaviour, their lifestyle or their manipulative demands.[1]

Nothing new under the sun

The roots of the Shepherding movement go back into numerous sources, primarily the writings of Watchman Nee, a Chinese believer who was imprisoned and later martyred for his faith by the Maoist government in China. We will be examining some of Nee's teachings that became formative for the leaders of the Shepherding movement.

Another source of input was the Latter Rain, through the writings and teachings of Ern Baxter, one of the 'Fort Lauderdale Five' who gave leadership to the Shepherding movement. As we have looked at the Latter Rain in depth earlier, we will only briefly touch on the areas of influence that the Latter Rain had on the Shepherding movement.

But the roots of the problem go much further back than Watchman Nee, or the Latter Rain. The problem of authoritarian leadership has been around for centuries. The prophets in the Old Testament regularly prophesied against the abuse that the Israelites were enduring under corrupt priests, false prophets and ungodly tyrants.

> Both hands are skilled in doing evil; the ruler demands gifts, the judge accepts bribes, the powerful dictate what they desire – they all conspire together. (Micah 7:3)
>
> Woe to those who make unjust laws, to those who issue oppressive decrees, to deprive the poor of their rights and withhold justice from the oppressed of my people, making widows their prey and robbing the powerless. (Isaiah 10:1–2)
>
> So the Lord will cut off from Israel both head and tail. . . the elders and prominent men are the head, the prophets who teach lies are the tail. Those who guide this people mislead them, and those who are guided are led astray. (Isaiah 9:14–15)

Jesus' words to his own disciples echo the same problem with the human tendency to want to have power over others: 'You know that the rulers of the Gentiles lord it over them, and their high officials exercise authority over them. Not so with you. . .' (Matthew 20:25–26).

The problem still exists today, in that people use a ministry position to gain power over others, or at the very least, the common understanding of what leadership looks like places leaders in a system which demands and rewards hierarchical control.

The irony is that most of these leaders would see themselves as servants, but the model of leadership that has been adopted is at odds with the servant example of Jesus. Brother Maynard is a respected Canadian blogger with roots in the Salt & Light movement in Canada, and he notes, 'It is not possible to hold the thoroughly hierarchical view of Church authority necessary to support the doctrine of spiritual covering and still exhibit New Testament servant leadership. The two are incompatible.'[2]

Peter also warned church leaders that they must act in a way that is 'not lording it over those entrusted to you' (1 Peter 5:3). J. Lee Grady strongly states: 'It is time we challenged authoritarianism and called it what it is: an illegitimate use of God's name and authority[3]. . . We expect bullying in the corporate world, but we should not tolerate it among church leaders.'[4]

To place the responsibility for authoritarian leadership solely on the Shepherding movement, or Watchman Nee, would be short-sighted. The problem of authoritarianism predates the church age that began at the Feast of Pentecost, going back into the earliest history of the people of God.

At the same time, the pervasiveness of the terms 'covering' and 'under authority' – backed up by 'touch not the Lord's anointed' – gives ample reason to look more closely at the most recent movements that have spawned authoritarianism (which was the last thing they had intended). To that end, we will examine some of Watchman Nee's teachings that in turn shaped the Shepherding movement, where the terms 'covering' and 'under authority' gained the prominence that we see continuing even today, long after the dissolution of the movement.

George Mallone observes wisely, 'In its extreme, it (Shepherding) is extortion and domination of the worst variety. Seen in its best light it is a response to the crass individualism of many North American Christians. The question that is being asked is, how are we to shepherd people unless they are responsive to our authority?'[5]

Watchman Nee

Watchman Nee's writings had a profound influence on the Shepherding movement, and the articulation of the ideas of covering and authority stem mainly from Nee's *Authority and Submission* (also published under the title *Spiritual Authority*). While Nee's most well-known writing is *The Normal Christian Life*, it is *Authority and Submission* that is the text that delineates the covering doctrine.

Watchman Nee was raised in a second generation Christian family, but it was not until he was 17 that Watchman became a professing Christian. His early influences were mostly Plymouth Brethren teachers and writers, although some of his later teachings do not reflect classic Brethren thought.

'In 1928, Watchman Nee settled in Shanghai where he based his own speaking and publication work, the Shanghai Gospel Bookroom, which published books by Watchman Nee and others. . .'[6] Nee's passion was for the local church, and many thousands of house churches in China can trace their lineage to Nee's influence and writings.

To be fair, it is important to consider that much of Nee's emphasis on authority was a product of his time and place in history. 'Nee's writings on spiritual authority and on the normal church life reflect the kind of Asian authoritarianism that prevailed before World War II.'[7]

Watchman Nee was imprisoned in 1952 during the Communist revolution in China, and remained in prison until his death in 1972. Because of Nee's steadfast faith in spite of his imprisonment, and his subsequent martyrdom, his writings have, posthumously, been given a significant platform.

While *The Normal Christian Life* does not normally raise eye-brows for most Christians, there are still some intriguing ideas that Nee puts forward, particularly his interpretation of the interaction between the 'soul' and the 'spirit' of a man. Nee believed that the spirit of a man was good, responding to God appropriately, but that the soul was in rebellion against submitting to God's authority. Referring to Adam's fall in Genesis 3, Nee suggests, 'It is not merely that man has a soul, but that from that day on the soul, with its independent powers of free choice, takes the place of the spirit as the animating power of man.'[8]

This wrestle between acting in the spirit (desirable), versus acting in the soul (basis of sin), dominates much of the rest of the writing of *The Normal Christian Life*. Nee applies this to the temptation of Jesus: 'That thing in Him which is in distinction from the Father is the human soul, which He assumed when He was "found in fashion as a man". Being a perfect Man our Lord had a soul, and of course a body, just as you and I have a soul and a body, and it was possible for Him to act *from the soul* – that is, from Himself.'[9] *(emphasis in original)*

This, according to Nee, was the basis of Satan's temptation of Christ – whether Jesus would act from his soul, or from his spirit. The debate regarding whether or not Jesus could actually have chosen to sin has been hotly contested, but most Christians would accept the idea that, in order for Jesus to have been 'tempted in all ways as we are, yet without sin' (Hebrews 4:15), the temptation would have to be truly 'tempting', and the possibility of succumbing a real danger.

The use of this 'spirit/soul' dichotomy is not uncommon in some charismatic circles – you often hear references to 'soul-ish' attitudes or even soul-ish prayers, meaning that some people are acting, thinking or praying from their soul, not their spirit. In some ways, it is another form of Gnosticism, where the body (flesh) was seen as evil and the spirit was good; in this instance the same approach is used regarding the soul versus the spirit. While not wanting this to become a rabbit trail to the whole issue of submission and authority, it is helpful to recognise that this idea from Watchman Nee *does* impact the issues of covering. Simply put, when people question the inappropriate use of authority that too often results from the doctrines of covering and authority, the questioner is usually dismissed as being 'in rebellion', or acting soulishly.

In *The Normal Christian Life*, Nee also puts forth the idea that Christians cannot be used by God until they have achieved some level of spiritual purity. (Some of Nee's apologists suggest that Nee had, in classic Wesleyan fashion, achieved perfection and completely overcome Satan.) Nee takes this to the extent that he suggests that whether or not we are 'raptured' with Christ depends on our preparedness:

> If I mistake not, this is the one passage in the New Testament that tells of our reaction to the rapture call. We may have thought that when the Son of man comes we shall be taken up automatically, as it were, because of what we read in 1 Corinthians 15 . . . Well, however we reconcile the two passages, this one in Luke's Gospel (17:31–32) should at least make us pause and reflect; for the emphasis is here very strongly upon one being taken and the other left. It is a matter of our reaction to the call to go, and on the basis of this a most urgent appeal is made to us to be ready.[10]

Again, this is not meant to divert us from our discussion of submission and authority. However, it should be pointed out that the emphasis on possibly missing what God was doing has also been used to keep people from questioning leaders. While Nee takes it to an extreme – missing the Second Coming – many charismatics have been effectively silenced by suggestions that they were acting soulishly and therefore might be passed over in the next great move of the Spirit.

Nee on spiritual authority

Throughout the text of *Submission and Authority*, it becomes immediately clear that the concept of submitting to authority is the lens through which Nee read the entire Bible:

> In the old creation and in the new creation, the order of precedence is the basis of authority. Whoever is created first is the authority. Whoever is saved first is the authority. For this reason, wherever we go, our first thought should be to find those to whom the Lord wants us to submit.[11]

Nee based this understanding on authority being the primary concern of God, and that this authority was bound up in God's very essence. Much like his creation of a binary opposition between spirit and soul, Watchman Nee also separated God's holiness and authority into different categories:

> Violating God's authority is a matter of rebellion; it is more serious than violating God's holiness. Sin is a matter of conduct; it is easy to be forgiven of sin. But rebellion is a matter of principle; it is not easy to be forgiven of rebellion.[12]

This elevation of rebellion as the highest sin – with the built-in threat that receiving forgiveness for rebellion is somehow more difficult than receiving forgiveness for sin – serves to place an inordinate amount of pressure on those who accept this teaching to make sure that they do not stray out from under the authority that is placed above them.

Watchman Nee believed that God had appointed 'delegated authorities' to express his authority on earth, and absolute, unquestioning obedience to these delegated authorities was required. Nee went as far as to state that rebellion against delegated authority was the same as rebellion against God, because all authority comes from God: 'Not only did (Eve) transgress God's commandment, she also disregarded Adam's authority. Rebellion against God's deputy authority is rebellion against God Himself.'[14]

Nee saw this hierarchical approach to authority as being of first and foremost importance whenever Christians were gathered: 'When a few brothers are together, they should know how to line themselves up immediately . . . With us there should never be right or wrong, good or evil. Wherever we go, we should first know who is the authority. If you know who you have to submit to, you will spontaneously know what position you should occupy in the Body, and you will stand in your proper position.'[13]

The reason behind Nee's insistence on submitting to delegated authority was that he envisioned that this hierarchy of submission was actually present in the Trinity itself. Nee believed that Jesus only became 'Lord' after his ascension and that, previously, Jesus was not considered to have the attributes of lordship – because he had not yet earned them through living a life of submission on earth.

Being God is (Jesus') original position. But His attainment of the position of Lord is based on what He has done. When He laid aside His divine form to fully maintain the principle of submission and subsequently ascended to the heavens, God accorded to Him the position of Lord . . . This lordship was not originally present in the Godhead.[15]

Even salvation was contingent on submission to delegated authority. Nee taught that only those who were in submission to their leaders truly understood – and had experienced – salvation. Hence the need for absolute obedience and submission to any earthly delegated authority (determined by how long others had been Christians, and also their chronological age).

If we want to learn submission to God, we should know to whom the authority of God is entrusted. If we understand God's authority as being only in Himself, it is very likely that we will offend God's authority more than half of the time . . .[16] Man's rebellious nature likes to submit to God's direct authority but reject God's appointed deputy authority.[17]

This troubling statement seems to negate the Reformation doctrine that Christ is mediator between God and humanity, without the need for additional human intermediaries. The teaching regarding delegated authority (or 'under-shepherds' as the Shepherding movement would refer to it) turns the clock back on the Protestant Reformation, and is reintroducing the idea of a hierarchical system of intermediaries. The idea of mutual submission to each other as equal parts of the body of Christ is rejected.

For Watchman Nee, submission to delegated authority was an unquestionable protocol: 'Today many ask, "Why do I have to submit?" They also ask, "Why do I have to submit to you? I am a brother, and you are a brother." Actually, men do not have a right to say such things.'[17]

It is important also to recognise that Nee did not take the responsibility of being a delegated authority lightly. He was concerned that delegated authorities, like the Old Testament kings and priests, could become corrupt and misrepresent God's authority: 'It is imperative that an authority represent God properly. Whether in wrath or in compassion, he should be like God all the time. If we are wrong, we should confess that we are wrong; we should never drag God into our mistake.'[18]

While it is commendable that Nee would want delegated authorities to be willing to admit error, it remains disturbing that he still assumed that 'in wrath or in compassion', an authority was even capable of 'properly' representing God.

Attaining status as a delegated authority

The request in Matthew 20 of James and John (through their mother) for the seats on the left and right of Christ is a significant part of Watchman Nee's teaching on who may occupy those seats of authority.

Jesus used the request of James and John to highlight that the disciples were not to seek to lord it over their brothers and sisters, as the rulers of the Gentiles did. However, Watchmen Nee turns this passage around to mean just the opposite:

> James and John thought that they would acquire the place merely by asking. But the Lord told them that it was not a matter of asking but a matter of drinking the cup and partaking of the baptism. . .[21]

This is why the Lord asked James and John, 'Are you able to drink the cup which I drink'? It seems that the Lord was saying, 'If a man wants to draw near to Me and receive a place in glory above that of the other children of God, he must be like Me, yielding to God's will and taking it as the unique goal. Only such ones can come near to Me and sit at My right and left hand.'[22]

Jesus was saying no such thing. He was using this opportunity to teach his disciples that they should eschew such desires for hierarchical power positions in favour of mutual service towards each other. To be great in the kingdom is to be a servant, not to seek the status of 'delegated authority'.

Watchman Nee also held out the possibility to those who followed his teachings that they could aspire to have those seats which James and John coveted:

> If the Lord gave the right and left places to James and John, these two seats would have been gone for the past two thousand years of church history . . . The Lord did not grant their request, and the two seats are still available. Some among us may still have a chance to take those two seats.[23]

One of the responsibilities that anyone seeking the two seats must be willing to accept is that '. . .we must learn to bear all of God's children upon our shoulders. May the Lord make us gracious persons, those who can tolerate all of God's children and who can bear His children upon our shoulders.'[24]

This kind of thinking should set off alarm bells for those familiar with Scripture, as Jesus is the only one who deserves this position, but keep in mind that it makes sense if you accept the idea of delegated authority in the first place. But aside from not being a biblically sound idea, the acceptance of this paradigm often results in giving leaders power over the body that they have no right to have; power that creates temptations towards authoritarianism which they seem incapable of resisting.

As J. Lee Grady notes, 'Rather than see their role as that of a servant to encourage, strengthen and equip the people of God, authoritarian leaders inflate their own importance and view themselves as somehow "owning" the people God has entrusted to them for spiritual oversight.'[25]

Hebrews 13 is a passage often cited to support this idea; we will spend some time dissecting these verses in the post-charismatic part of this section. Watchman Nee, however, takes this 'ownership' motif a step further by suggesting that those who have attained the status of delegated authority will have unique insights into the hearts and motives of the people under his authority (I am deliberately using non-inclusive language here because only men were allowed to be leaders in both Nee's and the Shepherding movement's understanding of covering and authority).

'If a man has met authority [learned submission and become a delegated authority], any transgression in others will be detected by him immediately. He will see through many lawlessnesses and realize many rebellions. He will then come to know that the principle of lawlessness abounds everywhere, in the world as well as in the church.'[26]

This type of omniscience is usually reserved for God. However, the suspicion that many controlling leaders exhibit towards those in their churches might make more sense, knowing that they're expecting to be able to easily discern people's transgression, rebellion and lawlessness.

Nee takes this to an interesting extreme: 'It is also right for us to leave the denominations to stand as the testimony of oneness in the local church . . . Today's denominational organizations are overthrowing the Lord's glory. This is a blasphemy to the Lord.'[27]

Lastly, Nee taught that delegated authorities had special revelatory knowledge of God's will that was not available to the average believer. As such, these delegated authorities had the responsibility to tell other believers under their care what God's will for them as individuals was: 'A person becomes an authority because of his knowledge of God's will, God's mind, and God's thoughts . . . God appoints a person to be a deputy authority because such a person knows His will and His thoughts more than others.'[28]

Another area that affects the later Shepherding movement and leaders today who employ an authoritarian approach to discipling is Nee's insistence on aloofness on the part of the delegated authority from the rest of the body:

> But if we vindicate ourselves to anyone, we are in effect making him our judge. If we seek understanding from anyone, we are falling under that person's feet. Hence, we must never vindicate ourselves and must never seek understanding from anyone.[29]

In other words, leaders who buy into this paradigm never have to defend, explain or be accountable for anything they say or do. They are unassailable. This is a dangerous position for the leader to be in, and even more so for those who have been convinced to submit their lives to such a leader.

This type of aloofness is also seen in some leaders who pride themselves on their professional and scholastic accomplishments, but here Nee is advocating a distance between shepherds and those following them that destroys the fabric of community, and leaves the delegated authorities vulnerable as a result of isolation and spiritual pride.

> In order for us to learn to be an authority, we can only fellowship with the brothers and sisters to a certain extent . . .[30] It will strip us of excitement. We will no longer dare to joke around the brothers and sisters . . .[31] We cannot enjoy what others enjoy, and we cannot rejoice in what others rejoice in. (God) has to separate the holy from the common. . .[32]
>
> Authority is based on separation. Without separation there is no authority. If you crave the company of others, you cannot be an authority. The higher an authority stands, the greater is the separation . . .[33] Authority manifests itself in separation and distinction.[34]

This runs contrary to the most prominent metaphor of the church that is found in the Bible: that of the body of Christ, all submitted to the lordship of Jesus, and mutually submitting to each other out of reverence for Christ. As George Mallone reminds us, 'Contrary to what we would like to believe, elders, pastors and deacons are not in a chain of command, a hierarchical pyramid, which puts them under Christ and over the church. The leaders of a biblical church are simply members of the body of Christ, not an elite oligarchy.'[35]

However, as the recent (1970s and 1980s) history of the charismatic movement has shown us, these ideas of delegated authority, hierarchical power, and a clergy/laity divide do not easily go away. As was mentioned earlier, Watchman Nee did not originate these ideas; even Jesus had to actively teach his own disciples against this kind of approach.

It is sad to hear the protest, 'Don't you know Watchman Nee was martyred for his faith?' used in an attempt to silence anyone who questions his teachings, as if martyrdom equates God's stamp of approval on anyone's teachings. Significantly, Nee's writings were used to give credence to the Shepherding movement which began to coalesce within a year or so of Nee's martyrdom in China, circa 1972.

The Shepherding movement

The Shepherding movement did not start out intending to be a 'movement'. The five men who decided to enter into an accountability pact with each other were responding to the recognition of their own human weaknesses, and humbly choosing to be transparent and accountable to each other.

However, if you use the phrase 'shepherding movement' around anyone who is familiar with what it later became, the reaction is typically coloured by references to controlling, abusive, hierarchical power trips. What happened?

As J. Lee Grady points out, 'Since the renewal blossomed in the late 1960s, many groups that began with vibrant faith degenerated quickly into legalism and authoritarianism.'[36] There were many sociological as well as spiritual reasons for this troubling trend. The turbulence of the 1960s had left many exhausted and looking for stability and rest.

The failure of the 1960s revolution to achieve its most cherished goals – ending the war in Vietnam, enlightenment through experimentation with drugs and the occult, and a new era of world peace and love – left many young people disillusioned. But even as the sixties were drawing to a close, God was supernaturally orchestrating a significant revival among the emerging generations of that day, and particularly among the hippies and counter-cultural groups that had just recently been some of the harshest reactionaries against Christianity.

Literally thousands of counter-cultural young people became Christians in just a few years – they were called Jesus People and Jesus Freaks, and the movement was quickly dubbed the Jesus movement, and even featured on the cover of *Time*. Calvary Chapel, Costa Mesa, became one of the most well-known centres for this revival among the emerging generations. Similar to the post-charismatics of today, 'the Jesus Movement was non-traditional and characterised by an emphasis on community, contemporary music, outreach activism, use of indigenous media and parachurch structures.'[37]

However, as exciting as the Jesus movement was in terms of thousands of the emerging generations turning to God, there arose the problem of discipleship (spiritual transformation) among an entire generation that was the forefront of the growing trend of the 'un-churched' – meaning that many, if not most, of these new converts had zero previous involvement in a church.

> The 1960s cultural revolution, with its anti-institutional orientation, had been carried into the Jesus movement revival and left many young people 'leaderless' . . . The Jesus movement fostered a generation of energetic and idealistic young Christians in need of spiritual accountability and discipline.[38]

While to suppose that the entire Jesus People revival was charismatic in theology and experience would be inaccurate, the influence of Calvary Chapel, and later the Vineyard movement (an offshoot of Calvary Chapel), meant that a significant number of these Jesus People were charismatic in their understanding and practice of the faith.

This raised a sociological problem that many did not take into account at the time. David Moore, in his helpful book *The Shepherding Movement: Charismatic Ecclesiology and Controversy*, writes: 'Since the Charismatic Renewal in part was a reaction to a lack of spiritual experience in the historic churches, many Charismatics responded not only by leaving their churches, but also by casting off any sense of ecclesiastical polity, tradition, or restraint, making themselves vulnerable to confusion and deception.'[39]

So, then, we can see three sociological phenomena that shaped the fabric of the charismatic renewal, including the Jesus People, that set up the kind of situation where a leadership and discipling vacuum would emerge:

- A society that was in turmoil and wanting some sense of stability in the midst of significant cultural change
- A movement of charismatics who, in their zeal to throw off dead systems of church, had not developed a robust ecclesiology in its place – they had an instinctive distrust of denominational and clergy authority
- An influx of counter-culture young people, with passion and zeal but little knowledge, who shared a similar distrust of authority

An aside just here would be to point out the chilling similarity between the societal and ecclesiastical situation of the early 1970s and the dynamics that are present now in the early twenty-first century. It is this writer's contention that we may face another, possibly more damaging, version of the Shepherding movement if we do not learn from history's mistakes, and pro-actively develop a biblically sound understanding of authority and discipleship. Some of the more abusive leadership styles that exist today use the term 'mentoring' instead of 'shepherding', but the tactics of control and the demand for conformity are the same.

Even as the 1960s were drawing to a close, older Christians were already recognising the need for helping these young believers to become disciples, and not just converts. These older Christians were deeply concerned that these new believers could end up falling away from the faith as in the Parable of the Sower and Seed, when the cares of this world or persecution would cause these tender plants to shrivel and die.

One of these concerned believers was Eldon Purvis, a Christian businessman, who felt a deep concern for the lack of spiritual depth that he was aware of in the charismatic renewal of the 1960s. 'From these Charismatic meetings Purvis and others became increasingly aware that there was a need for "some kind of teaching mission" to tell others about the Holy Spirit's power. From this vision came the birth of the Holy Spirit Teaching Mission (HSTM).'[40]

The HSTM began in earnest in 1965, and began holding conference in Fort Lauderdale, Florida, that same year. It quickly became a significant centre of the charismatic renewal, with many well-known Pentecostal and charismatic speakers addressing the conferences, including David du Plessis and Dennis Bennett, whose book *Nine O'Clock in the Morning* (co-written with his wife, Rita Bennett) had become a classic text for the charismatic renewal and beyond. The primary motivation was to provide a teaching ministry, and as such Purvis and his colleagues were seeking to fulfil the mandate to be spiritual fathers (1 Thessalonians 2:10–12). The HSTM also made use of television and was granted its own broadcasting licence in 1968.

> Of greater significance, the HSTM started *New Wine* in the spring of 1969. Purvis invited Don Basham and Derek Prince, both living in Ft. Lauderdale, to serve with him on the magazine's editorial board . . . Beginning with the magazine's second issue, Charles Simpson wrote a monthly Bible study, 'Breaking Bread', and also joined the editorial board in early 1970 along with Bob Mumford. At Purvis' invitation, Mumford moved to Ft. Lauderdale in August 1970.[41]

What makes this significant is that these four men – Prince, Basham, Simpson and Mumford – would become widely referred to, along with Ern Baxter, as the 'Fort Lauderdale Five', who were the acknowledged leaders of what would later become the Shepherding movement.

However, not long after the introduction of *New Wine* magazine (not to be confused with the present-day renewal conference and confederation which started in the UK), Eldon Purvis – the undisputed leader of the HSTM – was accused of 'serious misconduct', which he later admitted to, as well as confessing other problems. The HSTM's board called the four teachers associated with the ministry – Prince, Basham, Simpson and Mumford – to meet with them to work through the crisis.

It was during this time that the four teachers began to forge the bonds of relationship that would prove to be the genesis of the Shepherding movement: 'As the four men discussed and prayed regarding the problems surrounding the crisis and particularly the unfortunate situation with Purvis, they recognized their own weaknesses . . . One by one the men acknowledged their own vulnerability to misconduct and confessed their fears and temptations to one another. The four knew they needed accountability and protection.'[42]

The four men decided to form a mutual accountability group for themselves. They all had independent teaching ministries, although they were also commonly linked through *New Wine* magazine, but recognised that as human beings who lived in the reality of Romans 7, they needed each other as a safeguard against falling into sin.

However, as well-known teachers, with the added platform of a magazine and a regular conference, word spread of their commitment to each other. 'Because these men had hammered out a special covenant among themselves, submitting their lives and ministries to one another, they taught that all Christians, in order to grow spiritually, should likewise submit themselves to a personal pastor or "shepherd".'[43]

It should be noted that the initial accountability covenant was a bond of mutuality. The change towards each person needing a personal shepherd – quite different from a mutual accountability – was the beginning of a change that would later lead to the hierarchical structures that the Shepherding movement became most noted for.

As David Moore notes in retrospect, 'From this milieu a church movement was born as they tapped into a leadership vacuum within the Charismatic Renewal. Hundreds of leaders came running to find a pastor.'[44] Suddenly, the four teachers were thrust into the spotlight as the leaders of a new paradigm of leadership which they themselves were still fleshing out. They had intended to encourage believers to be in accountability or 'covenant' relationships with each other, but the vacuum of leadership quickly pushed them into developing an ecclesiology to give language to this concept.

The mutuality of the original Fort Lauderdale Five gave way to a discipling method – which they saw as flowing in the same manner as John Wesley's Methodist small groups – that quickly raised some suspicions that these leaders were covertly (or unwittingly) moving towards developing a charismatic denomination, with themselves as the leaders.

From the beginning, there were concerns about the association of the four teachers. Prince and Basham had a strong emphasis on deliverance ministry, including the controversial question of whether or not a born-again, Spirit-filled Christian could be demonised (literally, 'have a demon', not synonymous with demon possession) – both Prince and Basham taught that Christians could indeed be demonised.

Leaders such as du Plessis and Ralph Wilkerson expressed concerns to Mumford and Simpson about their association with the 'demon-chasers' (Prince and Basham), but 'These five very different men were drawn together because they were like-minded in their concern for the spiritual maturity of the Charismatic believers.'[45]

> According to Prince: 'We saw a lack of spiritual growth in many Christians . . . Thousands of people were coming into the Charismatic Renewal, but most had little or no knowledge of Scripture, or how to live in the Spirit.'[46]

The Fort Lauderdale Five did not become a quintet until 1974, with the connection that the four teachers made with Ern

Baxter, who approached them at one of the early conferences and asked to be directly included in their accountability group. As a fifth teacher, Baxter fitted in immediately. Despite the unsought label 'Fort Lauderdale Five', the five teachers were never all living in Fort Lauderdale at the same time. But four of them did, and the *New Wine* magazine was based there, which gave impetus to the name sticking.

Ern Baxter brought an interesting mix of theological ideas to the group; Baxter was a Reformed pastor in a Pentecostal denomination, and had been a part of the Latter Rain Movement, as well as one of the Bible teachers travelling with William Branham in the 1950s. Baxter also functioned as Branham's campaign manager during his seven years of travelling with Branham. The Latter Rain influence on the Shepherding movement came primarily through Baxter.

Bob Mumford was but one of five teachers, all of whom were considered gifted, but his personal charisma and eloquence resulted in him being the figurehead of the burgeoning movement, although the others' influence, teaching and writings remained considerable.

As Prince was quoted above, the lack of perceived spiritual growth in the charismatic renewal (including the newly minted Jesus People) was disturbing to the teachers, who felt a sense of burden and responsibility to address this leadership vacuum. However, the high profile association of four (later five) high profile conference speakers caused some concern that they were gearing up to start their own denomination.

While some of the focus was on Mumford and Simpson joining with the 'demon chasers', Basham and Prince, the concerns went beyond that issue . . . As a consequence of the suspicions regarding their association and other issues that challenged the Charismatic Renewal's unity, Basham, Mumford, Prince, and Simpson were instrumental, along with Dennis Bennett, Harald Bredeson, and David du Plessis, in starting an annual 'Charismatic Leaders Conference'.[47]

The original intent of this Charismatic Leaders Conference was to provide an opportunity for charismatic leaders from across a wide spectrum of denominations to join together for fellowship and teaching; the second issue was to demonstrate that the Fort Lauderdale Five were not starting their own denomination, which the inclusion of Bennett, Bredeson and du Plessis should have indicated.

However, the vacuum in leadership created a situation in which the anticipated numbers were dwarfed by the deluge of conference participants. 'Expecting 75 charismatic pastors and lay leaders, the conference drew, by word of mouth, an attendance of over 450. The second, in June 1974, held at Montreat NC, drew over 1,700 pastors and leaders.'[48]

Watchman Nee's influence became evident very early on. After the spring Church Growth Ministries Conference in Miami in 1972, the next issue of *New Wine* included this quote:

In past years God has laid the emphasis of teaching on the Baptism in the Holy Spirit, Water Baptism, The Gifts of the Spirit, and other topics usually associated with the Charismatic movement. This year the message came through loud and clear on a new area: AUTHORITY. God is beginning to place in His Church the authority that has been truly lacking for so many years. Along with this came a new understanding of the home and family relationship, divine order in the church, and a believer's personal relationship of submission to God.[49]

Nee's concept of delegated authority quickly became a central part of a strategy that consisted of essentially three parts:

1. A recognition of the need for submission to God's delegated authority. 'Another significant article in *New Wine* was Charles Simpson's "Covering of the Lord" in the October 1972 issue. This article was a direct result of the HSTM leadership crisis in 1970 and focused on the "covering" or protection provided by submitting oneself to God's delegated authority in the home, church, and civil government.'[50]

2. An emphasis on the five-fold ministries – apostle, prophet, pastor, teacher and evangelist – as the key to equipping the body to be effective in ministry and grow in maturity. Like the Latter Rain movement, there were assumptions made that the leaders of this movement were the apostolic and prophetic foundation. 'Specifically, he (Prince) emphasized the roles of apostles and prophets as present-day ministries. Prince also presented an idealistic view of "one city, one church" concept in which Christians should congregate not by any one denomination, but by geographical groupings of "cells" or house churches, in which leaders emerge.'[51]

3. The house church (or cell group) as the primary vehicle for these shepherding relationships to be practised. Each house group leader would be likewise submitted to another leader above him (women leaders were not allowed), and so on, up the hierarchical chain to the translocal Fort Lauderdale Five.

Idealism was quite common among the leaders in the early months; it seemed to them that God was allowing them a precious opportunity to assist the charismatic renewal into a season of greater spiritual maturity. The developing ecclesiology that would give impetus to this ministry would be the house church or cell group. 'Along with Basham, Mumford and Prince, Simpson became more convinced that house churches were central to New Testament ecclesiology and were the missing dimension in contemporary church practice.'[52]

The concept of house churches as a primary building block of the growing Shepherding movement was initially seen as a helpful way to allow a relational basis to develop. In light of this, while there was emphasis placed on apostles and prophets in the five-fold ministry, there was also a strong emphasis on the pastoral role in the maturation of the body.

> They saw shepherds as the most important of God's delegated authorities in mediating his government on the earth. Jesus as the Great Shepherd delegated to 'undershepherds' the care for his sheep. This concept of Shepherding was a logical next step in implementing the ecclesiologically oriented principles of authority and submission, covering, and fivefold ministry offices . . . Discipleship emphasized the need for mentoring by a more mature leader, and house groups provided the venue for building the accountability and community the four teachers believed so essential.[54]

The goal of these house groups, as they submitted to their delegated authority (under-shepherd), was simple: 'Believers were not to be casual church participants who simply attended meetings. Each believer was a vital participant in the church. . .[55] They hoped their teachings on submission to a shepherd and the importance of Christian community would help charismatic leaders draw independent charismatics into practical, committed church participation.'[56]

With the influence of Ern Baxter, the Latter Rain concept of a conquering end-times army became grafted into the teachings that were already heavily influenced by Watchman Nee's *Authority and Submission*. In *Thy Kingdom Come*, Ern Baxter wrote: 'Drawing from Psalm 110, the movement taught that Christ was to remain seated in heaven until his enemies in the earth were subdued by the activity of the redeemed community . . . whereby he would establish God's sovereign right to reign in his own redeemed earth.'[57]

The teachings of the Shepherding movement continued to develop into a stronger hierarchy of delegated authority – the Five would have shepherding relationships 'translocally' with other leaders, who would in turn be shepherds over others, and so on. As this happened, some Christian leaders began to express concerns. At the same time, the fervor in the movement was becoming increasingly apocalyptic. 'At one of the evening sessions, after Derek Prince had challenged the men, most of the 60 present made life or death "military-type" commitments to the leaders.'[58]

Part of the problem – in hindsight – that began to develop was the extent to which the leaders defined the practical outworkings of this shepherding relationship. 'The movement taught that submission to a shepherd provided spiritual "covering" by being in right relationship to God's delegated authority in the church. The shepherd assumed responsibility for the well-being of his sheep. This responsibility included not just their spiritual well-being, but for their full development emotionally, educationally, financially, vocationally, and socially.'[59]

The phrase that was employed – which may sound familiar to some – was having 'permission to speak into their lives'. The understanding was that the people being shepherded, by requesting a discipling relationship, were giving permission to the shepherd to 'speak into' every aspect of their personal lives. This differs from giving advice when requested; the under-shepherd was 'responsible' to speak into anything that he thought might be problematic in the lives of his sheep.

If we recall Watchman Nee's assertion that delegated authori-ties would have the God-given ability to discern the thoughts and motives of those being discipled, and that the shepherds would also have the ability to know God's will better than those being shepherded, it is not difficult to see – again, in hindsight – how this understanding of the discipling relationship would become controlling and abusive. 'The movement's leaders failed to realize fully the strong desire people have to belong, and that many of their followers committed to the system without recog-nizing how it would work functionally.'[60]

Shortly after the 'military-style' commitments made in 1975, well-known Christian ministries began to publicly denounce the Shepherding movement. Initially, the first two that spoke up were the 700 Club's Pat Robertson, and the head of the Full Gospel Business Men's Fellowship International (FGBMFI), Demos Shakarian.

> For what he called 'cultic' excesses, Robertson forbade Mumford and the others to appear on CBN-affiliated radio or TV stations and ordered that all CBN tapes of the teachers be immediately erased. . .[61] At about the same time, Full Gospel Business Men's Fellowship International (FGBMFI) founder Demos Shakarian

joined the controversy by forbidding the five teachers or any teaching on shepherding or discipleship in any FGBMFI chapter.[62]

In the controversy that ensued, there were many accusations and counter-accusations. Bob Mumford expressed concerns that the Five were being publicly charged with serious error, yet had not been previously contacted in private to address these concerns. To Mumford, this meant that their critics had violated the teaching of Matthew 18 on handling discipline within the body.

A meeting between all of the concerned parties, as well as other recognised leaders within the charismatic renewal, was called in the early part of 1975, in Minneapolis. Of central concern was a letter that Pat Robertson had published, which 'contained a long section contrasting the Shepherding teachings with Scripture and making serious charges of "another Charismatic heresy in the order of the manifested sons, the latter rain and Jesus only teaching of the former days"'.[63]

'"The shoot-out at the Curtis Hotel", as the meeting became known, was heated, with accusations flying back and forth, and accomplished little toward reconciliation and understanding.'[64] In an incident which would have been humorous but for the extreme acrimony that typified the meeting, an extremely upset Dennis Bennett at one point got up to leave the room, but accidentally went into a broom closet instead of choosing the exit door. After some crashing around, Bennett came back into the room and left by the appropriate door.

(Brick) Bradford summarized the previous day's proceedings, saying that Robertson needed to publicly 'ask forgiveness for his handling of the situation that [contributed to the] controversy'. He called on Christian Growth Ministries (CGM) leaders to 'temper teaching in regard to controversial doctrine'. Bradford asked for a re-establishment of communication and recognition between ministries.[65]

Bradford's words were well intentioned, but the sides were entrenched enough, and upset enough, not to heed his admonition. Don Basham later referred to the meetings as 'a time of almost total frustration',[66] while Pat Robertson publicly announced: 'My concern is for the gross doctrinal error and resulting practice which has been harming the body of Christ nationwide, and yet has been covered up by a cloak of deception of which we saw only part in Minneapolis.'[67]

One of the immediate results of the Curtis Hotel meetings was that Basham, Baxter and Simpson all wrote letters to those they were shepherding and urged them to exercise caution in how they applied shepherding principles, as they felt that there was some legitimacy to the accusations being made against them.

In words that would be restated over the years, Mumford wrote: 'These instances, as far as I know, are occasions of immature use and application of spiritual authority. Misuse and abuse are always wrong. However, the principles I understand to be correct and Biblical. I am not embarrassed to say "we have not gone this way before", and some mistakes are unavoidable. We have, as well, sought to walk in all candor, openness and adjustment from responsible leadership – charismatic and non-charismatic.'[68]

When well-known healing evangelist Kathryn Kuhlman also took a public stand against the Shepherding movement, the spotlight on this movement only got brighter. Kuhlman stated, in part, that the 'doctrine of discipleship and submission must be stopped or it's going to bring absolute destruction to the great Charismatic movement'.[69]

Jack Hayford, the well-known Foursquare pastor of Church on the Way in Van Nuys, California, was of the opinion that some of the judgments against the movement were unnecessarily harsh, but was also concerned that the Fort Lauderdale Five had not adequately addressed some legitimate concerns, because they felt their accusers had not brought their concerns forward in an appropriate way. Hayford felt that they were dodging the real questions, even if they were correct about some of the accusers.

Chuck Smith, the pastor of Calvary Chapel of Costa Mesa and one of the Jesus movement's most high-profile pastors, also strongly rejected the tenets of the Shepherding movement. 'In answer to Mumford's request for "time and patience to demonstrate the fruit of what are presently new Biblical concepts", Smith emphatically told him there already was more than enough evidence to reject the movement's teachings as Satan's deception.'[70]

'(Dennis) Bennett feared that the movement was setting up a new hierarchy to be God's government in the last days.'[71]

And therein lie some of the reasons why the Shepherding movement was not refuted as quickly as some thought it should have been. Some people were concerned about the heavy-handed discipling methods that put people in an extreme dependence on their 'shepherd', while others thought that discipleship was a needed component but were worried that the movement was trying to set itself up as a denomination. Others recognised the potential for abuse inherent in the discipling teachings, but the concern about a new denomination being formed eclipsed these concerns.

After a meeting with David du Plessis, where he called the Five to recognise that there had been problems with the practice of some of their shepherding concepts, the movement's leaders issued the following statement in 1976:

> We realize that controversies and problems have arisen among Christians in various areas as a result of our teaching in relation to subjects such as submission, authority, discipling, shepherding. We deeply regret these problems, and insofar as they are due to fault on our part, we ask forgiveness from our fellow believers whom we have offended. We realize that our teachings, though we believed them to be essentially sound, have in various places been misapplied or handled in an immature way; and that this has caused problems for our brothers in the ministry. We deeply regret this and ask for forgiveness. Insofar as it lies in our power, we will do our best to correct these situations and to restore any broken relationships.[72]

Another complicating factor is that the Five were recognised teachers whose commitment to Jesus was without question. The accountability that existed between them was testimony to their integrity as Christians and as leaders. Whenever meetings were called to address some of the concerns, many of those concerned could not bring themselves to denounce brothers in the Lord, even if they couldn't agree with some of their emphases.

> The consensus of the [1976 charismatic leaders conference] meeting was that allegations of heresy were unfounded, that there was no reason to question the integrity of the teachers involved, and that, while many doctrinal differences remain among the groups represented, those differences fall within acceptable limits.[73]

However, immediately after this statement was released, Oral

Roberts University professor 'Dr. Ervin wrote to Kevin Ranaghan in April 1976 and challenged the Ann Arbor statement that said the movement's doctrines fell within acceptable limits'.[74]

All of this contributed to creating a feeling of being persecuted for truth's sake among the Fort Lauderdale Five and those closest to them. The ferocity apparent in some of the attacks made it seem like it was a form of spiritual warfare – possibly even direct demonic attack – which only served to strengthen and encourage the movement leaders to hold firm, although they did take steps to curb some of the fringes.

Bob Mumford met with numerous leaders in attempts to mitigate some of what were perceived to be legitimate concerns. '(Mumford's) group discussed authoritarianism, exclusivism, elitism, neglect of the female role, unbalanced use of metaphors, creation of a jargon, and minimal biblical support for the degree of headship they taught.'[75]

Meanwhile, the number of participants in the 'shepherding track' at the annual Charismatic Conferences continued to grow – as many as 4,600 pastors and leaders at one point, easily dwarfing the main conference workshops.

While some continued to suspect that a new denomination was being created, others more charitably suggested that this movement was not attempting to begin a new denomination, but still warned them that this would be the unavoidable end of their work. Oral Roberts University professor Charles Farah 'believed that the movement had certain institutional features that would inevitably lead to a denomination, even if the leaders did not want it'.[76]

The Five, because of their strong Restorationist view

(influenced by the Latter Rain contributions of Ern Baxter), were ardently anti-denominationalist, yet after hearing the same accusations repeatedly, began to take steps to defuse these fears. '(Simpson) wrote in a 1976 newsletter: "In the interest of hearing God, we are dismantling our property, offices, or concentration of influence here in Pascagoula that might smack of a headquarters for a new denomination." '[77]

The Shepherding movement's influence, meanwhile, had become quite international in its scope. For example, 'Bob Mumford had a strong relationship with English and Canadian church leader Barney Coombs . . . However, according to Coombs, Mumford's leadership was personal and did not directly involve the churches Coombs led in England and Canada.'[78]

The beginnings of the British movement began to emerge in the 1950s. As we have seen, Arthur Wallis's book *In the Day of Thy Power* outlined a vision for revival that was to draw him into the company of other pioneers who were looking for a return to 'New Testament patterns of church life'. A 1958 conference saw Graham Perrins and other future 'Restoration' leaders gather to discuss the 'ordering of God's church and kingdom'.

The sixties saw widespread interest in speaking in tongues, healing and new styles of worship across the church spectrum in the UK, but it was in the seventies that the UK's own Shepherding movement began to emerge. Arthur Wallis drew together seven leaders of the 'house church' movement. These rapidly grew to 14, and it was this group that was to set the continuing agenda. Out of their friendships grew large-scale Bible weeks, and in 1974 Ern Baxter entered the scene. An attempt by the 'Fort Lauderdale Five' to solidify their authority in the UK by asking John Noble and Bryn Jones to 'submit' to their long-time friend Arthur Wallis was to prove disastrous as John and his associates declined. Fissures began to grow among the 14. Nevertheless the seed of the 'covering and submission' doctrines had been planted, and only began to wane when the US leaders took stock themselves.

As much as Mumford and the others were attempting to listen to their critics and address some of the legitimate concerns being raised about the discipling and submission teachings, the ship that was the Shepherding movement proved to be hard to turn. The momentum carried the group along despite the attempts to bring correction and balance.

> The other leaders shared Mumford's concerns, but they found it difficult to maintain their efforts to produce order, discipline, and maturity and, at the same time, avoid the aforementioned pitfalls. The very things they taught created a propensity toward an abuse of spiritual authority, especially among young immature leaders, or leaders who lacked character and integrity.[79]

The Shepherding movement felt a kinship with the Anabaptist understanding of the visible, believing community. Their emphasis on house churches and living separate from the world intersected smoothly with Anabaptist distinctives. The movement also felt that the persecution and misunderstandings that had plagued those radical reformers were very similar to the struggles and controversies that they were experiencing.

By 1980, however, the stress was taking its toll, and cracks were beginning to show in the solidarity of the Five, as evidenced by the following quotes:

The five teachers thereupon agreed to bring together all the movement's leaders for a Congress of Elders in Louisville, Kentucky,
expecting several thousand men. . . . Two months before the Congress, Mumford and Prince objected to the plan, feeling it was a
move towards becoming a denomination, which Simpson
adamantly denied was his intention. As a result of Mumford's and
Prince's concern, the Congress was cancelled. Simpson was
extremely frustrated, feeling that the other two men did not trust
him, and he released both Mumford and Prince from their commitments to him.[80]

Over the years, at least from 1977 on, Derek Prince had struggled with some of the movement's teaching. . . First, he felt the
movement was 'by most generally accepted standards' a denomination. Further, Prince said he did not feel there was an adequate
scriptural basis for the concept that 'every Christian should have a
personal human pastor', or 'the practice of a pastor overseeing
another pastor translocally' . . . The theological and geographical
distance between Prince and the other four teachers culminated in
March 1984 with Prince's formal disassociation from the Shepherding movement.[81]

The UK was to see similar convulsions. The divisions that arose
were characterised as differences over law and grace, with one
group of leaders having more relaxed attitudes over hot-potato
issues such as alcohol, tobacco and masturbation (to name but
three) than some of the more conservative leaders. But a reserve
over the covering and submission doctrines behind the Shepherding movement also widened the growing gaps between
members of the original band of 14.

The men who were wary of legalism were also wary of authoritarian behaviour generally. David Tomlinson, who at one time

was the leader of several dozen churches, remarked in *Restoration* magazine:

> No one has such authority that he cannot be questioned or challenged . . . It is important that those being discipled feel that they will be seriously heard and not merely swept aside.

Others simply turned their backs on the movement, to explore new expressions of church. Nick Butterworth and Maurice Smith, two early influencers, are reported by Andrew Walker in his book *Restoring the Kingdom* to have concluded that their friends were always trying to 'improve people'. In the mid-eighties they decided to abandon such principles and preach a message that Jesus is happy with people just the way they are.

There were also many defections from the ranks during that time: 'By 1980 many leaders and their followers were leaving the movement.'[82] This was due in part to the concerns being raised by other leaders, but also from a sense of disillusionment in the relationships with shepherds, and also not a little sense of conviction that some of the teachings were being abused.

> Mumford and Simpson, in particular, were faced with many situations around the nation where leaders were accused of abusing their spiritual authority. Many other leaders and churches were leaving the movement disillusioned because of what they thought were extreme teachings and practices.[83]

The combined effect of these defections, accusations and Derek Prince's leaving the movement brought the remaining four teachers to an almost inescapable crossroads. 'In April 1986, at a meeting in Chicago, Basham, Baxter, Mumford and Simpson decided to dissolve their structural and governmental ties together as a movement.'[84]

The Shepherding movement was officially at an end, but the teachings of covering, authority, and the concept of under-shepherds (delegated authorities) have continued to this day in many circles. Granted, some participants in the movement did not suffer the extremes of abuse that others did, and many would point to the positive fruit (e.g. Hosanna/Integrity, a major Christian recording company which produces many worship resources and recordings, began in the Shepherding movement), but the fatal flaw was not in the existence of the abuse, but in the foundational assumptions that gave credence to the teachings on submission and authority.

After the demise of the organisational structure of the movement, the Five registered a variety of post-Shepherding reactions. 'In June 1987, Basham affirmed the Shepherding movement's good points and also acknowledged the movement's abuses. He apologized to any who had been hurt by the movement. . .[85] In 1988, he suffered a massive heart attack (and) on 27 March 1989, Basham died after suffering another heart attack.'[86]

Ern Baxter continued to teach for a while, but failing health (he was the oldest member of the Five) slowed him down quite a bit. 'Baxter's health declined rapidly into the summer of 1993, and he died on 9 July.'[87]

Charles Simpson remains the major inheritor of the Shepherding movement, although he has reformed the movement under the name of Fellowship of Covenant Ministers and Churches (FCMC), which 'carried on many of the central themes of the Shepherding movement. . . discipleship, account-ability, covenant, male government, kingdom of God, house groups, and servanthood. . .[88] Today, Simpson believes that he and those who continue in association have corrected many of the movement's extremes.'[89]

Derek Prince took a very different response to Simpson's. 'After his departure in 1983–84, Prince seldom referred to his longtime relationship to the Shepherding movement. He publicly wrote in 1995 that he believed the movement was guilty of the Galatian error: "having begun in the Spirit, we quickly degenerated into the flesh". . .[90] "I don't believe now, looking back, it was ever God's intention to start a movement. . . I think God wanted us to relate to one another as brothers."' [91] Prince died in 2003.

The most significant statement coming out of the post-Shepherding movement came from its most readily identifiable spokesperson: Bob Mumford. The cover of *Charisma* magazine had an excerpt from Mumford's statement, which confirmed what the critics had been saying for some time, and which started the process of healing for many who had been injured in the movement.

After a season he described as 'deep conviction from God' and counseling with leaders, including Jack Hayford, Bob Mumford issued a strong public statement of apology in November 1989: 'This statement of apology has two known motivations. First, I feel as though I have offended the Lord Himself, resulting in His resistance and conviction. Secondly, I am deeply convinced that only by my stating the truth can those who have been adversely affected be healed and released. The following statement represents my personal convictions, and I do not presume to speak for any other person. . . Accountability, personal training under the guidance of another and effective pastoral care are needed biblical concepts. True spiritual maturity will require that they be preserved. These

biblical realities must carry the limits indicated by the New Testament. However, to my personal pain and chagrin, these particular
emphases very easily lent themselves to an unhealthy submission
resulting in perverse and unbiblical obedience to human leaders.
Many of these abuses occurred within the spheres of my own
responsibility. For the injury and shame caused to people, families,
and the larger body of Christ, I repent with sorrow and ask for your
forgiveness.'[92]

Mumford received hundreds of letters of support, including a
letter from Dennis Bennett, affirming Mumford's courage to make
a public apology. Bennett also apologized to Mumford for his own
antagonism during the controversy.[93]

With Mumford's broken and humble public statement of repen-
tance, the Shepherding movement was laid to rest in the public
mind. While there were still many people recovering from being
a part of the movement, even Mumford's statement of repen-
tance proved to be a part of their healing over time.

However, as has been stated several times over in this section,
the concepts that the Shepherding movement popularised during its hey-day of the 1970s have not been laid to rest with the
dissolution of the movement. These ideas are still very much
alive and well in many charismatic circles, and probably would
rank as the no. 1 reason that many have chosen to call themselves 'post-charismatic'. Hype and abuse of spiritual gifts are
also prominent reasons for the exiting of many charismatics, but
that usually manifests itself in weariness and disillusionment.
The impact of the shepherding emphasis on covering and submission runs far deeper, as wounds that need healing, which
accounts for the much deeper visceral reaction to the movement's teachings.

We will now turn our attention to deconstructing the major tenets of covering, submission and spiritual authority.

Post-charismatic

We have seen that, although the Shepherding movement was dissolved quite some time ago, the concepts of spiritual covering, being under authority, and 'touch not the Lord's anointed' have continued to be used in exactly the same manner as the Shepherding movement. Again, the abuse of 'authority' is consistently one of the most oft-voiced reasons given by post-charismatics to explain why they have left; even their revulsion at the hype of 'charismania' comes second.

The more extreme application of the Shepherding concepts, even after 'Mumford admitted that the Shepherding emphasis was heresy',[94] included leaders taking over virtually every aspect of their followers' lives. 'Rather than see their role as that of a servant to encourage, strengthen and equip the people of God, authoritarian leaders inflate their own importance and view themselves as somehow "owning" the people God has entrusted to them for spiritual oversight.'[95]

This misunderstanding of their role as pastoral leadership resulted in situations where the pastors/shepherds themselves were brought into considerable bondage, believing that God would require from them an accounting of how their followers had lived. And for those in their churches, it was equally a source of bondage – to the leader. The verse that is often used to support this idea was Hebrews 13:17:

> Obey your leaders and submit to them, for they keep watch over your souls as those who will give an account. Let them do this with

joy and not with grief, for this would be unprofitable for you. (NASB)

By spending a brief amount of time looking at this verse, we can demonstrate a very different way of applying Hebrews 13:17.

1. Obey is the Greek word *peitho*, which can mean 'to persuade, to be persuaded by, to co-operate with, to have confidence in, to trust, and to obey'.

2. *Hegeomai*, from which we get the word 'leader', can be translated as 'to have authority over' or 'to go before, to lead'. When coupled with the word *peitho*, it's a realistic interpretation to suggest that the writer of Hebrews was instructing the people to trust or co-operate with those who 'go before' them. This sounds less like a hierarchical chain of command, and more like giving respect to those who have been walking with Jesus a bit longer. Or it could mean what others have suggested: being under the authority of those God has placed above you. Perhaps digging through the rest of the key words can put this in a larger context.

3. *Hupeiko* – submit – can mean one of two things: to yield to authority, or to resist no longer as combatants. So far, we could interpret this verse to say 'yield authority to the leaders above you', or 'have confidence in those who have gone before, and stop fighting (being combative)'.

4. 'Keep watch' is a phrase that comes from the Greek *agrupneo*, which can be translated 'to be sleepless, to watch' or 'to be circumspect, attentive'. Either way you want to translate this one, it speaks of 'leaders' as those who are

genuinely committed to the spiritual health of those around them.

5. 'Give an account' – *apodidomi* – can mean 'to deliver (sell)', but I don't think leaders sell us back to God. Next possibility? It can also mean 'to give back, restore', but I'd be on shaky ground if I suggested that anybody is going to 'give back' people to God; last time I checked, Jesus is the only Mediator between God and humanity. It can also mean 'to pay off a debt'; hmmm. . . that doesn't fit the context either. Finally, it can simply be translated as it usually has been: 'render (give) an account'.

So we could look at this verse and apply it like this: 'Have confidence in those who have gone before, and stop fighting (being combative) with them, because they are there to be attentive to your spiritual growth, and they answer to God for how they lead. So don't make it tough on them, because then nobody wins.'

Or, as this verse has been translated in Eugene Peterson's *The Message*: 'Be responsive to your pastoral leaders. Listen to their counsel. They are alert to the condition of your lives and work under the strict supervision of God. Contribute to the joy of their leadership, not its drudgery. Why would you want to make things harder for them?'

The bottom line is that this verse cannot be translated to mean that leaders are accountable for how people think, believe, or behave. Leaders are accountable for the manner in which they lead, not for how people follow. This kind of thinking only leads to a performance-driven bondage for the leader and anyone who is considered a follower.

An intriguing bit of context for this verse is found earlier in the same chapter of Hebrews, where we read: 'Remember your leaders, who spoke the word of God to you. Consider the outcome of their way of life and imitate their faith' (Hebrews 13:7).

The context that this verse provides is that there is a clear implication that we are to actually evaluate the lifestyles of leaders, and follow their (good) example. Many 'covering' proponents use Hebrews 13:17 and add the phrase 'it doesn't say "obey" if your leader is good – it just says "obey". . .' However, a mere ten verses earlier, we are encouraged to imitate our leaders as we see an example of faithfulness.

Of course, we could easily read a phrase like 'consider the outcome of their way of life' and apply it in a way that was more about fault-finding than looking for good examples of faith. A suspicious and critical mindset, whether in leadership or in the broader gathering, is the antithesis and destroyer of true community.

In context, both of these verses point towards a community dynamic more than a hierarchical one. If we were to pair them sequentially, we would read:

'Appreciate your pastoral leaders who gave you the Word of God. Take a good look at the way they live, and let their faithfulness instruct you, as well as their truthfulness. . . Be responsive to your pastoral leaders. Listen to their counsel. They are alert to the condition of your lives and work under the strict supervision of God. Contribute to the joy of their leadership, not its drudgery. Why would you want to make things harder for them?' (Hebrews 13:7, 17 *The Message*)

Covering

As many critics of the Shepherding movement are quick to point out, the term 'covering' – when used in the Bible – does not have the same meaning that it was given by the movement. The idea of the covering was one of protection – initially, protection through accountability that was mutual, but as we have seen, it quickly degenerated into viewing submission to leaders as being the protection.

Most post-charismatics would understand that mutual accountability is a good thing. But they would stress the 'mutual' aspect much more strongly. As one writer put it, when someone asks 'Who are you submitted to?', they can just as easily ask – and often are asking – 'Who controls you?'

An interesting aside to take note of: while the Shepherding movement was gaining both popularity and notoriety among charismatics in the late 1970s and early 1980s, the Bill Gothard Institute in Basic Youth Conflicts was also becoming a dominant movement within non-charismatic denominations. In ways very reminiscent of the Shepherding movement, Bill Gothard emphasised the 'covering' idea, although he extended the covering concept even further than absolute submission to church leaders, to include a rationale that married women must not be employed outside the home – and therefore not under the covering of their husband – lest they be easy prey for Satan.

Gothard was also accused of heavy-handed authoritarianism, and many churches that adopted the Institute's teachings produced similar spiritual casualties, who – disillusioned and wounded – eventually freed themselves from Gothard's teachings but are still in recovery (those who didn't give up on their faith as a result of the abuse).

It should not be surprising that there was a non-charismatic version of shepherding occurring at the same time; the societal changes that helped to shape the vacuum that produced the Shepherding movement were at work everywhere, not just in the charismatic movement. What is truly disturbing is that so many charismatic, evangelical, and fundamentalist churches and denominations were so easily sucked in.

As I mentioned earlier, Derek Prince, some years after the dissolution of the movement, observed, 'I don't believe now, looking back, it was ever God's intention to start a movement. . . I think God wanted us to relate to one another as brothers.'[96] The mutuality of the original four teachers in submitting to each other could have functioned as a great example for other Christians to follow. But by attempting to build a theological justification to place other believers *under* them in accountability – again, in the words of Prince – 'the movement was guilty of the Galatian error: "having begun in the Spirit, we quickly degenerated into the flesh."'[97]

Post-charismatics believe in the dynamic of community and the value of house churches – ironic when you consider that the Shepherding movement also placed such a high emphasis on house groups. Post-charismatics, however, have at times removed themselves so far from authoritarianism that the status quo of non-leadership becomes an equally controlling system.

Authority

Most post-charismatics question why they are expected to submit to certain church leaders as authorities, when there is nothing about these authorities (other than their ecclesiastical position) that engenders trust – a key component to any kind of relational accountability.

Many who advocate Watchman Nee's understanding of 'delegated authority' are doing so because they need some theological pretext to justify why they want people to submit to them. They do not see that authority – the ability to speak into someone else's life – is based on trust, not position.

During the height of the Shepherding movement's influence, the Assemblies of God produced a statement in response to the problems that were arising out of the movement, *The Discipling and Submission Movement (Assemblies of God Position Paper, 1976)*. In this document, the authors wisely pointed out that the goal of the five-fold ministry is to equip the body to be mature; in other words, to work themselves out of a job. To use the Ephesians 4 passage to justify an increase in control over individual believers actually sets up a system that works directly against developing Christian maturity.

> However, when they rely altogether on another person to protect them from all error, they will cease searching the Scriptures and fail to develop their own ability to withstand false teaching.[98]
>
> Thus believers need more than a human shepherd to protect them. They need to develop their own ability to search and understand the Scriptures under the guidance of the Spirit, who alone can lead into all truth (John 16:13).[99]

Inadvertently, George Mallone touched on this in *Furnace of Renewal: A Vision for the Church*: 'In its extreme, it is extortion and domination of the worst variety. Seen in its best light it is a response to the crass individualism of many North American

Christians. The question that is being asked is, *How are we to shepherd people unless they are responsive to our authority?*[100] (*emphasis added*)

The question post-charismatics would immediately respond with is, 'Why does discipleship (apprenticeship to Jesus) depend on your authority?' As Todd Hunter (President of Alpha USA) pointed out, 'What does it mean to lead people who are supposed to be following Somebody else?'

Is it possible to disciple people without having to have them answerable to us? Can we 'give people authority' based on their character and our relationship with them, without having to relinquish (or be asked to relinquish) our own individuality?

Does 'authority' equal power and control? Or is the five-fold ministry (apostle, prophet, evangelist, pastor, teacher) meant to function outside of a hierarchical model?

Protecting the flock?

An argument that is often employed in defence of Shepherding-influenced leadership styles is that the pastor is to protect the sheep from false teachers. The belief is that, without appropriate pastoral oversight, individuals and groups will fall into doctrinal error or excesses. In reality, this *is* a biblical function of elders in the local church, but to extrapolate it in such a way as to require subservience to a leader is absurd. Post-charismatics would be quick to point to entire churches and denominations which have changed their understanding of doctrine and practice (and are no longer considered orthodox), and would also consider the authoritarian nature of Shepherding teaching to be doctrinal error in itself.

The Assemblies of God position paper also identified this

problem in its response to the Shepherding movement: 'Both Paul and Peter warn against false teachers, but the New Testament does not indicate that the answer is to get a human shepherd who will protect the believer.'[101]

Perhaps the most bizarre reinterpretation of Scripture that I have heard in defence of a shepherding-style understanding of hierarchical authority was Jesus' lament over Jerusalem: 'For I tell you, you will not see me again until you say, "Blessed is he who comes in the name of the Lord."' (Matthew 23:39; Luke 13:35).

Somehow, this verse is twisted to mean that unless believers give absolute, unquestioning submission to their leader – who 'comes in the name of the Lord' – these believers will be unable to see God.

When I challenged this interpretation of Jesus' lament over Jerusalem, the only response I was given was: 'Hey, it's the clear teaching of Scripture; you're not arguing with me, you're arguing with God's word. Rebellion is like the sin of witchcraft, so if that's what you want to choose. . .'

A close second would be the time I listened to a guest speaker use Matthew 10:24 – 'A student is not above his teacher, nor a servant above his master' – to bolster her assertion that leaders must be obeyed without question, since they are above us. The context of this verse is Jesus warning his disciples that if he was being persecuted, they could expect persecution as well. It is definitely not a statement on leadership.

In regards to the issue of accountability within the body, the Assemblies of God also recognised that 'The Bible does teach a submission to our leaders and to one another in love. But this is a matter of mutual concern and consideration for one another.

The Bible also recognizes the need for leadership, but Jesus warned that whoever would be first should be the servant of all. There is no room in the church for anyone to lord it over another or over God's heritage (1 Peter 5:3).'[102]

The irony is that the Shepherding movement had fully intended to function as a relationally based ministry. Yet, as some would point out, it almost appears as if there is an inherent deficiency in any attempt to organise and administer any kind of group – call it a fatal flaw of human nature, or whatever, but at times it seems that it's impossible to create any level of organisational structure that does not eventually become rigid and authoritarian.

> The Shepherding movement emphasized the relational organic nature of the church . . . The irony of this ongoing relational emphasis was that the movement seemed to function as a highly organized and structured oligarchy until its eventual breakup.[103]

The new apostolic reformation

While the concepts of covering and being under authority continue to be used in some charismatic circles, in addition, a new movement which calls itself the New Apostolic Reformation (NAR) has recently been gaining momentum. C. Peter Wagner is often associated as one of the main proponents of this movement due to his prolific writing ministry which has devoted several titles to this movement: *ChurchQuake!*, *The New Apostolic Churches*, *Spheres of Authority*, *Apostles and Prophets: The New Foundation for the Church*, and so on.

In his book *Spheres of Authority*, Wagner presents a stunning revisionist approach to recent history, when, acting out of a Restorationist paradigm (that the 'offices' of apostle and prophet have been lost due to prejudice in the church, but God is restoring them), he states: 'The Latter Rain embraced the ministry of apostles and prophets. Not surprisingly, they were condemned by their first cousins, so to speak, the Assemblies of God because they threatened the status quo.'[104]

Wagner quotes an Australian Assemblies of God minister, David Cartledge, who makes the indictment against the American Assemblies of God of being 'pentecostal cessationists'. Wagner makes no mention whatsoever of the heretical doctrines that led to the rejection of the Latter Rain, and turns the movement into a sort of martyr for the Restorationist cause.

In describing the dynamics of what he is calling 'The Second Apostolic Age', Wagner proposes the following: 'Apostolic-type churches make a different set of assumptions concerning the local church pastor:

- The pastors cast the vision. Not the congregation.
- Pastors major on leadership and minor on management.
- Pastors make top-drawer policy decisions and delegate the rest.
- Pastors build a solid management team of both elders and staff. The pastor is not subject to the authority of this team, but the team serves at the pleasure of the pastor. The staff members are employees of the pastor, not of the church.
- Pastors are called for life.
- Pastors choose their successors.'[105]

In language that is startlingly reminiscent of the Shepherding movement, Wagner envisions 'translocal apostles' having authority over churches and pastors that voluntarily choose to be part of the network of the New Apostolic Reformation. 'Local churches are autonomous, and, as I have said, pastors are the leaders. They decide whether or not to place themselves under the "spiritual covering" of a translocal apostle based solely on their personal relationship with the apostle.'[106]

If that sounds somewhat akin to the Shepherding movement's line of reasoning, it's probably because the terms are virtually verbatim from the teachings of that movement. In a statement that raises a red flag of warning in my mind, Wagner says of these apostolic 'coverings': '(These pastors) are convinced that they would not be able to reach their full destiny in serving God apart from their submission to the apostle. This allows them not only to contribute financially to the apostle's ministry, but also to be cheerful givers.'[107]

Wagner believes that all the five-fold 'offices' (a term which is often seen as hierarchical in nature and which we will deconstruct in Spirit and Praxis) should still be in operation today, as the stated purpose of the five-fold ministries is to produce maturity and completeness in the body. The argument for their continuation would be that the body has not yet achieved the maturity and unity that Ephesians 4 mentions. I would concur with his assessment about the necessity of the present-day function of all the five-fold ministries (or Ascension Gifts as they are sometimes called), but as will become evident in the next section, I do not believe the Scriptures portray a hierarchical, positionally authoritative approach and application of the five-fold ministries of Ephesians 4:11–16.

PART TWO

SPIRIT AND PRAXIS

Towards a reconstructed praxis

Is it possible to be a part of, a catalyst within, or a functioning member of a group that is *not* led, inspired, directed, and at times interrupted, by the Holy Spirit of Jesus?

Can we expect to build communities of faith, with a missional focus and flavour, without being able to hear the voice of God for ourselves? Or will we – in our sincere and understandable desire to avoid charismania and questionable teachings and practices – find ourselves on the wrong side of Psalm 127:1?

Unless the Lord builds the house, its builders labour in vain.

With an understanding that we are committed to avoiding the extremes and rabbit trails that have been detailed in the previous sections, we now need to reconstruct an understanding of how to live as post-charismatics (in the cultural sense) in four main areas:

1. A biblical view of authority and the five-fold ministries that is not hierarchical and controlling
2. The role of faith, and what it means to be living by faith; to be people characterised by faith
3. A view of spiritual formation (discipleship) that goes beyond the typical weekly crisis-event of 'ministry/altar time' but without eschewing genuine Spirit-initiated crisis-events
4. A new vision for being 'communities of the Spirit', including a community-based model of the place and use of spiritual gifts

First, let's have a look at Jesus' understanding and teaching regarding how the community of faith is to understand authority and how it is to be used.

FIVE-FOLD RECONSIDERED

Retro-view

Frank Viola has written one of the most well-known books on the rejection of the covering teaching, *Who is Your Covering?* In the introduction of Frank's book, you can find one of the most oft-quoted statements in this discussion: 'Let us widen the question a bit. What do people really mean when they push the "covering" question? I submit that what they are really asking is "Who controls you?"'[1]

For many who have experienced some level of abuse from these left-overs from the Shepherding movement, there is an immediate resonance with the word 'control'. Many post-charismatics have developed a 'won't get fooled again' posture towards anything that even hints at authoritarianism and hierarchical power structures.

And when authoritarian leaders are questioned or – by the more daring of Christians – confronted about their abuse of leadership, the common response is the quote 'touch not the Lord's anointed', which is usually understood to refer to the saga of David and Saul. The typical application of this understanding is to suggest that abusive leaders (as the Lord's anointed) must still be absolutely submitted to, and never questioned, leaving the results to God. The use of this phrase is interesting for a couple of reasons, the first being that by invoking the example of David and Saul, the authoritarian leader is thereby likening him/herself to Saul, whom God rejected. The community, then, would represent David, whom God had chosen to replace Saul for his disobedience.

I would not want to be guilty of promoting the reverse error – thinking that all leaders represent Saul and all non-leaders are

David – but it's safe to say that using the example of David and
Saul as a tool for keeping people 'under covering' presents a
whole new set of problems (unless no one checks the context of
the verses). Of course, if by invoking this phrase the authoritarian leader can win the acquiescence of the congregation, they
won't mind being 'Saul'. The status quo is maintained.

The second reason is that the actual biblical phrase 'touch not
my anointed ones' comes from 1 Chronicles 16:22; this passage
is the first psalm that King David gave to his worship leader
Asaph (a percussionist, according to 1 Chronicles 16:15), to be
a part of the celebration when the Ark was returned to Jerusalem
from Obed-Edom. It should be noted that, even in English,
'anointed ones' is plural, not singular, and in this psalm (part of
which is also found in Psalm 105:1–15), the 'anointed ones'
were the whole assembly of God's people, not their leader(s).
The irony is that in these passages, God rebukes those in
leadership against doing harm to his anointed community of
people.

J. Lee Grady has strong words for authoritarian leaders:
'. . .because the pagan idea of leadership pervades our churches,
many of us are in constant pursuit of celebrity status in the
Kingdom of God.'[2] What makes the current understanding of
leadership more akin to paganism than Christianity? Simply
this: Jesus has taught us clearly and specifically how the body is
to be in relationship to each other, and we haven't followed his
instructions.

'Our Western philosophy, so steeped in competitive tradition,
has done plenty to squelch true fellowship and love in our
churches.'[3] And the lack of love between those who claim leadership giftings (Romans 12:8 speaks of the Holy Spirit gifting

people with 'leadership') and those who are thought to be 'followers' testifies to this reality.

You will find many post-charismatics, including some independent charismatic house churches that still teach the 'spiritual submission' understanding of house church ecclesiology, who claim, quite sincerely and without guile, that the Holy Spirit is the leader of their group, and not any man or woman.

Perhaps my own experience is not yet broad enough, but I have yet to find a group that does not have at least one person functioning as a leader within it. It has been noted that the real test of community comes when there is sin in the camp that has to be dealt with. If I could create a litmus test for discovering who the leaders are in these leaderless groups, it would be: 'Introduce a new idea or direction in any house church, and see who everyone looks to for validation or rejection of the new idea. That's who the leader is.'

Many post-charismatics have also come up against the ecclesial brick wall that results from an inappropriate understanding and use of 'accountability'; they have, at some point in their journey, confessed some weaknesses and struggles with sin to someone in leadership at their local church. The Bible supports the idea of confessing our sins to each other, so that we can be set free (healed) from the effects of sin in our lives (James 5:15–16). However, many later found themselves on the hamster wheel of being 'not ready to be released' into ministry by their leaders. Admitting weakness to their leaders has resulted in them being forever banished to the 'damaged goods' category; the leaders have used this intimate knowledge (given in trust and in keeping with scriptural teaching) to maintain control over the penitent.

One of the best ways to discern between whether one is experiencing 'conviction of the Holy Spirit' (John 16:8) or condemnation has always been to examine the fruit: if it's truly conviction from the Spirit, we are drawn to become closer to God, but if it's condemnation, we feel that we must hide from God.

To extrapolate that simple test to 'accountability', allow me to suggest that the fruit will likewise help us to discern the difference between appropriate and inappropriate use of accountability: does it produce freedom, or another type of performance-oriented bondage?

'Leadership' has become a dirty word for many Christians – whether post-evangelical, post-colonial or emerging/missional church – and like all of these other expressions of Christ's body, post-charismatics need to sort out what leadership looks like according to the Scriptures. An old saying that I first heard in Bible college was, 'The answer to bad theology is not "no theology", it is to recapture good theology.' The same principle applies to how we deal with inadequate, and at times abusive, models of leadership – we need to reconstruct good and biblically based leadership models.

Let's return to George Mallone's 1981 observation on the Shepherding movement. He said:

> In its extreme, it is extortion and domination of the worst variety. Seen in its best light it is a response to the crass individualism of many North American Christians. The question that is being asked is, 'How are we to shepherd people unless they are responsive to our authority?'[4]

While Mallone was clearly rejecting the shepherding emphasis, the question he raises hits us on two levels. The first is the obvious one that George is bringing to our attention: how does discipleship take place? The second level, which is an unintentional nuance on George's part, is the idea that we need to 'get' people to be responsible to 'our authority' in order to 'shepherd' them. How do you 'get' people to submit to your authority, without using manipulation and control? Or is there another way of seeing it?

Let's look again at that admonition in the Assemblies of God denominational white paper regarding the Shepherding movement:

> Both Paul and Peter warn against false teachers, but the New Testament does not indicate that the answer is to get a human shepherd who will protect the believer. . . Thus believers need more than a human shepherd to protect them. They need to develop their own ability to search and understand the Scriptures under the guidance of the Spirit, who alone can lead into all truth (John 16:13).[5]

Pulling these three concerns together, we can see the following dynamics that need to be addressed:

1. Assemblies of God – people need to develop their own ability to be led by the Holy Spirit; leadership is there to help them move in this direction
2. George Mallone – but how do leaders get people to listen and develop this maturing ability?
3. Frank Viola – but leaders are all about 'controlling' people, and only God should be the Leader

Todd Hunter asked, 'What does it mean to be leading people who are supposed to be following somebody else (Jesus)?' Perhaps the best starting point for reconstructing a post-charismatic praxis is to look at Jesus' use of his authority, and how he taught his disciples (apprentices) to function in the use of the authority that he gave them (and us).

Jesus and authority

One of the most famous passages of Scripture that describes the earthly ministry of Jesus is Philippians 2:5–8:

> Your attitude should be the same as that of Christ Jesus: Who, being in very nature God, did not consider equality with God something to be grasped, but made himself nothing, taking the very nature of a servant, being made in human likeness. And being found in appearance as a man, he humbled himself and became obedient to death – even death on a cross.

In this passage Paul writes of Jesus emptying himself of his divine prerogatives – as King of the universe – and becoming the suffering servant that Isaiah prophesied about (Isaiah 53). The theological term is *kenosis* – taken from the Greek word *kenoo* which is translated 'emptied' in Philippians 2:7 – the idea that Jesus actually gave up some of his divine attributes while on earth. Certainly, he was no longer omnipresent while confined to the normal limitations of a human body.

However, theologians like Wayne Grudem suggest that this emptying was not that Jesus relinquished certain attributes as much as it was a focus on him willingly becoming the servant of a creation over which he was the Creator. Grudem's warning is that the *kenosis* theory, as advocated by German theologians in the 1800s, potentially forces us into a position where 'we could no longer affirm Jesus was fully God while He was here on earth'.[6]

Grudem would suggest that the appropriate understanding of this verse in Philippians, as was commonly held in previous centuries, is that Jesus was at all times fully God, but willingly chose to limit himself in the expression of his deity.

When one reads the Gospels, there appears to be evidence that Jesus had indeed given up some of his attributes in a way that contradicts Grudem; Jesus was certainly not omnipresent in a physical sense, and there were times when either he was not omniscient (all-knowing), such as when the disciples questioned him about the timing of his second coming, and Jesus responded that he didn't know; only the Father knew (Mark 13:32).

With respect to Grudem's interpretation of Philippians 2:7, it is probably best to stay on the side of affirming the full deity of Jesus in the incarnation – after all, it was precisely the understanding of Jesus being fully God and fully Man that was the subject of many of the early church councils, when various heresies were floating around which denied some aspect of Jesus' nature.

While holding on to the tension presented by Jesus' actions in the Gospels, Grudem points us in a helpful direction – the willingness of Jesus to be the servant to a people who should have been serving him. The focus of the Philippians passage is on the servant attitude that Jesus exhibited; indeed, the focus of the whole first half of this passage (Philippians 2:1–11) is on Christians seeking to imitate the servant attitude towards each other.

Authority in action and teaching

With this understanding that Jesus was deliberately choosing to walk the road of humility and servanthood, it is still astounding to see the level of authority he claimed and exhibited, even in his servant-walk of incarnation.

Certainly the people who heard Jesus were often amazed at the authority which he exuded. Those who heard him teach commented on how he had an authority about him that the teachers of the law did not (Matthew 7:29; Mark 1:22), and even commented, 'A new teaching, and with authority! He even gives orders to evil spirits and they obey him' (Mark 1:27).

His disciples saw his authority exemplified in his miracles of healing (Matthew 4:23–24), deliverance (Mark 1:32–34), and divine provision (like the feeding of the five thousand in Matthew 14:15–21, Mark 6:35–44, Luke 9:12–17 and John 6:1–13), and his calming of the storm on the Sea of Galilee, which caused them to exclaim, 'What kind of man is this? Even the winds and the waves obey him!' (Matthew 8:27).

The Pharisees, it must be remembered, wanted Jesus dead because he threatened their self-perception that they were the rulers of Israel. They recognised an authority in Jesus that they could not compete with, no matter how many times they tried to trap him (Matthew 15:1–9, 22:15–22, for example), and they were afraid and angry at him.

Just after his baptism by John the Baptist, and hearing the blessing from his Father as the Spirit descended on him 'like a dove' (Matthew 3:13–17; Mark 1:9–11; Luke 3:21–22; John 1:32–34), we read in the three Synoptic Gospels about the temptation of Jesus at the hands of Satan (Matthew 4:1–11; Mark

1:12–13; Luke 4:1–13). Much has been written on the application of these temptations of Jesus for everyday believers, but it would not be a stretch at all to see one aspect of the temptation of Jesus as being a test of how Jesus would use his authority as the incarnational servant:

- Changing stones to bread – stepping out of his role of depending on his Father and misusing his authority as Creator
- Jumping off the Temple – playing games with his authority (accepting a dare from Satan to 'prove' his position as beloved Son)
- Bowing to Satan – to abdicate his authority (and the plan of his Father) by worshipping (giving authority to) Satan

Without taking this servant hermeneutic too far, there is something significant in even the temptation of Jesus as it relates to how he used his authority while taking on the form of a servant.

Jesus' claims of authority

For someone who had willingly humbled himself to be a servant, Jesus still overtly claimed that he was an authority on more than one occasion. As many who have read the Gospels have already noticed, Jesus seemed to go out of his way to juxtapose himself with some of the 'greats' in the Old Testament – with himself always coming out the greater.

The Tabernacle was the resting place of God's glory until the completion of Solomon's Temple (1 Kings 8:1–66), and even in Jesus' day it was the centre of Israel's worship (despite the depiction of God's glory leaving the Temple as found in Ezekiel 10, there was still the hopeful expectation of the return of his glory in Ezekiel 43:1–5). Yet Jesus, when questioned about his disciples breaking Sabbath laws, goes beyond defending his disciples to make the claim that he was greater than the Temple, and Lord of the Sabbath (Matthew 12:1–8).

Solomon, the son of David who was granted a gift of wisdom as king of Israel, who was also the one whom God appointed to build the Temple in the first place, also comes up short when Jesus speaks of him. When the Pharisees demanded that Jesus do a miracle for them to 'prove' his authority, he declines – although he had just healed a demon-possessed blind and mute man (Matthew 12:22) – but goes on to say that he is greater than Solomon (Matthew 12:42).

Jesus further outraged the Pharisees and teachers of the law by claiming not only that he was greater than the patriarch Abraham, but that he was 'I Am' – Yahweh (John 8:52–59), and that Abraham was overjoyed when he saw Jesus' day (time) come. The Jews knew what Jesus was saying, which explains their response of picking up stones to kill him – a proper response, if Jesus hadn't been telling the truth.

So, Jesus clearly has established himself as an authority in the minds of the people and his disciples (the ones who did not desert him when he continued to upset their preconceived ideas about the Messiah – John 6:66–68), and even in the minds of the Jewish leaders who could not trap him and wanted him silenced – at any cost.

Jesus has also demonstrated his authority over those afflicted with demonic spirits, over sickness, and over death by raising Jairus' daughter (Luke 8:49–56) and his friend Lazarus (John 11:41–44).

Jesus also overtly claimed authority in numerous areas of his ministry:

- The authority to expand upon accepted interpretations of the Old Testament, in his teaching that we have come to call 'The Sermon on the Mount' – 'You have heard it said. . . but I say unto you. . .' (Matthew 5:21–48)
- The authority to forgive sins, which the Pharisees objected to after a paralysed man had been lowered through the roof so that Jesus could heal him (Mark 2:3–12)
- The authority to pronounce judgment on cities (Korazin, Bethsaida, Capernaum) that had not received him or his proclamation of the kingdom of God (Matthew 11:20–24) and even Jerusalem itself (Matthew 23:37–39)
- The authority to pronounce judgment on the Pharisees for not only rejecting him, but using their positions of influence to dissuade others from becoming followers of Jesus as well (Matthew 23:1–36)
- The authority to take up a home-made whip and drive the money-changers out of the Temple, over-turning tables and accusing them of making his Father's house a 'den of thieves' as he did so, and to silence his Pharisaical critics when they tried to protest (Matthew 21:12–13; 23:27; Mark 11:15–18; 27–33; Luke 19:45–48; 20:1–8)

By this point, it may seem amazing to describe Jesus, as the Philippians 2 passage does, as becoming 'nothing' and a 'servant', when he clearly claims, exercises and is recognised as having incredible authority. Perhaps more amazing still would be what his full authority might look like when he is revealed as King of kings and Lord of lords.

However, the key dynamic for an understanding of how authority is meant to function among the gathered body is not only to look at Jesus' understanding and use of his own authority, but to also look at how he taught his disciples (apprentices) about what kind of authority he was giving them, and how it is to be expressed even today, in the gathered body, in the advancing kingdom.

Apprentices and authority

Perhaps one of the most oft-quoted scriptures – after John 3:16, of course – is the 'Great Commission' of Matthew 28:18–20:

> Then Jesus came to them and said, 'All authority [Greek *exousia*] in heaven and earth has been given to me. Therefore go and make disciples of all nations, baptising them in the name of the Father and of the Son and of the Holy Spirit, and teaching them to obey everything that I have commanded you. And surely I am with you always, to the very end of the age.'

This short passage has been the driving force behind much of the evangelistic energy of recent centuries. There was a time, of course, when churches did nothing 'outside the walls' because the church building was perceived to be the most appropriate place for people to hear the gospel.

The treatment that John Wesley received from the Anglican Church in his day was indicative of this mindset – Wesley's preaching in the fields and in homes was seen as treating the gospel with contempt, and Wesley endured much verbal and even physical abuse because of it. Even Wesley himself initially struggled with the idea of preaching outside the church, at one point remarking, 'I could scarce reconcile myself at first to this strange way of preaching in the fields . . . I should have thought the saving of souls almost a sin, if it had not been done in a church.'

In recent years, of course, there have been many examples of revival meetings held not just in churches but auditoriums, and evangelistic crusades held in sports stadiums, as well as innumerable examples of musical groups, drama teams, movie-makers and even street corner preachers going outside the walls of the church in order to preach the gospel to every creature.

The connection between evangelism and authority is found in Jesus' words to his disciples in the Great Commission: He gave them authority to preach the gospel, and to teach those who became followers of Jesus.

The Greek word *exousia*, which we translate as authority (or authority and power in the King James Version), can be taken to mean:

1. the power of choice; liberty of doing as one pleases
2. physical and mental power (ability or strength which one possesses or exercises)
3. the power of authority (influence) and of right (privilege)
4. the power of rule or government
(Source: The NAS New Testament Greek Lexicon).

When thinking of this word as it concerns Jesus, any or all of the above definitions would fit. The significance for his apprentices is that this same word that describes Jesus' authority also describes the authority that Jesus has given us.

Examples of the use of this word include: the crowds recognising an authority in Jesus' teaching that their scribes didn't have (Matthew 7:29), Jesus' words regarding his authority to forgive sins as well as heal (Matthew 9:6), and the interaction between Jesus and the Pharisees about his authority (Matthew 21:23–27).

The same Greek word is used regarding the secular authorities of the day, the governor (Luke 23:20), the local puppet-king, Herod (Luke 23:7), and any authorities that the disciples would be dragged before on account of Jesus (Luke 12:11).

Authority over what?

It is vitally important to understand that while the secular authorities had power and control over people, the authority given to the disciples by Jesus did not.

Jesus himself certainly had authority over people, as they referred to him as Rabbi, which means 'teacher' (Matthew 26:25; Mark 10:51; John 1:49), and Lord (Matthew 14:28–29; 17:4; John 6:68), and Jesus referred to himself as both when with his disciples at the Last Supper (John 13:13). But when we read of authority being given to the disciples (apprentices), that authority does not include power over people; rather it includes power for preaching the good news of the kingdom, and power over sickness and the demonic – in other words, the proclamation and demonstration of the advancing kingdom of God.

As mentioned earlier, the most oft-quoted passage pertaining to the advancing kingdom is Matthew 28:20, where Jesus gave the disciples authority to preach the gospel and teach the new disciples all of his teachings (commands – which would include his prohibition of any of them presuming to lord it over others, according to Matthew 20:25–27).

A parallel Great Commission passage is Mark 16:15–18, which is in a somewhat disputed part of the New Testament, as 'the most reliable earliest manuscripts and other ancient witnesses'* do not contain this passage of Scripture (*New International Version notes on this passage and also John 7:53 to 8:11).

Charismatics tend to use the Mark passage more often than the one in Matthew, while conservative evangelicals usually have a preference for the Matthew version. Charismatics, of course, like Mark's inclusion of tongues, miracles, and signs and wonders as being inherent in the preaching of the gospel. Evangelicals are more likely to prefer Matthew for the opposite reason, and will use the 'most reliable earlier manuscripts' argument to call the miraculous into question.

But evangelicals would also be the first to say 'don't build a doctrine based on only one verse'; the biblical witness regarding Jesus' proclamation and demonstration of the good news of the kingdom, as well as the example of the apostles throughout the book of Acts, would suggest that a non-miraculous understanding of preaching the gospel of the kingdom is an *eisegesis* of Matthew's wording. In addition, Luke's Gospel also records Jesus giving the disciples 'authority to tread on serpents and scorpions' (Luke 10:19) – an undisputed portion of the New Testament – which must be taken into consideration.

What is very consistent between both Matthew and Mark (widely believed to be the oldest Gospel written, which then served as source material for the writers of the other Synoptic Gospels – Luke and Matthew), is that neither of these commissioning statements from Jesus includes any bestowal of his authority over people. Jesus remains Lord and Shepherd, and there is no conferring of his lordship to any 'delegated authorities' or 'under-shepherds'. Jesus remains the Authority.

This is an understanding that Paul expands upon in his writings on the body of Christ (1 Corinthians 12:12–17): that Jesus is still the Head (authority), and everyone else is a member of his body, although with varying functions as the Holy Spirit graces people with spiritual gifts for the common good (1 Corinthians 12:7). We will look at this in more detail in 'Community of the Spirit'.

There are two other instances recorded in the Gospels where Jesus conferred authority on some of his followers. The first is found in Luke 9:1–2: 'And he called the twelve together, and gave them power and authority over all the demons, and to heal diseases, and he sent them out to preach the kingdom of God, and to heal the sick.'

The parallel passage in Matthew 10 recounts the same story: authority to preach, authority to heal, and authority over unclean (evil) spirits. In Matthew's account, the twelve were commissioned and immediately sent on this mission; hence the understanding of apostle as being a 'sent one' on a mission for Jesus.

In Luke's account, the twelve who would later became apostles (except for Judas, of course) witnessed more miracles and heard more of Jesus' teaching before being sent out, but the authority was identical: preaching the gospel, healing the sick, and authority to set people free from demonic bondage. Unique to Luke's Gospel is the second passage which recounts the second sending out of seventy-two of the disciples:

> After this the Lord appointed seventy-two others and sent them two-by-two ahead of him to every town and place where he was

about to go. He told them, 'The harvest is plentiful, but the workers are few. Ask the Lord of the harvest, therefore, to send out workers into his harvest field.' (Luke 10:1–2)

Jesus instructs them to heal the sick (Luke 10:9), and later, 'The seventy-two returned with joy and said, "Lord, even the demons submit to us in Your name"' (Luke 10:17). So, in this second instance in Luke's Gospel of a commissioning of workers for the harvest, we see identical authority given to the seventy-two as was given to the twelve soon-to-be apostles. Later, as Luke recounts for us throughout the book of Acts, this circle of those empowered for the Great Commission would continue to expand beyond the original twelve.

Two things stand out strongly in all of these passages which deal with Jesus bestowing authority on his apprentices:

1. The authority is given in connection with them participating in the advancement of the kingdom – evangelism, and
2. No authority over other apprentices is even slightly hinted at. The authority was the message, the healing, and the deliverance from demonic spirits.

Significantly, in both Luke's and John's Gospels, the disciples are commanded to wait until the Holy Spirit is poured out before taking on the Great Commission. In Luke, Jesus refers to the promise of the Father, and that they will be clothed in power before being sent out as witnesses (Luke 24:48–49). Luke picks up this same command to wait for the Spirit in Acts 1:5 and again in Acts 1:8.

In John's Gospel, we read of Jesus inviting 'all who are thirsty' (John 7:37) to come to him, and that whoever came would be given the promise of the Holy Spirit, who had not been poured out at that time (John 7:39). In language reminiscent of Luke's writing, John is anticipating the coming expansion of the circle of those who would get to 'do the stuff' – participate in the advancing kingdom. Even after his resurrection, we read in the Gospel of John that Jesus told his disciples that they would be sent, just as he had, and that their reception of the Holy Spirit was part of and prerequisite to that sending.

Finally, in preparation for his impending death at the Last Supper, Jesus shows all of his apprentices, past and present, what 'taking the very nature of a servant' looks like, when he washes his disciples' feet.

> Jesus knew that the Father had put all things under his power, and that he had come from God and was returning to God; so he got up from the meal, took off his outer clothing, and wrapped a towel around his waist. After that, he poured water into a basin and began to wash his disciples' feet, drying them with the towel that was wrapped around him. . .
>
> When he had finished washing their feet, he put on his clothes and returned to his place. 'Do you understand what I have done for you?' He asked them. 'You call me "Teacher" and "Lord", and rightly so, for that is what I am. Now that I, your Lord and Teacher, have washed your feet, you also should wash one another's feet. I have set you an example that you should do as I have done for you. I tell you the truth, no servant is greater than his master, nor is a messenger greater that the one who sent him. Now that you know these things, you will be blessed if you do them.' (John 13:3–5, 12–17)

Usually, when people are trying to make a point, they go from a lesser argument to a greater one. Jesus himself used this way of reasoning with people when he said things like, 'If you then, though you are evil, know how to give good gifts to your children, how much more will your Father in heaven give the Holy Spirit to those who ask him?' (Luke 11:13).

This time, however, Jesus does just the opposite. The ultimate Authority takes on a level of servanthood that his disciples had not yet caught on to. Imagine the chagrin they must have felt as Jesus washed their feet, and then reminded them that, as Lord and Teacher, it would have been more appropriate that they wash his feet (although not stated explicitly, it would have been foremost in the minds of the embarrassed disciples by this point). Jesus was emphatically clear about his intent in this living parable: they were to serve, just as he had, and not fall again prey to the attitudes that prompted his teaching on authority in Matthew 20:25–28.

With this ultimate example of servanthood in mind, armed with the understanding that our authority as apprentices does not include authority over each other, and knowing that the circle of participants in the advancing kingdom would be expanding with the unique ministry of the Holy Spirit in the whole of the body, we can now turn our attention to the place of the five-fold ministries (Ephesians 4:11–16) in the gathered body of Jesus Christ.

Five-fold reconsidered

During the same evening that Jesus washed his disciples' feet, we also find the most direct teachings of Jesus regarding the work of the promised Holy Spirit, who would soon be poured out at the Feast of Pentecost. Jesus had mentioned the Spirit before, such as when he warned the Pharisees about the unforgivable sin of attributing the work of the Spirit to satanic activity (Matthew 12:22–32; Mark 3:20–30), and also at the end of his parable about the neighbour who comes at night with a request for food (Luke 11:13), but this evening would mark a much fuller disclosure from Jesus as to the work of the Holy Spirit in the body.

Jesus makes it clear that it is to the benefit of the disciples (and us) that he returns to the Father, so that the Holy Spirit could be sent. The indwelling Holy Spirit empowers the individual Christian in a remarkable new way; whereas in the Old Testament we read of people who were anointed by the Spirit at different times (Samson, Solomon, David, Samuel, Elijah and the rest of the Major and Minor Prophets, for example), now everyone becomes indwelt by the Spirit.

At the Last Supper, Jesus describes the Holy Spirit repeatedly as the *parakletos* (usually transliterated as paraclete), a word which literally means 'one who comes alongside'. Various Bible translations have given different meanings to this term, including counsellor, helper and comforter. While all of these meanings are possible – and perhaps the best way to view the paraclete understanding of the Spirit's work is to recognise that all the possible definitions in English are simultaneously accurate – what stands out is the 'coming alongside' nature of the Spirit's work. Jesus remains the Head of the body, and the Spirit – while indwelling us – is also in some way 'alongside' us, pointing to Jesus, empowering us to follow him, purifying us, and gifting us to co-operate with the Spirit in the advancing of the kingdom of God.

During this evening, Jesus first tells his disciples that the Spirit will be the Spirit of truth. Some early church fathers interpreted this to be a personification of wisdom that fit into their

Platonist worldview, but Jesus in this passage (John 14:15–27) seems concerned more with his disciples' understanding that the Spirit of truth will instruct the disciples but also bring to remembrance what Jesus had already taught them (cf. Jesus' instruction in Matthew 28:20 that the disciples should teach 'all that I have commanded you' to new disciples).

Jesus also reminds his disciples that his leaving would be necessary before the Spirit was sent (John 16:5–15). As we noted earlier, the circle of those who were commissioned to preach, heal, and deliver people from demonic bondage had already been widened from twelve to seventy-two. The coming of the Spirit to indwell each believer was necessary for widening that circle indefinitely to include every follower of Jesus. Again, Jesus remains the Head, but the entire body is filled with the Spirit of Jesus, enabling the body to act as the Head wills.

Jesus lists several aspects of the Spirit's work: convicting people of sin and righteousness, guiding the disciples into truth, speaking to us what he hears from the Father, and bringing glory to Jesus by sharing his thoughts and plans with us (cf. Jesus' declaration that his disciples are friends, not servants, 'because a servant does not know his master's business' – John 15:15).

We will be developing a post-charismatic understanding of spiritual gifts in the gathered body later, but it is important at this juncture to grasp the implication of the widening circle of those who get to 'do the stuff', and that the Spirit who distributes spiritual gifts according to his will for the benefit (common good) of the body (1 Corinthians 12:7, 11) does so as a paraclete – one who comes alongside.

The significance of this when it comes to the issue of the five-fold ministries found in Ephesians 4:11–16 is that, if the Spirit acts as a paraclete, and gifts people in order to see the body – of which Jesus is the only Head – come to maturity, then it stands to reason that the five-fold ministries – apostle, prophet, evangelist, pastor, teacher – should function as paraclete (alongside) ministries. This is also in keeping with Jesus' command that the disciples should never seek to lord it over each other, but to serve as Jesus had when he washed their feet.

In addition to being listed in what have come to be termed the five-fold ministries of Ephesians, the gifts of apostle, prophet, and teacher are also included in two other gift-lists in the New Testament (Romans 12:6–8 and 1 Corinthians 12:28).

The Romans 12:6–8 passage is interesting, as the gifts of prophecy and teaching are clearly placed on the same par as gifts of serving, encouraging, giving and mercy. There is nothing to suggest in this list of gifts that there is a hierarchical or 'office' function. In the Romans passage, the emphasis is on exercising the gifts by faith, and let us also recall the very well-known beginning of this passage: 'offer your bodies as living sacrifices' as a 'spiritual act of worship' (Romans 12:1), and to 'not conform any longer to the pattern of this world' (Romans 12:2). In the context of this passage, it is hard to imagine that one would somehow interpret this to mean that the prophet or teacher was somehow given authority over others. 'But because the pagan idea of leadership pervades our churches, many of us are in constant pursuit of celebrity status in the Kingdom of God. . .'[7] All of us in the charismatic renewal need a swift return to these simple truths of self-denial. We need to learn humility.'[8]

The emphasis in 1 Corinthians 12:28–29 is that all of the gifts are necessary, and that since all of us are (equal) parts of the body, none of the gifts has even a hint of elevation of importance in the body. True, Paul begins the list in verse 28 with God having appointed 'first apostles, second prophets, third teachers', followed by miracles, healings, helps, administration and tongues; the following verse, however, reveals a key element to understanding these gifts as *parakletos*: not everyone has all the gifts, and all are necessary – there is no indication that some gifts are more necessary than others.

In many charismatic churches, the Ephesians 4 passage has somehow taken on, in the minds of some, a certain level of hierarchical authority as the five-fold ministries became labelled 'offices' (with the implication that authority and governance is part of the office) that is inconsistent with the rest of the New Testament's teaching on spiritual gifts, and particularly the nature of the Spirit who gives them. As Len Hjalmarson notes, 'It seems the phrase is mostly used in charismatic circles as part of a package that sells a certain understanding of authority . . . hierarchical and positional, founded around office and status in the community.'[9]

Ephesians 4:11–16

As we unpack this passage of Scripture, it would be helpful to keep in mind that, as Brother Maynard reminds us, 'the gift is not given to an individual, but to a corporate group, the church'.[10] When any of the gifts of the Spirit are expressed through an individual, it would be inappropriate for that person to find and define their identity by their gift. The gifts are manifested through people, but they are given to the church.

Perhaps the main reason that people want to interpret the five-fold ministries as 'offices' of authority is because of the inclusion of 'apostle' in the list; the fact that the other gift list that includes apostles (1 Corinthians 12:28–29) is set in the broader context of the whole body, not a select group of ministers, is curiously not referenced very often.

The word 'apostle' in Greek is *apostolos*, and can be translated in several different ways – delegate, envoy, messenger, agent – and all of these interpretations are found in the New Testament. It becomes apparent that there are the twelve 'Big A' apostles, as well as a larger number of 'small a' apostles in the New Testament. The original twelve (eleven actually, since Judas committed suicide after betraying Jesus) were seen as the 'Big A' apostles: they were eye-witnesses of Jesus' resurrection (as were over 500 others who were not considered apostles in the same sense), had authority to make decisions on behalf of all Christians (e.g. Paul's instructions to the various churches in Corinth, Galatia, etc.), and in some cases, wrote Scripture.

> However, besides the Twelve, the New Testament text appears to clearly designate such persons as Paul, James the brother of Jesus (1 Corinthians 15:7; Galatians 1:19), Barnabas (Acts 14:14), Andronicus and Junias (probably a woman) who were 'outstanding among the apostles' (Romans 16:7).[11]

While there is some debate whether Andronicus and Junias were actually apostles, or simply held in high esteem by the apostles, it is clear that Paul, Barnabas and James the brother of Jesus were considered apostles. None of them were part of the original twelve, so we now have clear biblical record of at least 15 apostles, and perhaps more, if Andronicus and Junias are included.

The significance of this is that while the Twelve hold a special place in the history of the church – since they are pictured as twelve foundations of the New Jerusalem (Revelation 21:14) as well as being considered the foundation, along with the prophets, upon which the church was established (Ephesians 2:20) – there are other apostles in the New Testament that function differently from the Twelve.

Referring to the Greek *apostolos*, from which we get the word 'apostle', Wayne Grudem notes, 'In the broad sense, it just means "messenger" or "pioneer missionary".'[12] In this regard, there is biblical evidence that there can be ministry that is apostolic in nature without necessarily being a 'Big A' apostle in the same sense as Jesus' disciples (who wrote Scripture, although not all the apostles functioned in this way, either).

> The early church did use the word apostle from time to time for other than those who had witnessed the Resurrection. However, the term is used in these cases in its generic sense of dispatching representatives on an official mission on behalf of the senders.[13]

One of the issues raised at the beginning of this section was from the Assemblies of God, who made the statement: '(People) need to develop their own ability to search and understand the Scriptures under the guidance of the Spirit, who alone can lead into all truth.'[14] The function of the five-fold ministries, according to the same passage in which they are listed, is 'to prepare God's people for works of service, so that the body of Christ may be built up' (Ephesians 4:12).

It is impossible to ignore the recognition that many who claim 'office' gifts do so in a hierarchical, position-of-authority manner, and consider themselves experts in ministry whom others must submit to. This is contrary to an understanding of the five-fold ministries as a Paraclete-inspired paraclete ministry.

The fundamental problem with the hierarchical understanding of the office gifts is that it misunderstands the nature of service in the Kingdom. Jesus was among us as one who serves, and He was demonstrating how Kingdom leadership works: not to lord it over, but to serve. Rather than taking a title or position, Jesus exhorts leaders to humble themselves and become the least among those they serve.[15]

The goal of the five ministry gifts is helping the body become more mature. As such, these gifts have no other option but to function as serving under, not over, the rest of the body. It is also significant that nothing in the three biblical passages that mention these gifts gives any indication that there is a governmental function or role inherent in them: 'The five-fold ministries are not here equated with elders, nor are they charged with leading or ruling the church – just equipping them.'[16]

The word that we often translate as 'equipping' is *katartismos*, which has also been translated as 'preparing' (NIV) and 'perfecting' (KJV). It is used only once in the whole New Testament, and means 'complete furnishing, equipping'. Equipping for what? Works of *diakonia* (service). It's hard to imagine that equipping someone to 'serve' could be done in any other ethos than that of the Master who washed his disciples' feet, and gave the Paraclete to come alongside.

When the Jerusalem Council resolved the schismatic debate over whether the Gentiles should keep the Jewish law, the issue was decided by 'the apostles and elders' (Acts 15:4,6,22).[17]

It's intriguing to note that it wasn't just the apostles who decided this issue when the inclusion of Gentile believers brought about a cultural identity crisis for the fledgling church.

The apostles, together with a group of anonymous leaders referred to only as elders, made a group decision. If any group of apostolic people had the 'right' to make an autonomous decision, it would have been the original apostles in Jerusalem, yet they worked in concert with the elders of the Jerusalem church.

'Prophets, while never appointed to ruling functions in their capacity as prophets like overseers/elders, did exercise spiritual influence with the apostles and elders in the belief and practice of the Early Church.'[18] What cannot be ignored is that, in a body where Paul wrote that he wished everyone could exercise the gift of prophecy (1 Corinthians 14:1, 39), he never appointed prophets, nor instructed any of his church planters to appoint prophets; elders were appointed, but they appear to be the only ones given any mandate for governance.

What about elders?

If the five-fold ministry gifts are not meant to function in a governmental fashion, then is there any need for elders and leaders any more?

There are those who would contend that church history and the plain teaching of Scripture requires a complete renunciation of anything remotely resembling oversight by individuals (or a group of individuals) within a local gathered body. However, 'leadership' is one of the listed gifts in Romans 12:6–8, as are the gifts of apostle, teacher, encouragement and mercy. And not only did Paul make a habit of appointing elders in every church, but he instructed his colleagues Timothy and Titus to do the same, and even provided some helpful criteria in discerning and selecting them (1 Timothy 3:1–13; Titus 1:5–9).

When C. Peter Wagner argues for a continuation of apostolic ministry, it is possible, as we have seen, to agree with him but refine our understanding of how apostolic ministry is meant to function and the Spirit in which it is to function. The same is true for leaders and elders: there is an undisputable gift of the Spirit called leadership, and the example of Paul was that elders were to be appointed 'in every town, as I instructed you' (Titus 1:5), but is it possible that how they are meant to function in the Spirit is different from the manner in which many have experienced them?

One of the 'duties' of the elders, according to Paul's instructions, was to safeguard the gathered body from false teaching brought by false apostles – in the common vernacular, we might call them 'wanna-be' apostles. Significantly, 'in the early church, false apostles did not pioneer ministries; they preyed upon ministries established by others'.[19]

Paul warned the Ephesian believers before his last trip to Jerusalem that false apostles would show up, and that some of them would even come from within the body, whose ultimate motive would be 'to draw away disciples after them' (Acts 20:30). Recognising that people still have the tendency to want to 'lord it over' others (Matthew 20:25), Paul knew that false apostles would enter or arise from within, in order to directly contravene Jesus' clear instruction that they were not to act in such a way.

When looked at through this lens, the admonition that an elder be 'able to teach' (1 Timothy 3:2) and able to 'encourage others by sound doctrine and refute those who oppose it' (Titus 1:9) makes even more sense than it does on the surface. If the elder can teach, it means that elder knows the content of the message – invaluable knowledge if one is responsible to keep the 'safe place' a safe place. Paul saw that, beyond the danger of false teaching itself, these false apostles had a goal of deceiving people so that they would follow them, and lording it over them.

Therefore, part of the role of those entrusted with oversight includes guarding against false teaching, according to Paul's admonitions to Timothy in particular (1 Timothy 1:3–7; 4:11–16) and Titus (Titus 1:10–14), and particularly the cryptic part of instructing Titus to 'have nothing to do with' divisive people (Titus 3:9–11).

The two-sided coin that elders or overseers are responsible for has, on one side, guarding against false doctrine, and, on the other side, guarding against false apostles whose goal and intent was to gather their own followers.

It should be pointed out that the qualifications for elders and deacons in both 1 Timothy and Titus are moral guidelines that presuppose the background acceptance of Jesus' instructions regarding servant leadership, and the Spirit's gifting of the whole body. Paul is building on the foundation of Jesus' teaching, not the other way around. These additional moral qualifications were important for a number of reasons, including the appointment of elders (*episkopos*, literally, 'curator, guardian, overseer') who were trustworthy on a relational level (notice how many of the qualifications have to do with relational integrity inside the body and out), and who would be less likely to seek to lord it over others.

It's also noteworthy that while Paul instructed that elders be appointed, and gives some helpful moral criteria, there is not a great deal of clear exposition of exactly how they went about being 'overseers'. Deacons were a little easier to figure out – even the word *diakonos* gives us a clue: it means someone who serves food and drink (i.e. waits on tables – cf. Acts 6:1–6, where the first deacons are commissioned to oversee food distribution). The word *diakonos* also carries the meaning of caring for the poor; it's essentially a hands-on responsibility for some aspect of service that the body has undertaken or a need they are responding to. However, as noted above, there are clear examples in Scripture of what Paul was instructing Timothy and Titus to do – what teachings they were to refute, and how to deal with wanna-be apostles. Then, more positively, they were instructed to teach on what a Christ-infused life should look like. All this came to constitute the ongoing function of those entrusted with eldership or oversight.

An early situation that required elders to be a part of decision-making is evidenced in Acts 15:1–35, where the elders and the apostles together are recorded as having to make the decision about whether or not the Gentile believers would be required to follow Jewish dietary laws. If this example is normative, then if false apostles tried to make inroads in a local gathering, the elders would work in concert with the other mature people in the body to deal with the situation.

One of the unavoidable aspects of being an overseer, given the responsibility to guard the 'safe place', sometimes includes the uncomfortable and unpleasant decision to exclude someone from the group. Whether the context is a small house church or a larger, more structured church, it's never a tidy, everyone-feels-the-same situation. People are inter-connected; they have friends, and if the gathering is even remotely functioning as it should, disrupting these close-knit relationships is a sensitive matter, needing much wisdom and a pastoral heart. These times can be dangerously prone to producing a reactionary backlash, resulting in the 'dissensions' and 'factions' that Paul warns are not signs of the kingdom (he calls them 'acts of the sinful nature' in Galatians 5:20), and tearing apart the fabric of organic community.

Yet not to exercise what many call church discipline when it is required can actually result in the destruction of the safe place. While the case of 1 Corinthians 5 (expelling a man who was in an incestuous relationship with his mother or step-mother) is an extreme example, the precedent is that, in the case of grievous and unrepentant sin, sometimes the only loving, Christ-honouring and community-guarding response is to exclude someone until they change their way of thinking and living. But also note that in 2 Corinthians 2:5–11 Paul instructs them to welcome the repentant person back into the community, echoing the redemptive spirit of Jesus' teachings in Matthew 18:15–35.

This only serves to underline the great importance for elders or overseers to be chosen and appointed based on their character and track record of serving the body, not based solely on their gifts, talents, or abilities in the business world.

Many have quoted the principle of 'character before gifting', and nowhere is this more crucial than in the lives of those who give oversight.

When functioning as it should, the role of elders and leaders was to safeguard (oversee) the purity of the teaching, as well as guarding the ethos of the community, while *at the same time* the five-fold ministries would be equipping and enabling people to come to a point of maturity where they could discern for themselves.

Leading without controlling

To address the three dynamics from the beginning of this whole section:

1. People need to develop their own ability to be led by the Holy Spirit; leadership is there to help them move in this direction.

The whole impact of the five-fold ministries of Ephesians 4, as well as the other gifts mentioned in 1 Corinthians and Romans, is to function in a non-hierarchical way, in order for the body to mature. Overseers are responsible for creating the 'safe place' in which these ministry gifts can function.

2. Yet, how do leaders get people to listen and develop this maturing ability?

Ultimately, leaders can't 'get' people to listen or mature; you can't put them into the position of being responsive to your authority without violating Jesus' clear teaching and the dynamics of the paraclete nature of ministry gifts. It's possible that this is simply part of the maturation process, as people have to engage their own mind, will and emotions in the journey of becoming more Christlike within the community. It's not unlike the oft-quoted movie *The Matrix*, where Morpheus at one point says, 'I can only show you the door, Neo. You're the one who has to walk through it.' Perhaps the old saying could be slightly adapted to say, 'When the student is ready, the *servant* appears.'

3. But aren't leaders all about 'controlling' people, and shouldn't God be the only Leader?

No, *some* leaders (false apostles) are about controlling (lording over) people, and while Jesus is the uncontested and only Head, we can't do away with leaders, elders and deacons without ignoring some pretty clear scriptural teaching. If elders, deacons, leaders, apostles, prophets, evangelists, pastors and teachers are acting as Jesus instructed and modelled, then the fear of controlling leaders is lessened.

It really boils down to 'trust' – post-charismatics have had their trust in leadership damaged, and while forgiveness of past bad leadership examples is where the healing starts, it will be the risk of trusting other people in the body again that will open doors for true community. There really is no such thing as a 'leaderless' group; that's not how God designed the body. A restructured praxis has no biblical option but to recapture the kind of community dynamic that is in keeping with the teaching and example of Jesus.

A pastoral friend, when speaking of the different models of church government that have existed for many years (Presbyterian, Episcopal, and congregational), commented that 'there is room for abuse in any system – the success of government depends upon the trustworthiness and heart of the pastor or elders'.[20]

George Mallone sums it up this way: 'Contrary to what we would like to believe, elders, pastors and deacons are not in a chain of command, a hierarchical pyramid, which puts them under Christ and over the church. The leaders of a biblical church are simply members of the body of Christ, not an elite oligarchy.'[21]

Which brings us full circle to Jesus' authority, the kind of authority he gave his apprentices, and the example of both Jesus' foot-washing servant attitude and also the *parakletos* (coming alongside) of the Spirit who indwells each member of the body, and gives the five-fold ministries (*not* offices) so that the whole body can be equipped and mature.

PEOPLE OF FAITH

Retro-view

In the close of our review of Word of Faith, there were a number of reasons given as to why post-charismatics were reacting against the movement:

- The lack of care for the poor and needy (based on the perception that the poor simply lacked faith for their own prosperity)
- An approach to spiritual growth that denied the reality of suffering (based on the perception that health, prosperity and 'victory' were the only valid signs of a mature Christian life)
- The performance-orientation of having to always strive to maintain the 'positive confession' – coupled with blaming lack of results on the inadequate faith of others – that created a very static, non-relational, contractual approach to God (i.e. there was no room for Jesus to answer or not answer prayer; it was all dependent on our faith or lack of it)
- Rejection of the doctrines of the Word of Faith movement out of a recognition that they are ultimately not supported by Scripture

At a deeper level, the Word of Faith movement challenges us with the question of how faith is supposed to work in the gathered body, and in the many individuals who make up the body. If we reject the Word of Faith emphasis, then do we relegate faith to an intellectual assent to the propositional statements of doctrine that define salvation? If Martin Luther's rallying cry of the Reformation still rings true – 'the just shall live by faith' (Romans 1:17) – what does that look like?

Whose story is it anyway?

Perhaps the first thing to address is our perception of how we interact with the advancing kingdom of God. Many people seem to unconsciously hold to the idea that, in the final analysis, 'it's all about me'. If you would ask a general question about this to any group, everyone would probably enthusiastically agree that it's all about Jesus, and perhaps even quote Matt Redman's thoughtful and honest song, 'The Heart of Worship'.

For many of us, however, the reality is that too often we are unconsciously adding Jesus to **our** story. We may even inadvertently use phrases like 'making' Jesus Lord of our lives (as if he needs our endorsement to be 'Lord'), not realising that we have bought into a way of thinking that suggests that in our busy and important lives, we've graciously given Jesus space as well.

I'm stating this somewhat provocatively in order to make a point: whenever we become followers of Jesus, we are stepping into a mighty, rushing river of God-history – the advancing kingdom of God – that predates us by literally thousands of years. We are not the centre of the story; Jesus is the centre of the story and in reality, we are being added to his story, and not the other way around.

If the story did indeed revolve around us, then the Word of Faith approach is not so strange. We could therefore talk in terms of 'operating the Holy Spirit' (Franklin Hall), of our 'right to demand healing' (E.W. Kenyon), or that 'prosperity is a major requirement in the establishment of God's will' (Kenneth E. Hagin). Assuming that, somehow, the story revolves around us will result in an unbalanced approach to prayer and faith from the very foundation of our understanding of God. The

Assemblies of God summed it up this way: 'This puts man in the position of using God rather than man surrendering himself to be used of God.'[1]

After a conversation with David Watson about the state of the charismatic renewal in 1980, John Wimber commented, 'Have we entered a post-charismatic era, or is the charismatic movement entering a new stage in its development?'[2] (Note: Wimber was employing the phrase 'post-charismatic' to mean 'non'-charismatic; some were suggesting in 1980 that the charismatic renewal was over.)

As the eighties progressed, Wimber's growing Association of Vineyard Churches focused on 'equipping the saints' as part of their overall ministry. Wimber's favourite phrase was 'everybody gets to play' – meaning that there should be no superstars doing all the work while the majority sat and watched. In a post-charismatic scenario (in the sense that I have been using the term), the role of faith becomes very important indeed, if 'everyone gets to play'.

During his earthly ministry, Jesus preached the nearness of the kingdom of God, healed people, performed miracles, cast out demons, and taught anyone who would listen, but he also modelled an interesting dynamic for his followers. Jesus showed us what living in dependence on the Holy Spirit looked like.

For example, Jesus emphatically stated that he only did what he saw his Father doing, or said what his Father was saying. Jesus lived in a radical dependence on his Father, and taught his disciples to emulate that example.

> Jesus gave them this answer, 'I tell you the truth, the Son can do nothing by himself, he can do only what he sees his Father doing, because whatever the Father does the Son also does.' (John 5:19)

By myself I can do nothing; I judge only as I hear, and my judgment is just, for I seek not to please myself but him who sent me. (John 5:30)

While speaking to the Pharisees, Jesus further stated, 'When you have lifted up the Son of Man, then you will know that I am the one I claim to be, and that I do nothing on my own but speak just what the Father has taught me . . . for I always do what pleases him.' (John 8:28–29)

And with his disciples at the Last Supper, Jesus used similar terminology: 'I am the vine; you are the branches. If a man remains in me and I in him, he will bear much fruit; apart from me you can do nothing' (John 15:5).

This sense of radical obedience to his Father's leading is not only a pattern for us to follow – since we do claim to be 'followers' of Jesus – but is also perhaps an explanation of why Jesus only healed one person at the Pool of Bethesda in John 5:2–9.

The Pool of Bethesda, near the Sheep Gate in Jerusalem, was reputed to have healing qualities for the first person who was able to get into the waters after they were stirred up supernaturally. John tells us that a 'great number' of blind, lame and paralysed people were lying around the pool, each hoping to be healed.

Jesus approaches only one of them – an invalid who had been waiting there for 35 years and had become embittered and self-pitying in his futile attempts to be the first into the pool. Even when Jesus asks him, point-blank, if he wants to be healed, the invalid doesn't give him a straight answer, only a frustrated excuse/reason as to why he couldn't be healed.

Despite this man's apparent lack of faith, in contrast to many other healings where Jesus heals because of the faith of the sufferer (blind Bartimaeus – Mark 10:46–52) or their family (Jairus – Luke 8:40–56), employers (the Roman centurion – Luke 7:1–10), and friends (the roof-wreckers of Mark 2:3–12), Jesus heals the invalid anyway, and then promptly leaves Bethesda. There is no biblical evidence that Jesus healed anyone else in a place where 'a great number' (John 5:3) were waiting and hoping for healing.

Considering that Jesus is recorded elsewhere as healing 'all' who came to him (Matthew 8:16; Mark 6:56; Luke 6:17–19), it seems striking that he apparently chose to ignore the needs of those around him, and healed only this one (apparently weak-in-faith, high-on-self-pity, no-positive-confession) invalid.

Unless, of course, that for reasons that only the Father knows, Jesus was acting exactly as he had been instructed to by the Father. We don't know what the rationale would be for performing only one healing in such a needy place, but if we believe that God's thoughts and ways are truly above our thoughts and ways (Isaiah 55:8–9), then our inability to explain the purposes of God should come as no surprise.

How does this tie into a discussion on the role of faith in a post-charismatic understanding? Simply this: the two polar extremes are (a) a Word of Faith paradigm that 'demands' that God perform healings (and financial blessings) on a contractual basis because of our faith, or (b) negating a reliance on faith and 'doin' the stuff' in our own strength and without genuinely being led by the Holy Spirit.

Jesus offers us a third way, a middle ground: taking great risks of faith, but only the risks that the Father is telling us (via the Holy Spirit) to take, and only taken as a response to the initiating of the Spirit.

Faith is spelt R-I-S-K

All through the New Testament, the same Greek word that we translate 'faith' (*pistis*) occurs over and over again. In some places, it is also used for 'believe' or 'believed'. For example, 'Does God work miracles among you because you observe the law or because you believe (*pistis*) what you heard?' (Galatians 3:5)

Pistis has two meanings, the first being that of conviction or belief, which when used in connection with faith in Jesus Christ, carries a connotation of trust and holy passion as well. The other meaning has to do with fidelity or faithfulness. Both meanings are generally applicable to the New Testament use of *pistis*; for example, the same word is used throughout the famous 'Hall of Faith' in Hebrews 11, as well as in the discussion of faith and works in James 2 (which we will deal with soon).

When any discussion is held regarding faith as it pertains to salvation, it has been an unfortunate tendency to devolve into endless debating and drawing apart into different camps surrounding the age-old predestination versus free will argument. When this happens, any pursuit of understanding about what 'living by faith' means – in addition to being 'saved by faith' – is often obscured.

When the discussion of faith remains stuck at the level of how salvation occurs, then certain Bible verses are hijacked or explained away, depending on one's viewpoint on the predestination/free will continuum. Pentecostals are generally Arminian, Third Wave are generally Reformed, and denominational charismatics tend to follow the doctrine of whatever denomination they are still a part of.

Some of these verses include Romans 14:23, where Paul, as he concludes his admonition regarding whether or not Christians should eat meat sacrificed to idols, comments: 'But the man who doubts is condemned if he eats, because his eating is not from faith; and *everything that does not come from faith is sin.*' *(emphasis added)*

This is a provocative portion of Scripture. The immediate implication of this verse is the central importance of faith in the daily following of Jesus. True, this begins with salvation, but living by faith appears to be a biblical assumption – an assumption that we can unintentionally overlook if we think of faith only in terms of salvation, or specific instances where we are praying for divine intervention (healing, provision, deliverance, etc.).

To keep this verse in context, we need to remember that Paul is speaking specifically to the question of eating meat sacrificed to idols, and the admonition that those whose faith is strong (mature), for whom the meat is a non-issue, need to be aware of the effect of their actions on those whose faith is weak (immature). This passage has often been used – or misused, in actuality – to address such 'grey areas' as the consumption of alcohol, Christian rock music and body art (piercings and tattoos), just to name a few.

Joe Aldrich, in his book *Lifestyle Evangelism*, suggests that many Christians are 'professional weaker brothers', whose faith is not weak at all, but who are merely playing judgmental games with other Christians. In order to enforce their own more conservative standards of Christian living, they use the 'weaker brother' argument as a manipulative tool to shame others into acquiescing to their agenda.

Generally, someone whose faith is truly weak (meaning

immature – if the same person is 'weak' ten years later, they aren't growing spiritually), is someone who will question or doubt the validity of their own faith because of seeing other Christians participating in something that they don't feel the freedom to do. That is very different from a professional weaker brother who questions the validity of the faith of those participating, all the while feeling spiritually superior because of their non-participation. These people should perhaps be referred to passages such as Colossians 2:6–23.

Paul's conclusion in Romans 14:23 is that the weaker brothers and sisters should not eat the meat – but it's also safe to assume that this will no longer be a problem for them once their faith becomes stronger (mature).

The context of this verse is that faith – weak and strong, immature and mature – was being expressed in community. Faith has a personal element to it, of course, but the idea of 'living by faith' takes place best in the body. Living in a community of faith takes faith – the risk lies in the choice to remain open and welcoming in spite of the pain that happens when imperfect people deal imperfectly with other imperfect people. As King David once lamented: 'Even my close friend, whom I trusted, he who shared my bread, has lifted up his heel against me' (Psalm 41:9).

Another verse that speaks of living by faith, but is often overshadowed by the Calvinism-Arminian debate, is Hebrews 11:6a: 'And without faith it is impossible to please God.' The rest of that verse suggests that it is tied to salvation, since it speaks of God rewarding those who seek him; Arminians nod enthusiastically at this verse, while Calvinists quickly page over to Romans to counter the idea that anyone seeks God.

As is often true, it is the context of this verse in Hebrews 11 that gives us a clue as to what it means to live by faith, as well as being saved by faith. Throughout the whole Hebrews 11 'Hall of Faith', each and every one of those listed as being faithful earned that accolade because they lived their whole lives in light of what they believed God had promised, even without physical evidence to back it up: 'Now faith is being sure of what we hope for and certain of what we do not see' (Hebrews 11:1). It was not just an intellectual assent to propositional statements regarding the faith; it was a certainty in God that enabled them to make life decisions that would make no sense to a non-faith mind.

Noah's building of the ark, Abraham leaving his homeland and later almost sacrificing his son Isaac, Moses refusing a life of ease in Pharaoh's palace in order to lead the Israelites through the wilderness, Rahab risking her life to hide the Israelite spies in Jericho, and Gideon's army of 300 taking on thousands of Amalekites (to name just a few) – all have something in common: their faith caused them to do outrageous things in the eyes of others.

Many charismatics have long understood that 'Faith is spelled R-I-S-K', and that is an element that post-charismatics will have to seriously consider as they reconstruct how their communities of faith will function. Too much of what is occurring in the emerging/missional church today could be viewed as being done in the strength and ingenuity of people, with or without the Holy Spirit being involved. As Bob Girard looked around his church 35 years ago, his heart-breaking assessment was: 'It wasn't *Acts*. It was a testimony to the good things people can do – *all by themselves.*'[3] *(emphasis in original)*

The very real danger that post-charismatics face, as they detox themselves from 'charismania', is that the resultant communities of faith will be simply communities, whether faith is involved or not. By that, I do not mean that salvation by faith won't be important to these groups, but I do mean that we are at risk of losing what it means to live by faith if there is no element of risk-taking in our communities.

Part of creating communities of faith that function as a 'safe place to take risks' will include the cultivation of the *charismata* – the 'gracelets' we call spiritual gifts. While we will deal with this more fully in 'Community of the Spirit', suffice it to say for now that there are gifts of the Spirit which can only be exercised in the midst of risk-taking faith – healing and prophecy, for example.

In this context, faith also functions to remind us that we are not in control of our lives, and that our life's direction is not our own to determine. Following Jesus' example of only doing and saying what we see the Father doing – which includes the risk-taking of learning to hear the voice of God – means that we are relinquishing control, our own need for safety and predictability, and stepping into the reality of being Spirit-led instead of pro-gramme-driven. We will more closely resemble those Jesus spoke of: 'The wind blows wherever it pleases. You hear its sound, but you cannot tell where it comes from or where it is going. So it is with everyone born of the Spirit' (John 3:8).

In the conclusion to the Parable of the Widow and the Unjust Judge, Jesus sums up by asking, 'However, when the Son of Man comes, will he find faith on the earth?' (Luke 18:8) At first, this seems like a strange way to end this parable, when the purpose of the parable was clearly stated in the beginning: 'Then Jesus told his disciples a parable to show them that they should always pray and not give up' (Luke 18:1).

The juxtaposition of the unjust judge with a justice-loving God is not uncommon to Jesus' teaching style. He often used the lesser-to-greater approach in helping his disciples understand what his Father was like. Another example would be Jesus saying, as he summed up his teaching on prayer, 'If you then, though you are evil, know how to give good gifts to your children, how more will your Father in heaven give the Holy Spirit to those who ask him!' (Luke 11:13)

What Jesus is emphasising, much as the hall of faith in Hebrews 11, is that there was a tenacity of conviction, usually resulting in action of some sort, characterising this deeply held faith. It was risk-taking in light of God's character, and in response to his leading through the Spirit.

There is a rich sense of excitement in being able to point to something in the midst of a community of faith, and say without reservation, '*God* did that.' While some post-charismatics will be relieved to simply avoid the over-promising of what being a Christian can mean in this life, to miss out on the genuine activity of the Spirit, which can be explained only by the intervention of God, would be a tragedy.

Faith = verb: James 2

A faith that can be spoken of as being spelt 'R-I-S-K' assumes a certain amount of action; living by faith cannot be conceptualised as merely a mental activity – it must have a real-life application in order to truly be consistent with Paul's words, 'I have been crucified with Christ and I no longer live, but Christ lives in me. The life I live in the body, I live by faith in the Son of God, who loved me and gave himself for me' (Galatians 2:20).

Again, as Galatians 2:20 points out, it's all about Jesus and his story, and our Spirit-led role in that story.

No other passage on the topic of the interplay between faith and works (or faith in action) has been debated as much as chapter 2 in the Epistle of James. Martin Luther was so disturbed by the emphasis on 'works' in James that he seriously questioned its inclusion in the Bible, although to his credit, he did not actually attempt to have it removed.

This was similar to John Calvin, who thought that the Revelation of St John was not truly a part of the Bible. Calvin, like Luther, did not demand that the book be excluded from newer copies of the Bible being printed, but Revelation remains the only book in the entire Bible that Calvin pointedly declined to write a commentary about.

Luther's concern was that the emphasis on works in James might lead some to believe that they could somehow 'earn' their salvation by their actions, and not solely by faith in Jesus. Considering the emphasis of the Roman Catholic Church at that time, including the sale of indulgences to the common folk with the promise that these indulgences would shorten their time paying for their sins in purgatory later, it is not all that surprising that Luther was particularly sensitive to anything that might seem to contradict his assertion that 'the just shall live by faith' (Romans 1:17; Galatians 3:11; Philippians 3:9; Hebrews 10:38).

In the context of warning his readers not to show favouritism towards rich people, nor to ignore the needs of the poor, St James (the brother of Jesus, although James does not trumpet this fact in the letter) frames his discussion of the interconnect-edness of faith and works.

As mentioned earlier, faith is the Greek word *pistis*, meaning a deeply held conviction that included a sense of fidelity. The word translated 'works' is *ergon*, which can be an occupation, a product that is created by someone, or an act (deed). It literally means 'work' – an action that we undertake.

The context of James' discussion is very important. He has just finished admonishing his readers to:

- humbly accept the word planted in them (1:21)
- recognise that being only a 'hearer of the word' is a form of deception, if the hearing does not include 'doing' (1:22)
- remember that pure religion that God accepts is concerned with orphans and widows, and not being polluted by the world (1:27)
- avoid giving special attention to rich people, which is a sign of being polluted by the world, as is treating poorer people with contempt (2:1–8)
- be warned that fawning over the rich and despising the poor is equally as sinful as murder and adultery (2:9–11)
- speak and act as merciful people, because mercy triumphs over judgment (2:12–13)

With the echoes of being doers of the word, and to not show favouritism based on socio-economic standing ringing in his readers' ears, James then launches into the whole faith/works discussion. He begins with the rhetorical question regarding the genuineness of the faith of someone who has no 'deeds' (NIV) or 'works' (KJV, NASB) – the question is constructed in such a way as to lead to a negative response: *no*, faith without works cannot save.

It is interesting but perhaps not surprising – since James was just writing about not looking down on poor people – that the application that James suggests as an example of faith at work is related to caring for the poor.

Charismatics have been good at 'speaking blessing' over other people, and intercessors have often being deeply committed to praying against poverty, and binding and casting out the demons of poverty and hopelessness. And certainly, there is a sense of faith required to invest time praying for poor people and against the spiritual forces of darkness that are doubtless at work behind the scenes.

Rather than seeing intercession and ministry to the poor as an either/or situation, it is probably more biblically accurate to view them as partners in ministry. There is a need for people to pray in faith that God will overturn structures and disarm the enemy – but if these same intercessors hide behind their prayer meetings and do not get involved in hands-on ministry to the poor, we have the same problem that James is warning us against.

In *Loving Our Neighbor's Welfare*, Amy Sherman writes, 'Often the church has been guilty of a cheap benevolence that wants only to *help* the poor, but isn't willing to *know* them.'[4]

James reminds us through this example that knowing about needs within the body of Christ – as well as outside – puts us immediately into the position of needing to exercise our faith by helping those in need. This may be as simple as the reality that we, ourselves, may barely be scraping by financially, and therefore to help out will require a risk-taking act of faith on our behalf as well.

James puts the stakes on this very, very high: 'In the same way, faith by itself, if it is not accompanied by action, is dead' (James 2:17). The Greek word for 'dead' is *nekros*, which literally means 'a corpse'. There's no way to sugar-coat the implications of James' assessment of faith without works – it's not useless, it's not deficient, it's not lacking in some way; it's a corpse, rotting in a grave somewhere.

It's amazing, at times, the lengths people will go to in order to find a way to excuse themselves from this passage. Some – mostly in the Word of Faith movement – would blame the poor for being poor; they just need to claim the prosperity that God guarantees them. Others will attend conferences and prayer meetings till they have nothing else on their weekly schedules, and conclude that their intercessory work was doing their part.

Still others, in concern to not be perceived as believing in salvation by works, write off all ministries to the poor as being 'social gospel' – meaning that the gospel has been eclipsed by the works of caring for the poor. They maintain – in opposition to the rest of James 2 – that 'faith' is dependent solely on having correct doctrine.

I think that if more self-proclaimed intercessors and prayer warriors (I don't know about you, but I'm much more comfortable with people who just pray lots and pray for people, but don't feel the need to be identified and recognised as 'intercessors') spent time with the poor directly, 'knowing' them, their prayer times would be more focused and fervent. 'When we allow ourselves to be touched with the brokenness and pain of our needy neighbours, then an oh-so-needed holy discontent will begin to grow within us . . . There's not supposed to be discrimination. There's not supposed to be destitution. There's not supposed to be child abuse. There are not supposed to be hunger and privation. *We are spiritually impoverished by this absence of agitation.* We need the holy discontent we can gain by participating in the suffering of our neighbours.'[5] (*emphasis added*)

Missional post-charismatics have the opposite trap before them. Many post-charismatics have recaptured the hands-on dynamic of being involved with the lives of their neighbours and in their cities, but as the pendulum swings away from the prayer-meeting-only mentality, the danger is that our efforts will be grounded in James 2 practicality, but prayerless and lacking any sense of expectation of miraculous intervention from God. (The 24–7 prayer movement appears to be a welcome exception, demonstrating a potent mix of expectant prayer and practical compassion.)

Not too long ago, I spent several years working in closed-custody (medium security) facilities for teenagers convicted of crimes that were violent, sexual in nature, or who were repeat offenders and/or an 'AWOL' (flight) risk. I also spent some time working with a school board as an outreach counsellor for teenagers who had been expelled from their schools. It was very hands-on, very James 2 in its practicality, but as time went on, the inescapable conclusion I came to was that, even in this brief lifetime – let alone eternity – these teenagers had zero hope at all, apart from a literal divine intervention. My prayer life for these teenagers was deeply affected by seeing the level of devastation in their lives. Before that, my prayers for the emerging generation would have been genuine and heart-felt, yes, but after those years, there was an entirely different understanding of Romans 8:27:

In the same way, the Spirit helps us in our weakness. We do not know what we ought to pray for, but the Spirit himself intercedes for us with groans that words cannot express.

The balance that our restructured communities and our restructured praxis need to find is one that firmly embraces intercessory prayer and the need for divine intervention, but at the same time is living in the day-to-day practice of noticing and responding to the needs of those around us.

James goes on to challenge us to demonstrate our faith without works – his premise and conclusion is the same: it can't be done. Faith by itself is not remarkable, as evidenced by James' somewhat sarcastic remark: 'You believe that there is one God. Good! Even the demons believe that – and shudder' (James 2:19).

James refers to those who believe that intellectual faith is enough as being 'foolish' (James 2:20). This is the Greek word *kenos*, which means 'devoid of truth', or at times 'empty-handed or lacking a gift'. However you want to apply it, *kenos* (foolish) is neither a compliment nor something to aspire to. James is making it clear that faith without action is an oxymoron with deadly consequences.

James concludes this short passage with the examples of Abraham and Rahab, whose faith was expressed in their actions – Abraham by being willing to sacrifice his own son Isaac, and Rahab by aiding and abetting the Israelite spies in Jericho (James 2:21–26). Both situations required a great deal of faith being spelt R-I-S-K. Their belief (conviction) in God was expressed by their actions, and God considered their faith-filled actions to be righteousness.

The absence of this risk-taking faith-in-action is spiritual death, according to James, when he concludes, 'As the body without the spirit is dead, so faith without deeds is dead' (2:26). As previously mentioned, this means 'a corpse'. A cadaver, slated for burial.

Again, it is not merely the hands-on nature of ministry that qualifies as 'faith expressed in deeds'. If nothing that we are involved in requires risk-taking, but instead can be done all by ourselves with or without the Spirit's empowering, we have not yet found that all-important balance. As John Wimber once wrote:

> A disciple is always ready to take the next step. If there is anything that characterizes Christian maturity, it is the willingness to become a beginner again for Jesus Christ. It is the willingness to put your hand in His hand and say 'I'm scared to death, but I'll go with You. You're the pearl of great price.'[6]

Faith = expectation

> The Lord replied, 'My Presence will go with you, and I will give you rest.' Then Moses said to him, 'If Your Presence does not go with us, do not send us up from here.' (Exodus 33:14–15)

In every ministry setting – be it an institutional church, house church, parachurch or whatever – the stories that give people the greatest sense of excitement, adventure and encouragement in the faith are the stories where there is no other possible explanation except: 'God did it.'

Nothing encourages people to take risks in their expression of the faith more than hearing others – regular, everyday folk whom they are in relationship with and trust – tell God-stories where he has clearly had a hand in whatever was happening. It is the sense of wonder that the paralytic felt in Mark 2:1–12, after his friends had torn a hole in somebody's ceiling, lowered him through it, and then he heard Jesus say 'Son, your sins are forgiven . . . I tell you, get up, take your mat and go home' – and then *actually being able to get up and do just what Jesus had told him to do.*

Or the many who came to Jesus with diseases and demonic oppression, who were healed and/or delivered (Matthew 8:16–17; Mark 1:32–34; Luke 4:40–41), and who went home that night completely changed. Try to imagine being a jaded synagogue attendee, raised on stories of God's miraculous acts in the history of your people, yet having never seen anything like that happen in your lifetime – *until now.*

In charismatic circles, 'faith' has often had the unfortunate assumption tied to it that said 'action' was human effort, and was indicative of a lack of dependence on the Holy Spirit. I once heard a well-meaning leader say that the greatest thing about the harvest that God was about to bring in, was that none of us needed to do anything but 'sit back and watch God do it' – anyone who suggested how we might prepare for such a large harvest was viewed as wanting to usurp God's sovereignty.

And the most oft-prophesied theme in many charismatic circles is the impending harvest that God is about to bring into the church. Of course, who in their right mind *wouldn't* want to see a large influx of people becoming followers of Jesus? But many post-charismatics are jaded by these seemingly endless promises of certain revival – a revival contingent upon the church somehow getting its act together enough to be worthy of it. And consequently, when the revival doesn't come as promised, the people are blamed for somehow not fulfilling conditions that God had stipulated – conditions that were often only revealed when the prophetic people were announcing that the church had failed and why the harvest was delayed or not coming.

I have heard people prophesy that entire cities – the Canadian city of Calgary in one case – had been *so close* to experiencing this harvest, but there wasn't enough unity or something, so God bypassed them, but now *our* city (Victoria BC, at the time) was where God would release the harvest that Calgary had missed out on. (I don't recall that they mentioned whether or not they'd informed Calgary about being bypassed.)

When the prophesied harvest failed to materialise (the summer had been the guaranteed time of its arrival), the prophetic people decided that somehow Victoria hadn't met the conditions, so God was taking his harvest elsewhere.

My own thought is that the God who poured out his Spirit at Pentecost on 120 discouraged and fearful disciples, and saw over three thousand become followers of Jesus in one day (Acts 2), and who was so eager to see the Gentiles accepted into the previously Jewish-only church that he couldn't even wait for Peter to finish his sermon before pouring his Spirit on the Gentiles (Acts 10:34–48; 11:15–18), doesn't sound like the kind of God who would be so stingy about releasing a harvest in our present day and age.

It is the jaded response to unfulfilled promises of revival that has resulted in many post-charismatics treading close to being functional deists – they go about the 'works of the kingdom', but with little or no expectation of God actually 'showing up' in their midst. In a blog entry entitled 'Over-Promising?' Jason Clark writes, 'I've also got memories of seeing dozens of people being prophesied over "I see you changing a generation". Given

that maybe one or two people have that kind of influence historically, there are a lot of disappointed people out there, who that
has not come true for.'[7]

In my own experience, it was somewhat mystifying that
everyone was being promised some level of 'superstardom' in the
great thing that God was about to do. I often wondered why no
one ever received a prophecy about denying themselves, taking
up their cross daily, as part of following Jesus (Luke 9:23–24).
Len Hjalmarson suggests:

> We have moved from Christianity as a lifestyle to event-driven
> Christianity. Recently Chad Taylor, of Timothy's House, a disciple-
> ship house in Boise Idaho, wrote 'What does it really cost to see a
> whole region shaken by God? Is it more than infrequent confer-
> ences and prayer meetings? Could it cost us our lives instead? Our
> dreams and aspirations? Would it require that we take up our cross
> and follow Him wherever He may be going?'[8]

The good news is that many post-charismatics would read
Chad's words and resonate with that desire. Many post-
charismatics are willing to invest themselves in the cause of
Christ, but not in the hyped, 'over-promising' way in which they
perceive that many charismatic churches are functioning.

But in order to keep this risk-taking, faith-as-verb approach
firmly rooted in the leading of the Spirit, instead of works done
only in our own strength, there needs to be an expectation that
God will intervene and use us in ways that defy natural explana-
tions. We *need* the stories where the only possible explanation is
'God did it'. And we will have a hard time living these stories if
we do not cultivate an attitude of expectation, in faith, that God
can and will intervene in supernatural ways.

For example, another area that is often over-promised is the whole area of healing. Word of Faith practitioners often blame the person who is not healed for not having enough faith. In their worldview, it is simply impossible to *not* be healed if one has enough faith, so any lack of healing is a sign of inadequate faith.

Post-charismatics are more comfortable with answers like 'I don't know' than many of their charismatic friends are, and that includes the question of why some people aren't healed. While there are numerous instances in the New Testament of where people's faith was clearly a factor in their healing, there are other instances where people of faith were not healed. For example, Paul's famous affliction from which he was not delivered (2 Corinthians 12:7–9), his leaving Trophimus sick in Miletus (2 Timothy 4:20), and even his admonition to Timothy to self-medicate some stomach troubles with a little wine (1 Timothy 5:23). It was certainly not because of Paul's lack of faith, but as in the situation with Paul's 'thorn in the flesh, a messenger of Satan' (which many believe to be some sort of physical impairment, possibly Paul's eyesight), and Jesus' actions of going to the Pool of Bethesda and healing only one person, there are some times when the sovereign plans of God are beyond our comprehension.

'Through his books *Power Healing* and *Power Evangelism* [John Wimber] taught an entire generation of Christians about praying with faith for the miraculous, all the while trusting in the sovereignty of God.'[9] It is this understanding of the 'already and not yet' aspect of the kingdom of God that guards us from over-promising, but at the same time allows us to walk in an attitude of expectation of divine accompaniment and intervention.

Wayne Gretsky, the 'Great One' of professional hockey fame, is recorded as having said, 'You miss 100% of the shots you don't take.' This can also be said of living by faith; we will miss 100% of the opportunities – divine appointments – that the Holy Spirit is bringing our way if we don't cultivate an attitude of expectation that God can and will 'show up', and seek to hear his voice, and then take the risk of acting on what he is saying to us.

If faith is to be understood as risk-taking, and also as an action based on confidence and obedience in God, an expectation of his presence in our destructured communities of faith is basically a prerequisite to truly being the body. Yes, we need to avoid – even renounce – anything that smacks of hype or over-promising, but at the same time, the words of Paul to the Thessalonians are true for us as well: 'Do not put out the Spirit's fire; do not treat prophecies with contempt. Test everything. Hold on to the good. Avoid every kind of evil' (1 Thessalonians 5:19–22).

SPIRITUAL FORMATION

Retro-view

The Wesleyan/Pentecostal view of the second blessing (with or without the accompanying evidence of tongues) has long created a subtle mindset within the Pentecostal/charismatic and Third Wave movements that spiritual growth – sanctification, holiness, maturity, spiritual formation – revolved around crisis moments of the Holy Spirit's intervention. During these times of miraculous intervention, the Spirit is expected to (and often does) impart something of Jesus into the person(s) seeking him in prayer.

And many of those who have walked in the charismatic realm, including those who now refer to themselves as post-charismatic, can tell exciting stories of their encounters with the Holy Spirit, which left them feeling humbled, comforted, accepted, strengthened, penitent and overjoyed – often, all at the same time.

The second-blessing understanding of the Spirit's work has often led to a weekly practice of 'altar calls' or 'ministry time' at the end of each and every gathering of the church. While regular prayer times that begin with the expectancy that the Spirit can and will powerfully minister in the gathered body are to be applauded, at the same time, it could be argued that the pendulum has swung too far in this direction. While some have made mocking remarks towards charismatics for having a 'may God zap you' approach to spiritual growth, there is some legitimacy to their criticism. The emphasis has been heavily weighted towards a crisis moment with the Spirit, and church gatherings were viewed as the most appropriate setting for these moments.

Many charismatics have looked at things like 'spiritual

disciplines' (more on this later) as being tantamount to works-based striving in our own strength. The concern was and is that if Christians spend too much time emphasising spiritual disciplines, the Holy Spirit would be reduced to a figurehead position in the Trinity. Their (understandable) concern is that we will cease to be truly Spirit-led, and instead put our faith and trust in our own efforts to better ourselves. Therefore, spiritual disciplines were held at arm's length, while many charismatics made a weekly pilgrimage to the altar, wondering why their lives weren't being miraculous transformed.

Post-charismatics run the opposite risk, generally caused by their weariness and disillusionment with what Brother Maynard once called 'the weekly crisis event at the front of the church'. Now the pendulum swings wildly to the other extreme of putting so much emphasis on spiritual disciplines that the Spirit is almost relegated to a theologically administrative role, instead of a vibrant presence whenever two or three are gathered in Jesus' name. This is exactly what their leaders and friends in the charismatic movement were warning about; when they see post-charismatics swing to the opposite extreme, this has served to solidify their opinion that spiritual disciplines are merely works of the flesh.

Holding a 'both/and' approach to being Spirit-led while employing spiritual disciplines will go a long way in balancing out the pendulum swing.

'Discipleship' has become one of those words that once had a rich heritage, but through overuse and misuse has lost much of its winsome meaning. Many today instead refer to 'spiritual formation' to describe the process by which we become more Christ-like in our character, attitude, words and actions. The root of discipleship/spiritual formation remains the same, regardless of which term we prefer to use: it refers to sanctification – our becoming more Christ-like as we imitate him and are changed from the inside out by him.

Part of this ongoing transformation includes the old-school term 'holiness'. Like discipleship, holiness has become a word that has lost a lot of its meaning in general usage. For many, the word 'holiness' conjures up images of legalism and dreary bondage, instead of the freedom and partnership with the Spirit which the Scriptures reveal.

Some groups have used holiness as a hoop to jump through in order to get what they want from God. Within the Word of Faith movement, holiness is tied to the positive confession – the (conservative) lifestyle is seen as a vital part of living lives that God can bless with healing and finances. This would include clothing styles, musical genres, participation or non-participation in 'grey areas', and even political agendas. In this regard, holiness as a lifestyle is interpreted as a prerequisite to receiving God's blessing – the proverbial carrot and stick approach.

The Latter Rain movement had its own input on holiness as well, particularly in the teachings about Joel's Army of nameless and faceless overcomers. What both groups have in common is an approach to holiness that is ultimately self-centred, and which tends towards a mercenary pragmatism. We pursue holiness, in this approach, in order to get something from God – health, financial blessings or being an overcomer in Joel's Army. I have even heard some speakers confidently proclaim that the second coming of Jesus is being delayed by the lack of holiness in the lives of the emerging generations (reminiscent of the emphasis we looked at earlier in the Shepherding movement, as well as Latter Rain, that stressed that Jesus must remain in heaven until the world is perfected, based on their interpretation of Psalm 110).

It appears that many of us are still adding Jesus to our story, instead of realising that we are joining his story, and are only unworthy servants who have the awesome privilege of being included in God's work of redemption throughout history (see Luke 17:7–9).

We have come a long way from the understanding of some of the saints of yesteryear. Many of them had an understanding of holiness and sanctification that was sought after simply for its own sake, and because Jesus had commanded it. Bernard of Clairvaux (1090–1135) wrote:

> On the lower plain of action, it is the reluctant, not the eager, whom we urge by promises of reward. Who would think of paying a man to do what he was yearning to do already? For instance, no one would hire a hungry man to eat, or a thirsty man to drink, or a mother to nurse her own child. Who would think of bribing a farmer to dress his own vineyard, or to dig about his orchard, or to rebuild his house? So all the more, *one who loves God truly asks no other recompense than God Himself.*[1] *(emphasis added)*

It is this understanding of holiness and sanctification – that God is both the source and the reward of those who are his followers and apprentices – that we need to recapture in a post-charismatic belief and praxis. As we look more at this whole area of spiritual formation, there are several key areas and issues raised by, variously, the Word of Faith, Latter Rain, and Shepherding movements:

- The need to develop an understanding of the co-operation between the Holy Spirit and our own human responsibility

- Recapturing a right concept of holiness and sanctification
- Understanding the role of spiritual disciplines and even suffering in our growing maturity in Jesus
- A re-examination of legitimate, Spirit-initiated experiences, crisis or otherwise
- The corporate (community) dynamic that lends itself more easily to actual spiritual formation taking place

Our goal is to follow in the footsteps of other believers in centuries past, who have learned how to live all of life in the presence of God, and not just during meetings, conferences, and church services. Brother Lawrence of the Resurrection stands as but one of many examples:

> Everything was the same to him – every place, every employment. The good brother found God everywhere, as much while he was repairing shoes as while he was praying with the community. He was in no hurry to make his retreats, because he found in his ordinary work the same God to love and adore as in the depth of the desert.[2]

Impartation and responsibility

In the early 1990s, I was a worship leader at a local GodRock youth church in Victoria BC. During this season, we saw many street youth impacted by what are typically referred to as 'power encounters' with the Holy Spirit. Our worship was raw, loud and passionate. Breaking all the accepted assumptions about youth ministry, we had fairly in-your-face teaching from the Bible, and ministry times of prayer at the end of every gathering in a hard-floored, halogen-lit recreation centre. As aesthetically pleasing venues go, it was horrendous – fire codes meant no candles, and there was only one on/off switch for the glaringly bright halogens. The floor was tiled, hard and cold. It was a sound technician's nightmare. The chairs were of the cheap wooden stacking variety. All in all, not a very conducive atmosphere.

But God's presence was very evident – even those who weren't yet followers of Jesus would remark about 'something' spiritual happening in the room – and GodRock quickly became a gathering place for many youth.

We also attracted quite a number of youth from other churches, who would drop in to participate, mock or ask questions about what was happening. With such a divergent gathering, it was only a matter of time till the following happened. . .

Just before starting a worship set, I was approached by some obviously concerned young people, who asked me if we could forego what we had planned to be speaking on later that night, in order to address a topic that had come to their attention.

'Believe it or not,' they said, 'there are people here that believe you can lose your salvation. Could you set them straight on that?'

And immediately after the worship set, I was approached by a different group of equally concerned teenagers. 'Hey, could you address a problem with some of the people here? There's a bunch who don't understand that they could lose their salvation. Could you set them straight?'

Whenever a discussion comes up about where God's unmerited intervention in our lives ends and our human responsibility to live lives that are Christ-like in character begins, the tendency is to polarise into extreme positions which appear, on the surface and to new believers, to be antithetical. And each group is intent on proving the rightness of their position and the semi-heretical nature of those who disagree with them.

Many of the concerns of the youth on both sides of the 'once saved, always saved' question at GodRock had more to do with the perceived (or possible) praxis of the opposing group, and less to do with the theology behind it (although you can't address praxis without at least some level of understanding of the theology behind it).

The teenagers who believed that salvation could be lost were (legitimately) concerned with the actions and attitudes of their 'opponents':

- A cavalier attitude towards living in a holy manner, because their eternal destiny was signed, sealed and delivered, so their actions didn't matter
- An almost mocking view of God because they had him contractually over a barrel, so to speak
- In the extreme, contempt of God because they knew they could do anything and 'get away with it' because they'd 'prayed the prayer'

Those teenagers who believed that they couldn't possibly lose their salvation had equally legitimate concerns about the actions and attitudes of their 'opponents':

- An attitude of striving and almost neurotic obsession with 'have I crossed the line?'
- A legalistic approach to their own personal lives that spoke more of self-improvement efforts, rather than trusting by faith in the finished work of Christ
- A judgmental, accusatory stance towards any other

Christians who didn't share their exact views on what most
refer to as 'grey areas'

Both groups had doctrinally sound, historically theological reasons for believing as they did. Both groups also had pretty accurate insights into the problematic areas of practising either
viewpoint to an extreme.

The real problem behind both groups, however, was that they
had an almost identical – and inaccurate – view of their relationship with God. *They viewed their relationship with God as a contractual one.*

For one group, the contract was unconditional – they'd
'signed on the dotted line' by praying a prayer of salvation, and
now God was obligated to uphold his side of the contract (eternal life) regardless of their behaviour. This understanding is true
of many Third Wave and some charismatic renewal groups, who
are Reformed (Calvinist) in their theology.

For the other group, the contract was conditional – God
would uphold his side of the bargain, but only if they upheld
their side by living lives of exemplary holiness, which again leads
to the whole historical record of the Wesleyan (Arminian)
influence on the Pentecostal movement, and some of the charismatic renewal groups.

It's hard to imagine how either contractual viewpoint, when
taken to an extreme, could actually help us live in the Great
Commandment: 'Love the Lord your God with all your heart
and with all your soul and with all your mind and with all your
strength' (Mark 12:30). Neither a spirit of legalistic striving, nor
one of smug complacency, is conducive to a vibrant, growing
relationship with Jesus.

How this relates to the interplay between the work of the Spirit within us, and our own efforts in holy living, is that like the example above, we can reduce the question of sanctification to a series of doctrines that either (a) put all the pressure on us to perform adequately, although God will help us, or (b) put all the responsibility back onto God, and we become passive – even negligent – because it's 'not my job'.

Neither approach takes a growing relationship with Jesus into account, other than some form of contractual understanding. Our motivation in sanctification is not to twist God's arm to do something for us or to usher in revival (although God may sovereignly do those very things in the midst of our journey) – we are pursuing a deeper relationship with Jesus *that results in us changing.*

There are two sides to Jesus' words, 'If you love me, you will obey what I command' (John 14:15). Obedience is proof of our love for Jesus; love is the motivation for obeying Jesus. Yes, obedience does not depend on love. For example, when a parent asks (commands) one of their teenagers to take out the rubbish, the teenager may obey, but the primary motivation is probably because the parent holds the car keys, not a sense of love and devotion.

Obedience to Jesus based on the reality of him being King and Lord is fine; however, this same King and Lord said, 'I no longer call you servants, because a servant does not know his master's business. Instead, I have called you friends' (John 15:15). A friend of mine, who blogs under the moniker Emerging Grace, summed it up this way:

> Those who truly know Him as a friend don't disregard or belittle His deity and Lordship. However, I pray that those who serve Him

religiously without experiencing Jesus as a friend receive a deeper revelation of Him.

Jesus also made loving God the highest priority of all Christians. Obedience out of duty or in recognition of Jesus' status as Lord is better than disobedience, to be sure, but it is not the ideal that Jesus Christ invites us to step into, nor will it draw us into a more willing co-operation with the Holy Spirit. Obedience based on our deepening love of Jesus is the ideal that maturing apprentices of Jesus will evidence.

Throughout the New Testament, the Greek word that is most often translated 'holy' is *hagios*, which simply means 'a most holy thing; a saint'. *Hagios* is always the Greek word in 'Holy Spirit', but it is also the favourite word of Luke, Paul, Peter, the writer of Hebrews, and John when referring to Christians as 'saints'. It's the same word, in each case, although Paul also widens its usage to refer to holy apostles and prophets (Ephesians 3:5), while Luke uses it to also refer to the Temple (Acts 6:13) and to Jesus (Acts 4:30), and most famously, John uses *hagios* when he writes, 'Day and night they never stop saying: "Holy, holy, holy is the Lord God Almighty, who was, and is, and is to come"' (Revelation 4:8).

The origin of *hagios* is the root word *hagos*, which literally means 'an awful thing' – here the word 'awful' means 'full of awe', not repulsive and undesirable as it is typically understood today.

To the writers of the New Testament, the Holy Spirit is considered someone that we should react to with awe, as is Jesus himself, as evidenced by the four living creatures in Revelation 4:8. It is no accident, nor is it lacking in significance, that the same word is translated 'saints' throughout the New Testament.

Even the command to 'be holy, because I am holy' (1 Peter 1:16) utilises the same Greek word *hagios*.

Why this repeated emphasis on the holiness of the Spirit (which he has in his nature), and why are followers of Jesus referred to with the same word? Surely all Christians already participate in the holiness of God simply because they've become followers of Jesus?

One of my favourite verses on this theme is Hebrews 10:11–14:

> Day after day every priest stands and performs his religious duties; again and again he offers the same sacrifices, which can never take away sins. But when this priest [Jesus] had offered for all time one sacrifice for sins, he sat down at the right hand of God. Since that time he waits for his enemies to be made his footstool, because by one sacrifice *he has made perfect for ever those who are being made holy.* (*emphasis mine*)

It is this last phrase that so succinctly summarises this section: '. . .because by one sacrifice he *has made perfect* [past tense] for ever those who *are being made holy* [ongoing tense].' We can stop agonising over whether or not Jesus is pleased with our performance – he considers us perfected already. At the same time, we can deliberately choose to co-operate with the Holy Spirit in the process of maturing, or sanctification, as we are being made holy.

The word in this phrase that is translated 'perfect' is *teleioo*, which means 'to make complete, to bring to a proposed goal'. It is the same Greek word that James employs when speaking of faith being made perfect by works in James 2:22. The word, when used in Hebrews 10:14, refers to the finality of our holiness in God's view.

The word that is translated 'holy' at the end of Hebrews 10:14 is *hagiazo*, which is from the root *hagios* that we've been looking at, and is usually translated as 'holy' or 'sanctified'. The King James rendering of this verse reads '. . .he hath perfected (*teleioo*) for ever them that are sanctified (*hagiazo*)'.

It is interesting to note that the traditionally Wesleyan/Arminian side of the charismatic movement seeks a second-blessing experience almost as a 'seal' of their salvation – a surefire sign that they are truly one of God's children; this is almost Calvinistic in its desire for a guaranteed certainty of salvation.

Conversely, most Calvinists have an understanding of sanctification that seems to strongly depend on people having free will in order to co-operate with the Holy Spirit. As one Reformed theologian, who is also charismatic, notes: 'If we grow in sanctification we "walk by the Spirit" and are "led by the Spirit" (Galatians 5:16–18; cf. Romans 8:14), that is, we are more and more responsive to the desires and promptings of the Holy Spirit in our life and character.'[4]

It's almost as though Arminians are looking for a little Calvinistic assurance, while Calvinists are advocating a little Arminian free will when it comes to sanctification.

The meaning of sanctification here, even when *hagiazo* is translated as holy, is one of being dedicated to God's purposes rather than one's own, or those of the world. Erickson comments on *hagiazo*:

> In this sense holiness refers to a state of being separate, set apart from the ordinary or mundane and dedicated to a particular purpose or use . . . It is in this sense that the New Testament so frequently refers to Christians as 'saints', even when they are far from perfect.[5]

So, while on one hand we can all relax a little, and not become legalistically paranoid about our personal holiness, on the other hand, if loving Jesus is truly our pursuit – loving him with all of our heart, soul, mind and strength (Mark 12:30) – then we will actively co-operate with the Holy Spirit in his transforming work of sanctification. As the late John Wimber wrote,

> Spiritual growth, then, is a product of the initiating, empowering work of the Holy Spirit, *and* of our active co-operation. He engages our minds, wills and emotions, and He expects us to respond. If *either* divine initiative or human response is missing, we will not grow.[6]

It is the both/and dynamic of co-operating with the Holy Spirit which frees us from a contractual approach to holiness and spiritual formation, and allows us to be Spirit-led in our embracing and developing in the area of spiritual disciplines.

To these we now turn.

Spiritual disciplines

> But solid food is for the mature, who by constant use have *trained themselves* to distinguish good from evil. (Hebrews 5:14)
>
> No discipline seems pleasant at the time, but painful. Later on, however, it produces a harvest of righteousness and peace for those who are *trained by it*. (Hebrews 12:11)
>
> For this very reason, *make every effort* to add to your faith goodness; and to goodness, knowledge; and to knowledge, self-control; and to self-control, perseverance; and to perseverance, godliness; and to godliness, brotherly kindness; and to brotherly kindness, love. For if you possess these qualities in increasing measure, they

will keep you from being ineffective and unproductive in your knowledge of our Lord Jesus Christ. (2 Peter 1:5–8)

The topic of spiritual disciplines often evokes very strong opinions, usually ranging somewhere between viewing the disciplines as a key to spiritual maturity on one hand, or looking askance at them as being works of fleshly striving or 'salvation by works'.

But if we approach the area of spiritual disciplines with the understanding that we are co-operating with the Holy Spirit in the process of sanctification (keep Hebrews 10:14 in mind), and that all true change within us will be his doing, then the disciplines need be neither the magic cure-all, nor legalistic striving based on human effort.

In referring to this process of becoming more and more 'set apart' for God's use, Dr Wayne Grudem notes, 'Although Paul says that his readers have been set free from sin (Romans 6:18) and that they are "dead to sin and alive to God" (Romans 6:11), he nonetheless recognizes that sin remains in their lives, so he tells them not to let it reign and not to yield to it (Romans 6:12–13).'[7]

When we also consider the verses listed at the top of this section, we see the recurring theme of being 'trained' and choosing to 'make every effort', so that we will be participating in the advancing kingdom effectively – being about Jesus' mission in the world.

Todd Hunter, president of Alpha USA, has this to say regarding the classical spiritual disciplines as 'training':

Apple trees easily and naturally produce apples. But no matter how hard they may try, no matter how much they may sincerely groan and 'religiously' agonize over it, they cannot produce pumpkins . . . The disciplines are 'indirect effort'. In practising them, we do what is currently under our control with the intent, hope and expectation that they will enable us to do what we dream of in our idealistic language. Watch 'The Karate Kid' with this in mind. You will see how Daniel-san learns karate in very indirect ways. By doing what he can – scrub floors, paint fences and waxing cars – he becomes the kind of person who can naturally and easily defend himself from even expert karate punches and kicks. Lesson: we cannot 'try' to be good (remember the apples and pumpkins); we must 'train' ('store up good in us') to be good.[8]

Many times, by exerting our own willpower, we can approximate and imitate spiritual growth. We try harder, work harder and pray harder, and think (for example) that we have learned self-control and kindness as we relate to those around us. Then, out of nowhere, somebody cuts in front of us on the road, and our reaction – whether verbal, our utilisation of a symbolic and universally recognised gesture involving a certain finger, or even just the internal 'road rage' that wells up within us – gives away what is truly beneath our carefully crafted and maintained spiritual veneer.

This reality points us back to the necessity to remember that it is a co-operative effort with the Spirit; it is not our own efforts, although we are involved in the process. Richard Foster, whose *Celebration of Discipline* still stands as a modern classic on the subject of spiritual disciplines, says it well:

Willpower has not [sic] defense against the careless word, the unguarded moment. The will has the same deficiency as the law – it can deal only with externals. It is incapable of bringing about the necessary transformation of the inner spirit.[9]

Wayne Grudem concurs on the need for the Spirit's work on a deep level: 'To be dead to the ruling power of sin means that we as Christians, by virtue of the power of the Holy Spirit, have power to overcome the temptations and enticements of sin.'[10]

The busyness of everyday life in the twenty-first century has a way of crowding out our awareness of the spiritual part of ourselves, and the work of the Holy Spirit in us. In our very individualistic society, there is no precedent or example to follow in listening to the voice of God. For post-charismatics, many of whom have been 'trained' to expect that God speaks primarily (sometimes, only) through 'anointed leaders', a crucial discipline is simply re-learning to hear the voice of God for themselves.

The lack of congruence between the everyday work and school realm, and listening for the voice of the Spirit, means that we will have to train ourselves in this area – it will not come naturally. In *Celebration of Discipline*, Richard Foster writes, 'Christian meditation, very simply, is the ability to hear God's voice and obey His word . . . It involves no hidden mysteries, no secret mantras, no mental gymnastics, no esoteric flights into the cosmic consciousness. . .[11] In His intimate relationship with the Father, Jesus modelled for us the reality of that life of hearing and obeying.'[12]

As was noted in 'Five-fold Reconsidered', part of Jesus' earthly ministry included providing an example of what a life dependent on knowing what the Father is doing or saying is like. Therefore, the first disciplines that we should focus on are ways that we can hone our ability to hear what the Spirit is saying to us.

Foster lists as inward disciplines: meditation, prayer, fasting and study; I will not be going into great detail on each of the disciplines that Foster writes about, but some points should be made.

Different personality types (and schedules) will make these easier or more difficult for different people. Regardless of the approach we take to these disciplines, the goal behind them is to become more adept at hearing what God is saying, and then acting in a way consistent with what we are hearing.

Many of us are very aware that Paul spoke for everyone when he wrote in Romans 7:

> I do not understand what I do. For what I want to do I do not do, but what I hate I do . . . For what I do is not the good I want to do; no, the evil I do not want to do – this I keep on doing . . . What a wretched man I am! Who will rescue me from this body of death? (Romans 7:15–24)

This is the essence of the battle with our sinful nature that holiness and spiritual transformation repeatedly come up against. It is very easy to become so weary from the battle that we conclude 'What's the point?' But we need to remind ourselves of Paul's conclusion to his honest confession of struggle in Romans 7:15–25:

> What a wretched man I am! Who will rescue me from this body of death? Thanks be to God – through Jesus Christ our Lord! (Romans 7:24–25)
>
> Therefore, there is now no condemnation for those who are in Christ Jesus, because through Christ Jesus the law of the Spirit of life set me free from the law of sin and death. (Romans 8:1–2)

While we understand that we continue to live in the wrestle that Paul was describing, by keeping Romans 8:1–2 in mind we can stop beating ourselves up for our failures, because God has already declared that there is no condemnation. Learning to walk in forgiveness (no condemnation) is a discipline itself for many Christians.

> Just as prayer for daily bread provides a model for a prayer that should be repeated each day, so the prayer for forgiveness of sins is included in the type of prayer that should be made each day in a believer's life.[13]

It's often been said that prayer is a two-way street, and charismatics – with the theological understanding that God still speaks today – have no problem with this idea of two-way communication. But as many critics inside and outside of the charismatic realm have noted, a certain lack (at times) of biblical literacy has resulted in some pretty bizarre teachings and practices being introduced that should not have been.

Foster writes, 'In prayer, real prayer, we begin to think God's thoughts after Him: to desire the things He desires, to love the things He loves, to will the things He wills. Progressively, we are taught to see things from His point of view.'[14] The best way to ensure that what we think God is saying to us is actually in line with what God is truly trying to communicate to us, is to train ourselves in knowing what the Bible actually says.

When many people hear someone encouraging them to 'read the Bible more', it often comes across as a dry time spent legalistically slaving over the Bible in study. However, the exact opposite is true, if we approach reading and studying (reinterpreted as 'becoming fascinated with') the Bible with an attitude of learning how to hear his voice through the Bible, and also as a trustworthy grid for understanding and putting into action what we feel the Spirit is saying to us (more on this later in 'Community of the Spirit').

As we learn how to partner with the Holy Spirit, we will discover an increasing desire to co-operate more fully. It's not unlike a brilliant guitarist, who spends many hours doing 'boring' scales and finger exercises, but as a result has a repertoire of skills and instinctual fretboard knowledge that comes almost automatically during an improvisational solo.

As Todd Hunter mentioned above, the disciplines are an 'indirect effort' that will pay off when we most need to respond almost 'automatically' in a Spirit-led way. For example, it will certainly be more beneficial to the person we are praying for if we are at ease and supernaturally natural in our prayer, rather than stumbling around, searching for the right words to say, as it becomes obvious that prayer is something we talk about, but don't do much of.

Suffering as discipline

A friend of mine used to joke: 'God, give me patience – *right now!*' He would point out that the book of James clearly tells us how God develops patience in us – by sending trials our way (James 1:2–4) – yet when the trials come in answer to our prayer for patience, we freak out and try to pray the trials away.

Part of our 'training', according to Hebrews 12:7–11, includes hardship and trials. We usually see discipline as 'punishment', and that is pretty plainly a part of what the writer of Hebrews is saying, but it's not punishment for the sake of being punitive. It's about learning through hard times, including our mistakes and intentional disobedience, lessons that we don't learn any other way. It's 'discipline' if we learn and grow through it; if we fail to learn, and mature, then it will continually feel like punishment.

It is interesting – and no doubt significant – that James prefaces his writing on faith and works with words about enduring trials and temptations (James 1:2–4, 12) as part of being 'perfected' (complete), and 'not lacking anything' (James 1:4). There just seems to be certain areas of our lives that we don't mature in during good times, but that trials and temptations – which drive us further into faith and dependence on God – are able to accomplish much more powerfully.

In 'Spirit and Praxis: People of Faith', we noted that the many saints in Hebrews 11 were praised for their great faith in spite of not receiving what they were waiting and believing for. We should also take note that these great saints of the faith – of whom it is written 'the world was not worthy of them' (Hebrews 11:38) – also have, as part of their faith résumé, a dark list of terrible things that they endured or experienced as they walked in that faith: mistreatment, torture, execution, imprisonment, flogging, stoning, being sawn in two, persecution and being killed by the sword.

The writer of Hebrews uses this list of the faithful to inspire us to embrace the race that we are running, and accept that part of that race often will include suffering. Paul had his famous 'thorn in the flesh', which didn't go away despite his prayer of faith, because God had a purpose – keeping Paul humble – for that thorn (whatever it was) to accomplish (2 Corinthians 12:7–10).

This recognition that hardships are sometimes part of God's maturing process in us puts to rest the fear that, somehow, any troubles we encounter are the result of our own actions. This was the assumption of the disciples with the man born blind (John 9:1–3) – their question was 'whose sin' led to the man's blindness – but Jesus refuted that idea, saying that the man's healing (to God's glory) was the focus, not finding someone to blame.

At the same time, Paul warns us in Galatians 6:7–8 that we reap what we sow, and Peter speaks of suffering for God being praiseworthy, but that if we're suffering because we're jerks, then it's not (general paraphrase of 1 Peter 3:17 and 1 Peter 4:12–16).

The whole discussion of the existence of evil is outside the scope of this writing, but suffice it to say that in an imperfect world, where all of creation is groaning (Romans 8:22), we will, as Jesus promised in John 16:33, 'have trouble'. However, the whole of that verse is a necessary and encouraging reminder: 'I have told you these things, so that in me you may have peace. In this world, you will have trouble. But take heart! I have overcome the world.'

Welcoming surprises

A healthy understanding and practice of spiritual disciplines will keep us from living in a 'may God zap you' approach to spiritual transformation, but if the pendulum swings too far to one side – and we all have the tendency to be pendulums that are a little too exuberant in our swings – we can and will end up in a performance-based approach to spiritual formation that, legalistic or not, will result in spiritual immaturity.

The Holy Spirit is the one with whom we are co-operating in this process. It is very important that we remember that we are, in our co-operation, not setting the agenda – the Holy Spirit is.

And we should not be surprised when the Holy Spirit sometimes does the unexpected. In fact, we should anticipate and expect that God will do 'immeasurably more than all we ask or imagine, according to his power that is at work within us' (Ephesians 3:20), and that Paul was not exercising exaggerated poetic licence when he wrote this.

In one sense, the Holy Spirit is always present, because one of God's attributes is his omnipresence, and also because each apprentice of Jesus has the Spirit indwelling them. On the other hand, there are many biblical examples where this omnipresent Spirit's presence became much more obvious than what was perceived as 'normal'. These times, where the Holy Spirit's presence becomes more tangible and demonstrative, are often referred to as the 'manifest presence' of the Spirit.

Just as we need to remember that we're being added to Jesus' story, and not adding him to ours, we need to keep in mind that the Holy Spirit is co-defined as 'Lord' and 'God' in the Trinitarian parts of the early church creeds. The Nicene Creed reads, in part, 'We believe in the Holy Spirit, the Lord, the giver of life, who proceeds from the Father and the Son, who with the Father and the Son is worshipped and glorified. . .' If, in our recovering of an application of the classical spiritual disciplines, we neglect the ongoing role of the Holy Spirit in both personal and corporate spiritual transformation, we will become functionally cessationist (i.e. believing that the charismatic phenomena ceased when the Bible was completed).

It has become almost trendy, in recent years, for groups and denominations that were formerly known for being cessationist in doctrine, to suddenly proclaim themselves to be non-cessationist. This change came initially out of (however belatedly) recognising that the teaching of cessationism was not truly biblically based, but quickly became a way of portraying oneself as 'open' to whatever God may want to say or do in any given gathering, including all of the spiritual gifts listed in the New Testament.

However, as many who attended or pastored at these newly non-cessationist churches discovered, there was a big difference between believing that the spiritual gifts were still available today, and actually allowing people to use their spiritual gifts. 'Being open' seems to be an end in itself and it seems that teaching, training and releasing people into their giftedness goes beyond the assumed boundaries of that 'openness'. Many of these churches were non-cessationist in their doctrine, but *functionally* cessationist in their praxis. There was lip-service to belief in all of the gifts, but resistance to their use, and at times, expulsion of any who dared to actually use their Spirit-given gifts, or encouraged others to 'eagerly desire spiritual gifts, especially the gift of prophecy' (1 Corinthians 14:1).

While the following quote from John Wimber was written specifically about divine healing, the principle is the same for all of the spiritual gifts, and even the expectation of the Spirit's manifest presence:

> Many of these people were not offended by the *theory* of divine healing; it was the *practice* of healing prayer that offended them. I was not entirely surprised by their reaction. As a church consultant I often saw a discrepancy between what Christians believed and what they practised.[15] *(emphasis in original)*

In 'Community of the Spirit', we will look at Spirit-given gifts in more detail, but for now, it is important that we see that, as post-charismatics, we are potential candidates for becoming functional cessationists. It will not be enough to hold an intellectual idea about the manifest presence of the Holy Spirit, if we look around our communities of faith in a couple of years' time, and realise that he hasn't made his presence felt among us recently.

There are many scriptural examples that could be put forward to demonstrate that the Spirit shows up both when we aren't expecting him, and even when we are (but he comes more powerfully than we anticipated).

Individually, there are many biblical stories of God showing up unexpectedly in people's lives: people like Abram (later Abraham) being called out of Haran (Genesis 12:1–5). Moses wasn't expecting God in the burning bush (Exodus 3:1–4); Gideon was hiding in a winepress and when 'called', used the opportunity to complain about how God was treating Israel (Judges 6:11–13); Samuel thought it was Eli calling him during the night (1 Samuel 3:1–18); and the apostle Paul thought he *was* doing God's work, till Jesus knocked him off his donkey with a new revelation and new marching orders (Acts 9:1–19).

These are but a few examples of God interrupting people's normal routines with his manifest presence; in the five examples above, it should also be noted that these encounters turned out, over time, to be the turning points in their lives and the lives of those around them.

There are also many biblical examples of people going about the Lord's work in some manner, consciously aware of his presence, and then being overwhelmed with an encounter with God that went above and beyond what they would normally anticipate.

Solomon would have expected that the dedication of the Temple would be a spiritually momentous event, but were any of those present prepared for what actually happened? 'When the priests withdrew from the Holy Place, the cloud filled the temple of the Lord. And the priests could not perform their service because of the cloud, for the glory of the Lord filled his temple' (1 Kings 8:10–11).

One of the most well-known New Testament passages in charismatic circles is Acts 2, the watershed moment which even non-charismatic theologians often agree marks the starting point of the church age. The disciples had been told by Jesus to stay in Jerusalem until the Spirit was given (Acts 1:4–5), and they were doing just that, but they had no idea what it would look like. They were expecting power to be Jesus' witnesses, but the rushing wind, the tongues of fire, speaking in other tongues, and the resultant three thousand people becoming followers of Jesus was far beyond what they would have imagined.

Paul and Barnabas were sent on the first of Paul's many missionary voyages when the Spirit interrupted one of the meetings of the church at Antioch: 'While they were worshipping the Lord and fasting, the Holy Spirit said, "Set apart for me Barnabas and Saul for the work to which I have called them"' (Acts 13:2).

And in the final book in the New Testament, the Revelation of John, we find John receiving the beginning of his revelation with the simple words, 'On the Lord's Day I was in the Spirit, and I heard behind me a loud voice like a trumpet. . .' (Revelation 1:10). Whether John was praying, worshipping or whatever, he says he was 'in the Spirit' and then the Revelation began.

Church history is full of many instances of the Holy Spirit

'showing up' (to use a popular phrase in the Vineyard movement during the 1990s) to both those who were actively seeking a deeper understanding and experience of the Spirit, and at times among people who weren't really seeking or expecting – or even wanting – anything beyond what they had seen or experienced to that point in their spiritual journey.

John Wimber, in his book *Power Evangelism*, provides a partial list of well-known leaders from early church history who wrote of their experiences of charismatic gifts and Spirit-initiated encounters, including Justin Martyr, Irenaeus, Tertullian, and Augustine, who initially rejected the more overt manifestation of the Holy Spirit, but changed his mind and later wrote in *The City of God* that we should expect the miraculous intervention of the Holy Spirit.

John Wesley's journals reveal numerous times where, during prayer times in homes, the Spirit would profoundly move: 'About three in the morning, as we were continuing instant in prayer, the power of God came mightily upon us, so that many cried out for exulting joy and many fell to the ground.'

Another of the most well-known leaders in the Great Awakening, Jonathan Edwards, is quoted by Guy Chevreau in *Catch the Fire*: 'To rejoice that the work of God is carried on calmly, without much ado, is in effect to rejoice that it is carried on with less power, or that there is not so much of the influence of God's Spirit.'[16]

The historical list could go on almost indefinitely. The point is simply that throughout post-Acts 2 history, the Holy Spirit has been working in his people to advance the kingdom. Sometimes people are expecting and praying towards this, and other times the Spirit 'ambushes' people.

But are these 'divine interruptions' an end in and of themselves? Post-charismatics tend to be leery of a mindset that sees the greatest good in simply attending more and more meetings and conferences, praying and waiting for the next great move of the Spirit to set things right. During the Toronto Blessing years in the mid-1990s, there were more than a few warnings that what came down was meant to go out. A 'bless-me' club mentality has often contributed to the post-charismatic exodus that we now see.

However, this 'bless me' attitude is not an automatic part of a revival setting, as Wes Campbell reminds us in *Welcoming a Visitation of the Holy Spirit*: 'Even a casual look into church history reveals how intricately tied to revival is the aspect of showing mercy.'[17] Post-charismatics would use the word missional, perhaps, but the meaning is the same and we should not lose sight of the reality that Campbell reminds us of. A true encounter with the Holy Spirit will result in the fruit of mercy and compassion to the disenfranchised.

Campbell goes on to point out that people who had been touched by the Holy Spirit and who went on to affect society around them included William Wilberforce (abolition of slavery), John Howard (founder of the prison reform John Howard Society), the founders of the Young Men's Christian Association (YMCA – ministry to the homeless and poor), Henri Dunant (founder of the Red Cross), Anglican minister Arthur Bloome (founder of the Royal Society for the Prevention of Cruelty to Animals), Lord Shaftesbury (who spear-headed the Ten Hour Act which addressed the lack of child labour laws), and George Muller (a great man of prayer who housed literally thousands of orphans).

There is no dichotomy or contradiction between earnestly seeking to see the Holy Spirit move in demonstrative ways, and ongoing acts of mercy and compassion. Being truly impacted by the presence of the Spirit will be personally enriching, to be sure, but Spirit-led acts of mercy and compassion – being missional – are the fruit of these encounters with the Almighty.

The question for post-charismatics is whether or not it is better to be 'surprised by the power of the Holy Spirit' (the title of an excellent book by Jack Deere), or if it is more advisable and biblical to be expecting and seeking to be available for the Spirit's manifest presence and ongoing ministry through the body.

The radical middle

Perhaps the best guiding principle for living in the tension – sometimes called 'the radical middle' – is found in Jesus' words to the Pharisees:

> Woe to you, teachers of the law and Pharisees, you hypocrites! You give a tenth of your spices – mint, dill and cummin. But you have neglected the more important matters of the law – justice, mercy and faithfulness. *You should have practised the latter, without neglecting the former.* (Matthew 23:23, *emphasis added*)

While this was a harsh denunciation of the hypocrisy of the Pharisees, the principle can still apply to the current discussion: it's a both/and scenario, not an either/or approach, that is called for. Spiritual disciplines are an important part of our spiritual growth, and they should not be seen as supplanting the work of the Spirit in our lives.

At the same time, the Holy Spirit is Lord. He can do whatever he wants, speak whatever he wants, and direct us – individually and corporately – in the ways that the Head of the body, Jesus, wants us to go.

It's easier, in some ways, to focus entirely on the crisis moments at the altar, and to bury ourselves in endless 'revival' meetings, waiting in anticipation for the next great move of the Spirit, as many charismatics presently do. It's equally easy for post-charismatics to roll their eyes at this mentality, and embrace a more hands-on approach via spiritual disciplines and acts of mercy and justice, and relegate the Spirit to the realm of stories about the old days.

It's much more of a stretch to co-operate with the Spirit in our formation; to embrace that we are viewed as holy even as we are being made more holy; to train ourselves via the spiritual disciplines *and* continue to not only expect and welcome, but to yearn for the manifest presence of the Holy Spirit.

And the healthiest soil for this understanding to grow in is found in *community* – other journey mates who are on a similar quest to learn what it means to be post-charismatic but not post-Spirit.

COMMUNITY OF THE SPIRIT

Retro-view

> And let us consider how we may spur one another on towards love and good deeds. Let us not give up meeting together, as some are in the habit of doing, but let us encourage one another – and all the more as you see the Day approaching. (Hebrews 10:24–25)

In his landmark book *Christian Counter-Culture*, John Stott wrote, 'For the Christian counter-culture is not an individualistic but a community affair, and relations both within the community and between the community and others are of paramount importance.'[1]

Being 'in community' as apprentices of Jesus is one of the deepest desires that most post-charismatics have. Conversely, the damage that many have experienced in less-than-healthy church and parachurch situations fights against this desire. Many post-charismatics that I have had conversations with are very vocal about their deep longing for authentic community, but are also fearful of taking the risks required to be in deep fellowship.

The whole area called 'accountability', as it has been influenced by the Shepherding movement, has been a source of much pain, to the point where the very term 'accountability' has become synonymous with hierarchical control and domination. People who have opened their lives to controlling leaders, in a sincere desire to grow spiritually, have often come away feeling as if they have experienced spiritual blackmail.

When those who have felt burnt by unhealthy accountability structures read verses like James 5:16 – 'Therefore confess your sins to each other and pray for each other so that you may be healed' – they struggle to reconcile this verse with what they've experienced.

The Latter Rain movement has created a different set of hurdles for those desiring community. The heavy emphasis on corporate worship (influenced by the Tabernacle of David understanding) to somehow 'get it right' so that God could move and inhabit the praises of his people, placed a different kind of performance-driven pressure on the gathered church. Many post-charismatics have become so fed up with the performance-orientation of this approach, and also with the hyped atmosphere, that they have opted for a much more passive, individualistic approach to worship, where demonstrativeness is viewed with suspicion.

The Latter Rain cannot be exclusively faulted for the jaundiced reaction to the charismatic gifts that many post-charismatics exhibit; the abuse of spiritual gifts has happened in many Pentecostal, charismatic and Third Wave streams, which have contributed to the downplaying of charismatic gifts that is prevalent among many post-charismatics (those who haven't completely given up and sought out more highly liturgical, non-charismatic expressions of the faith).

Just as many disillusioned Pentecostals have reacted against the pressure and hype associated with speaking in tongues. The Latter Rain's influence on the current prophetic movement, as well as the New Apostolic Reformation, is behind the scepticism towards the revelatory gifts like prophecy and words of wisdom and knowledge. Between the elitism surrounding the 'have's and the have-not's', grandiose prophetic pronouncements that have not borne fruit, and the elevation of prophetic people above the 'rest of us', it is not surprising to discover that many post-charismatics have become functional cessationists when it comes to hearing the voice of God.

Many post-charismatics who are currently in the process of detoxing from church have formed small clusters and house churches, often with other friends who have also left their former churches. In these less-structured groups, they are re-learning and enjoying the expression of community. Others have planted new churches or parachurch ministries, and have found new relational life in these settings. They have sometimes deliberately avoided, or most often simply neglected to pursue, an expression of faith that includes the more 'typical' charismatic elements.

The relief of being free from the unhealthy structures is at first so exhilarating that little thought is given to what place charismatic theology and practice might have in their new situations. There are also numerous examples of post-charismatics seeking out church fellowships that are non-charismatic in both theology and practice.

However, as the detoxing journey continues, and healing begins to take place, many begin to feel a pull to re-examine and explore from a fresh angle what elements – done differently – could, and perhaps *should*, be reincorporated into their faith and practice. And the starting place for many would be the question of how the community of faith called 'the body of Christ' should function.

There are a number of biblical metaphors that describe the church, including the military metaphor that Paul often uses in describing the Christian walk (2 Timothy 2:3–4) and spiritual warfare (Ephesians 6:10–18). Other biblical metaphors include the bride of Christ (Ephesians 5:25–27), a holy priesthood (1 Peter 2:4–10), a holy building/temple (Ephesians 2:19–22), and the body of Christ (1 Corinthians 12:12–27). While this is not an in-depth exploration of the many metaphors for the church in the New Testament, this partial list demonstrates that there is no one singular way of conceptualising what the church is.

Wayne Grudem reminds us, additionally, 'The wide range of metaphors in use for the church in the New Testament should remind us not to focus exclusively on any one. For example, while it is true that the church is the body of Christ, we must remember that this is only one metaphor among many. If we focus exclusively on that metaphor we will be likely to forget that Christ is our Lord reigning in heaven as well as the one who dwells among us.'[2]

With Grudem's cautionary remarks in mind, it is still very important, for the purposes of talking about being a community of the Spirit, to focus more on the body metaphor. The discussion in the previous section focused partly on the spiritual disciplines that individual apprentices of Jesus can employ. In this section, we will be looking at the corporate disciplines that can be engaged whenever two or three are gathered in Jesus' name.

A thorough discussion of all the possible elements of community would be a book (or books) in and of itself, but to counter some of the specific problems arising out of the influence of the Latter Rain and Shepherding movements, we will need to address:

- The kind of biblical character which provides a context of community that can be described as a 'safe place'
- How the 'safe place' becomes a place to 'take risks', in the areas of:

  ○ healthy confession/accountability

- ○ going beyond 'allowing' charismatic gifts, and encouraging pursuit of spiritual gifts
- • an understanding of how the issues of authority, living by faith, and spiritual transformation are best addressed and expressed in community

The metaphor of the body of Christ is an organic one, rather than institutional. In other words, no matter the size of the gathering, it is the people who make up the community who will determine the health of the gathering. We cannot but create 'intentional community'; it is not enough to deconstruct inadequate structures and models, we have to look at the question: What *kind* of people create healthy communities of the Spirit, and are we those people?

A safe place. . .

Over a quarter century ago, Richard Foster wrote in *Celebration of Discipline*: 'The carefree spirit of joyous festivity is absent in contemporary society. Apathy, even melancholy, dominates the times.'[3]

On the different occasions when I've been able to visit a newly post-charismatic gathering, I have seen a certain level of melancholy (from the feeling of being burnt out) and an apathy – at times even resentment – towards anything overtly spiritual.

One group that I was invited to visit a number of years ago was filled with bruised and hurting post-charismatics. Burnt out and still stinging from the wounds they incurred when they left their respective churches (or CLB – Church Left Behind – as many now refer to them), they were clinging together for mutual support and a safe place to talk about the things that were disturbing them about the church in general.

On one level it *was* a safe place for them – because of their similar experiences, there was no taboo on talking frankly about their concerns and disillusionment. But on another level, it tended to be a bristly and brittle community.

During a second visit to this group, a mutual friend showed up mid-way through the evening. He had been having a really bad day, and at one point during our conversation, he remarked, 'Man, I could really use some prayer.' Naively, I called out to some of the other members of the group nearby, saying, 'Hey, let's pray for this guy. He would really like some prayer.'

The room got all quiet and cold, and in the distance, I'm almost certain I heard the sound of shovels digging my grave. Nobody wanted to pray for anybody. The leader of the group (or at least, the owner of the house where they met) accused me of having a 'religious agenda', and made it clear that I was disturbing the group. Our mutual friend was not prayed for, and neither he nor I went to the group ever again. The group imploded a few months later.

I recognise that some people are so wounded by their experiences that anything remotely resembling 'church' brings up all kinds of bad memories and panicky feelings of fear. Their initial reaction is to run away and hide somewhere. Because of this awareness, I would be very cautious about jumping to any conclusions about the spirituality of the members of that group. Some people from a group such as this will eventually come alive again, as their detoxing journey continues; others will choose to stay in the cycle of woundedness and disillusionment. This particular event was almost a decade ago; many who were at the group at that time have had significant healing since that time, and would not hesitate to pray for each other today.

What makes a group a safe place? For some people, that means 'no conflict of any kind', which can often result in an oppressive herd mentality of conformity, where any differing ideas are seen as anti-community. But ultimately, the true test of a loving, safe community is not the avoidance of conflict or difference of opinion, but rather how people with different gifts and callings can deeply appreciate 'the other', where diversity is celebrated.

In 'Five-Fold Reconsidered', we invested a lot of time in examining how authority is supposed to function in the body of Christ. The inescapable conclusion is that apprentices of Jesus do not have the authority to lord it over each other. We also looked at the *parakletos* (coming alongside) nature of the Spirit's work in the church, and the implications for how, as apprentices, the five-fold ministries were for equipping and releasing others, not gaining hierarchical power. We need to keep this in mind as we continue to look at how all apprentices co-operate with the Holy Spirit in making a community a safe place.

A phrase from Paul's writings that crops up repeatedly on all sides of this discussion is 'speaking the truth in love. . .' (Ephesians 4:15); interestingly, this phrase is part of the larger passage discussing the five-fold ministries. Some people love to focus on 'speaking truth' as being love in action (which they read as licence to be harsh and judgmental with people), but the context of the passage suggests that love provides the credibility and ethos where truth can be spoken.

The famous love chapter of 1 Corinthians 13 has been talked about in so many different contexts – often romantically attached to wedding ceremonies – that it is easy to forget its original context was deliberately placed by Paul in between his teaching on the diversity in the body of Christ (1 Corinthians 12), and his instructions on spiritual gifts (1 Corinthians 14). It is difficult to look at this passage with fresh eyes, but try to read it from the viewpoint of creating a healthy community, not simply referring to us as individuals, but as communities.

> Love is patient, love is kind. It does not envy, it does not boast, it is not proud. It is not rude, it is not self-seeking, it is not easily angered, it keeps no record of wrongs. Love does not delight in evil but rejoices with the truth. *It always protects, always trusts, always hopes, always perseveres.* (1 Corinthians 13:4–7, *emphasis added*)

The last phrase of this passage sounds almost paternalistic, as if a loving parent is safeguarding the family dynamic. If there is any one trait that needs to be recaptured and safeguarded, it is the dynamic of trust. Many, if not most, post-charismatics have had their ability to trust others seriously damaged. But if post-charismatic groups can build on these verses as essential DNA to creating a healthy, safe place, then the ability to trust again can begin to be recaptured.

As much as it is our human nature to set up defensive walls around ourselves for protection, these same walls thwart our desire for community. They make trust and therefore vulnerability, transparency and risk-taking impossible. Too many of us have settled for an individualistic approach to our journey with Jesus (which our Western culture applauds), and yet because he has designed us to be in community, we will ultimately become dissatisfied with a 'just me and Jesus' approach.

The Trinity exists as a co-eternal community. Three Persons in one Godhead. This is a mystery that has been debated and defined for centuries, but what is clear is that the Father, Son and Holy Spirit exist in some sort of relational community. As people created in his image, we reflect that relational 'wiring'; it's part of us.

One of the greatest needs for building deep, authentic community is for everything to be permeated with an attitude and practice of extending grace. Many post-charismatics have been deeply disillusioned by their encounters with leaders who have embraced or been heavily influenced by the 'accountability' (control) teachings of the Shepherding movement. As Richard Foster notes, 'Perhaps the most menacing danger is manipulation and control by leaders. If corporate guidance is not handled within the larger context of an all-pervasive grace, it degenerates into an effective way to straighten out deviant behaviour.'[4]

These leaders have often unwittingly acted like the wicked servant in the Parable of the Unmerciful Servant in Matthew 18:23–35. They seem to have forgotten how great a debt they have been forgiven, and do not extend the same grace to others. It is very significant that this parable is attached to Jesus' oft-quoted teaching on accountability (Matthew 18:15–20). The problem is when people separate these two passages, choosing to scrupulously apply the 'legalities' of following the steps found in verses 15–17, but neglecting the redemptive posture of verses 18–20, and ignoring the look-in-the-mirror point of the parable of verses 23–35.

But on the redemptive side, Foster also tells us, 'But if we know that the people of God are first a fellowship of sinners, we are freed to hear the unconditional call of God's love and to confess our needs openly before our brothers and sisters . . . In acts of mutual confession we release the power that heals.'[5]

Confession is where the healing is. Accountability has been discredited in the eyes of many, not because they are rebellious, but because what has passed for accountability has instead become a means of controlling and devaluing people. Too many leaders, however well-intentioned, have turned the 'insider knowledge' of people's honest struggles into a justification for controlling them, and prevent them from any meaningful involvement in the community. Commenting on Jesus' words to 'judge not' in Matthew 7:1–5, John Stott had this insight:

> The censorious critic is a fault-finder who is negative and destructive towards other people and enjoys actively seeking out their failings. He puts the worst possible construction on their motives, pours cold water on their schemes and is ungenerous towards their mistakes.[6]

Ironically, this results in a lack of transparency and truthfulness, as people in the community quickly learn to 'fake it' in order to fit in. If they have struggles with sin, they will continue to fake it, because they have learned that their leaders are the last people who can be trusted.

In *The Discipling Dilemma*, Don Vinzant observes, '(The Catholics) found that personal domination and manipulation can easily run out of control when the person is both the confessor and the Spiritual Director. They began to require, therefore, that the confessor and the Spiritual Director could not be the same person.'[7]

What the aftermath of the Shepherding movement showed was that accountability at gunpoint doesn't work; it only produces spiritual casualties and robs people of both personal responsibility in their Spirit-led walk and also genuine body-life where mutual accountability can happen in a healthy way. The healthy response must look more like Foster's 'acts of mutual confession'.

It is the mutuality of accountability that helps to prevent a hierarchical system of control from taking place. James 5:16 says, 'Therefore confess your sins to each other and pray for each other so that you may be healed. The prayer of a righteous man is powerful and effective.' There is healing to be found in honest confession, prayer with others, and hearing 'the Lord forgives you' from our brothers and sisters in Christ. This stands in stark contrast to a view of accountability that gives one believer power and authority over another (which Jesus explicitly forbids).

This mutuality is simply the body functioning as it was intended to; Jesus is the only Head, and the rest of the body is arranged under him. Grudem reminds us, 'The metaphor of the church as the body of Christ should increase our *interdependence* on one another and our appreciation of the diversity of gifts within the body.'[8] *(emphasis added)*

Stott also suggests, 'In all of our attitudes and behaviour towards others we are to play neither the judge (becoming harsh, censorious and condemning) nor the hypocrite (blaming others while excusing ourselves), but the brother, caring for others so much that we first blame and correct ourselves and then seek to be constructive in the help we give them.'[9]

In short, the healthier community approach to what has been called accountability needs to reflect these values in order to follow the spirit of James 5:16:

- *It is invitational* – it cannot function arbitrarily as account-ability at gunpoint, enforced by hierarchical power, structure or demand

- *It is seasonal* – any ongoing accountability aspect of confession is governed by the issue at hand; it is not an ongoing, 'for life' appointment
- *It is mutual* – there is a trust level that has been built where confession can take place without the confession being turned into justification for lording it over other apprentices; it values the 'each other' dynamic that James speaks of
- *It is redemptive, not punitive*, in its intent and practice

The high importance of community – the safe place – in the New Testament cannot be understated. The writings of James, John, Peter, and especially Paul (since the majority of the post-Acts books were penned by him), return time and again to dealing with the necessity of creating a safe community for spiritual formation – including the discipline of confession – to take place.

Even a quick perusal of some of the 'one another' passages yields the following:

- Accept one another, then, just as Christ accepted you, in order to bring praise to God (Romans 15:7)
- Be kind and compassionate to one another, forgiving each other, just as in Christ God forgave you (Ephesians 4:32)
- But encourage one another daily, as long as it is called Today, so that none of you may be hardened by sin's deceitfulness (Hebrews 3:13)
- Now that you have purified yourselves by obeying the truth so that you have sincere love for your brothers, love one another deeply, from the heart (1 Peter 1:22)
- Dear friends, since God so loved us, we also ought to love one another. No-one has ever seen God; but if we love one

> another, God lives in us and his love is made complete in us
> (1 John 4:11–12)

The 'one another' verses are only one part of the New Testament's teaching on the importance of the body functioning as a safe place. Paul instructs us to have the same attitude as Christ – that of a servant (Philippians 2:1–8), and to have concern for the weaker brother (Romans 14). James warns against showing favouritism (James 2:1–10), and the need for taming the tongue (James 3:1–18). Titus is counselled by Paul not to allow divisive people to disrupt the community (Titus 3:10), and the same warning is written to the church in Rome (Romans 16:17).

The list of community-oriented verses could go on, but the pattern is clear throughout the New Testament that community is of highest value. Paul's metaphor of the body in 1 Corinthians 12:12–27 further develops the need for a mutual interdependence, and also sets the healthy context for the exercise of spiritual gifts and worship, to which we will now turn.

. . .to take risks

> Every day they continued to meet together in the temple courts. They broke bread in their homes and ate together with glad and sincere hearts, praising God and enjoying the favour of all the people. And the Lord added to their number daily those who were being saved. (Acts 2:46–47)

The early days of the New Testament church (*ecclesia* – gathering) would have been a treat to watch on DVD; to actually see the miracles, the healings, the numbers of people turning to Jesus. Even better, to have been there – to be part of that group that met daily in the temple and also in each other's homes, listening to the apostles' teaching, witnessing the miraculous, and enjoying the favour of all of the people, as thousands became followers of Jesus overnight.

It didn't last long.

First, the persecution in Jerusalem, resulting in a diaspora of believers in all directions; later, the systematic persecution of the Roman government that would last for three centuries, until Constantine led the church out of persecution but arguably into the more subtle captivity of institutionalism.

But at the time that the Epistles were being written, the early church had other issues on its mind. Gnosticism was an early heresy born of Greek dualism that was plaguing the church, denying the incarnation of Jesus as 'God in the flesh'. Legalism in the form of requiring Gentile believers to live as culturally observant Jews was dealt with at the Jerusalem Council (Acts 15:1–35). And in Corinth, the dangerous mixture of elitism and spiritual gifts needed to be addressed.

Throughout his first epistle to the Corinthian church, Paul confronted the various ways that elitism and the desire for prominence was ruining the dynamic of the church. The Corinthians were priding themselves on who their leader was: some were claiming Peter, Paul, or Barnabas, while others – perhaps akin to some house church proponents today – claimed that they followed no human leader, but only Jesus (1 Corinthians 1:11–17).

Paul rebukes all of these factions, because the issue wasn't really if they were following Jesus or a human leader – the issue was that they were being elitist and dismissive of others whom they wished to look down on (a short step from lording over).

Their practice of spiritual gifts was no less elitist and hierarchical, to the point where some – in exasperation and frustration, most likely – were advocating that spiritual gifts should be suppressed (1 Corinthians 14:29).

We have seen that the famous love chapter of 1 Corinthians 13 is strategically placed in the middle of the discussion of spiritual gifts and corporate worship, in order to emphatically underscore the necessary ethos in which worship and spiritual gifts can best function. The elitism and jostling for position that the Corinthians had fallen into was preventing a healthy community dynamic for worship and the expression of spiritual gifts.

One of the areas many post-charismatics are now beginning to wrestle with is the question of the *charismata* – grace gifts, or 'grace-lets' – in a post-charismatic setting. Many have, for a season of detoxing, been operating as functional cessationists, but are now beginning to revisit the question of spiritual gifts in their gatherings.

Many post-charismatics have been turned off by the hype that some have surrounded the gifts with, and also with the elitism that prefers and honours some gifts above others. John Wimber writes, 'Some people think of the gifts as trophies, merit badges, or advanced degrees. They supposedly indicate an elite status in God's sight and higher level of spirituality. This mistaken point of view might tempt some people to show off their spiritual gifts like karate black belts or Olympic medals.'[10]

While this is clearly an immature way of viewing spiritual gifts, Wayne Grudem takes this assessment a step further: 'If spiritual gifts are sought only so that the person may be more prominent or have more influence or power, this certainly is wrong in God's eyes. This was the motivation of Simon the

Sorcerer in Acts 8:19. . .'[11] And as many will recall, Peter basically told Simon that his destination was hell, based on his mercenary attitude towards the power of the Spirit.

Many current models of exercising spiritual gifts seem to accentuate the very attitude that Wimber and Grudem are urging us to avoid. Those with upfront gifts, particularly prophetic people, seem to be the ones on stage, microphone in hand, much more prominent than others. What has usually happened, which has produced the post-charismatic reaction, is that only a select few get to do the upfront ministry, and there is little to dispel the idea that somehow those on stage are special and more 'anointed' than those sitting in the audience.

There is also a sense of safety for those on stage, because people are less likely to address prophetic ministry that might be somewhat 'off'; this is particularly true in churches where 'touch not the Lord's anointed' has been taught and enforced. This has resulted in a culture where weighing prophecy (1 Corinthians 14:29) has been neglected, and the average person in the audience hasn't been taught how to discern for themselves. And for those behind the microphone, this lack of weighing produces a false sense of safety, over-confidence, and at times recklessness in the exercise of their gifts.

When the stage and the spotlight are no longer available, however, exercising spiritual gifts actually becomes more grassroots, and therefore safer, yet at the same time, more risky. Smaller, more intimate settings of house churches or new church plants don't have the same perceived glamour or power position. (Although it should be noted that there are some people who deliberately prey upon house churches and new church plants because they want people to acknowledge and follow them.)

These smaller settings are riskier simply because there's immediate feedback to prophetic ministry; both the one sharing the prophetic word, and the one receiving it, are in close physical proximity, within earshot of mutual friends, and will have either just finished a shared meal or be about to start one. The dynamic is quite different from a large meeting with all the church props. While some people can put on airs in just about any situation, the relaxed, grassroots dynamic is ideal for setting a more 'dialled down' attitude and expression (to employ a John Wimber phrase).

And there can be a much healthier dynamic of weighing prophetic words (1 Corinthians 14:29) in these smaller settings. 'In a community which practises relational Christianity, such testing (of prophecy) is quite possible. But within the realm of media Christianity, globetrotting superstars, and oligarchic leadership styles, such a check is not possible.'[12]

While these settings are therefore healthier in their practice of spiritual gifts, there is still a sense of risk-taking involved. These smaller settings can actually be intimidating, especially when the woundedness that most post-charismatics have experienced is added to the mix. For many who find themselves in this season of life, stepping back into the exercise of spiritual gifts is just as daunting as the very first time.

We will not be developing an in-depth treatise on all of the spiritual gifts, but for the purposes of this writing, it's important to reconstruct a foundational understanding of how to approach the release and function of spiritual gifts.

There are two key verses in 1 Corinthians that provide the framework for keeping the perspective and practice of spiritual gifts healthy and life-giving to those around us:

1 Corinthians 12:7

> Now to each one the manifestation of the Spirit is given *for the common good.* (1 Corinthians 12:7, *emphasis added*)

As Brother Maynard said regarding the five-fold ministries, spiritual gifts are given to individuals to serve the rest of the body. The 'common good' is the goal of the Spirit gifting anybody. As Wimber pointed out, spiritual gifts are not signs of God's preferential treatment, nor are they given for our benefit. They are given to be used for the common good of those around us. As soon as we lose sight of why we have spiritual gifts in the first place, we have already lost the sole reason they were given.

The Greek word from which we get the phrase 'common good' is *sumphero*, which means 'to bear or bring together', and this word comes from the root word *phero*, which means 'to carry a burden, to uphold (bear up)'. The inference is clearly that the gifts were not given for the benefit of the one gifted; spiritual gifts are given to enable us to build up others.

Our motivation for having spiritual gifts is not our own reputation, or desire for recognition or position, but rather the common good of the rest of the body. The gifts are given to the body, expressed through us as individuals, but the focus remains the body.

1 Corinthians 14:12

> Since you are eager to have spiritual gifts, try to excel in gifts that *build up the church.* (1 Corinthians 14:12, *emphasis added*)

Paul instructs us to 'eagerly desire' spiritual gifts (1 Corinthians 12:31; 14:1, 39); the word 'desire' is the Greek word *zeloo*, which means 'to burn with zeal, to desire earnestly'. Passivity towards spiritual gifts is not what Paul has in mind; we are to burn with zeal regarding spiritual gifts (perhaps the first and most difficult step for post-charismatics).

But this zeal for gifts is based on looking around the gathered body, and recognising that the body needs to be built up, to become more in tune with the Head. Spiritual gifts do not separate the body into the 'haves' and 'have-nots'. When they function as they were intended by the Spirit who gave them in the first place (1 Corinthians 12:11), the body is encouraged (built up). Some have suggested that spiritual gifts can be understood as 'situational gifting', where the 'best gifts' to be eagerly pursued are the ones that would address specific needs in that gathering. Certainly, this view would lend itself more readily to a servant dynamic within a community, although it would not be wise to limit our understanding of spiritual gifts as being situational only.

Again, a discussion of the whole list of spiritual gifts would be too long for the purpose of this writing, but let's look at prophecy as an example, since (a) Paul urges us to pursue this gift in order to be an encouragement to others, and (b) it's easily one of the most abused gifts, between bogus prophetic words (perhaps rightly called 'pathetic words'), and the elitism and theatrics that have often surrounded prophetic ministry.

While I would not want to arbitrarily limit prophetic ministry to a small group, I find that many post-charismatics are far more open to a grassroots expression of prophecy than they are to the 'globetrotting superstar' model (as George Mallone referred to it) which they are often reacting against and recovering from. Certainly, the humility of being an unknown person simply exercising their gift in a house group would give a greater credibility in the eyes of post-charismatics.

For years, Wimber encouraged the Vineyard movement to avoid loaded charismatic phrases such as 'Thus saith the Lord' when encouraging prophetic ministry, preferring to use a more invitational approach, such as saying, 'I think the Lord may be saying ——; what do *you* think?'

This does a couple of things: first, it is invitational. It invites the interaction of the person receiving the 'word'; passivity is not a good thing, as we are instructed by Paul to weigh prophetic words as a community (1 Corinthians 14:29), as well as individually. Second, it downplays the importance of the person delivering the prophetic word, which is in keeping with a more humble use of the gifts that the Spirit is releasing. As Brother Maynard has suggested, 'we are best to remember that prophetic ministry should be considered post-certainty. . . the small group expressions generally come forth couched in "maybe" which is much more comfortable to our postmodern, post-certainty culture'.[13]

Given that prophecy was tested within the meeting itself (1 Corinthians 14:29), there probably was a greater sense of humility than we might think pervading prophecy in the early church. It is easy to say 'thus says the Lord' when there are not spiritual people around to judge the word. But when such individuals are present, the environment for receiving prophecy changes.[14]

These 'spiritual people', of course, are the rest of Jesus' apprentices who are present when the prophetic word happens.

The safe place to take risks is very important for post-charismatics, who are genuinely seeking to find a healthy way of seeing spiritual gifts expressed in their community. Many have rejected the hyped-up, over-promising model of prophetic ministry that they previously knew, and have not pursued hearing the voice of God for themselves. The passivity of neglecting to cultivate one's own ability to hear from God is just as unhealthy as the passivity of allowing a select few (often self-appointed) prophets to direct the affairs of the whole community. Both result in a 'famine of hearing the words of the Lord' (Amos 8:11).

The same principle would apply equally to any of the other spiritual gifts listed in 1 Corinthians 12:8–11, 12:28 or Romans 12:3–8. Since the Bible assumes that we will eagerly desire spiritual gifts (with burning zeal), exercised in an ethos of the 'more excellent way' of 1 Corinthians 13, then creating the 'safe place to take risks' will include encouraging each other to use or (re)discover the gifts that the Spirit has given.

Celebration (sacred space)

The living room was full of people, as the sounds of lively conversation and regular outbursts of laughter filled the room. The kitchen table and counters were a riot of colour and aroma as the 'bring whatever' bowls, pots and dishes covered every square inch of surface.

A hearty fire was warming the main room, as more friends arrived at the front door, kicking snow off their shoes and laughingly commenting on the frost which suddenly adorned their glasses as they came in from the -40°F Winnipeg winter.

Downstairs in the modest bungalow, a profusion of musical instruments were scattered around the room; later that evening, they would all be in use as people celebrated together in exuberant song. During the whole evening, the relaxed atmosphere meant that people would move from the kitchen for food or drink, to the living room for conversation with friends, and to the basement, where the jam went on for a couple of hours. It was a house party in the best kind of way.

There must have been 50 people crammed into the modest little bungalow in the southside of Winnipeg that night. My wife, Wendy, and I were the only Christians in attendance. It was a gathering of friends and families of the Celtic rock band that I played bass with at the time.

One of my co-workers, a single mother in her early twenties, sports a short, spiked and bleached blonde haircut; various artistic piercings complete her 'look'. She is hard-working and trying to make ends meet for herself and her infant daughter. She has, at this point in her journey, zero interest in Jesus, although she has some interest in various new age ideas. But as she works – and she works very hard – she sings.

As I discovered while playing with the Celtic rock band, there was a whole subculture of common songs that were sung loudly along with the band, no matter what city we were playing in, or even whether we'd ever met any of these people before. The songs were old standards of East Coast Canadian, Scottish, Australian and Irish origin, but people knew them, word for word, and joined in with enthusiasm.

When people gather together to celebrate, they sing. When people at work are enjoying what they do, they sing (or hum, or whistle). When people drive alone in their cars, they sing; until they get to traffic lights, where everyone immediately adopts the requisite bored expression of staring straight ahead until the light changes. Then they can sing again, once they're sure no one can see them.

Human beings are wired to celebrate, and singing has always been a natural part of that celebration. Witness the Welsh rugby games, where old hymns of the Great Awakening are sung in pubs with gusto after the game. Despite the seeming incongruence of old hymns and the general drunkenness of these gatherings, the most natural, community-building and community-expressing reaction is to sing.

The church culture of the past few centuries has been built around the 'worship service'. No matter what the style, format, structure or theology, everything revolved around a worship service that happened once a week. But as many post-charismatics (and post-evangelicals, as well) can attest to, this worship service has lost something in the translation.

Many post-charismatics point to the worship service as being the chief example of hype within the charismatic movement. A friend of mine, who has been an elder for two decades in a Pentecostal church, bluntly referred to their worship services as 'spiritual orgasm' – the climax being when someone finally spoke in tongues. 'Then everyone breathes a sigh of relief, and we are "allowed" to move on to the offering and the sermon.'

Not all charismatic worship services are that event-driven, but many are, judging by the stories that are heard. The reaction that this has produced is a fairly predictable pendulum swing to the opposite extreme: post-charismatics have either ended up in churches where the corporate worship is very predictable (mildly charismatic liturgical churches seem to be particularly attractive), or they have developed an understanding of worship that sees all of life as worship, but greatly downplays the part that singing might play in that all-life worship.

Andrew Jones (the Tall Skinny Kiwi) blogged in 2003 about a

conference in France where speaker Stuart Murray had commented, 'Many (in the emerging church) are post-charismatic.
After twenty years, they would rather shoot themselves than sing
another chorus.' Murray also spoke of a post-charismatic reaction to 'the tyranny of joyfulness'.

This reaction is most likely a response to an overdose of what
British charismatics have referred to as 'happy-clappy syn-
drome'. Post-charismatics are not anti-joy, but they are reacting
to an inauthentic pretence of joyfulness that denies problems
and the mundane day-to-day activities of life.

Many post-charismatics have expanded their understanding
of worship to include all of life, not just specific events in a gathering of Christians at an appointed place and time. This reflects
the same kind of 'practising the presence of God' that Brother
Lawrence wrote about centuries ago. All of life is seen as being in
the presence of God, and therefore worship cannot be narrowly
defined as singing songs in church.

Foster comments, 'God's normal means of bringing His joy is
by redeeming and sanctifying the ordinary junctures of human
life . . . When the power of Jesus reaches into our work and play
and redeems them, there will be joy where once there was
mourning. To overlook this is to miss the meaning of the
Incarnation.'[15]

Paul writes:

> Therefore I urge you, brothers, in view of God's mercy, to offer
> your bodies as living sacrifices, holy and pleasing to God – this is
> your spiritual act of worship. (Romans 12:1)

Clearly worship encompasses more than just singing another
chorus. My father-in-law, Franz, was a rancher on the Canadian

Prairies, who understood how to 'practise the presence' and worship as he worked on his farm. Wendy tells stories from her childhood of Franz singing old German hymns – in German, of course – while driving his tractor through the fields. A soft-spoken person, Franz nevertheless had quite a bit of vocal power when he sang, which he employed in order to hear himself over the noise of the tractor.

As a child, Wendy could easily be sent on the errand of 'get your father for lunch', as she could immediately track which field her father was in by simply listening for the sound of his singing.

But at the same time, it should be said that Franz wasn't worshipping *by* cutting hay; Franz was worshipping *while* he was cutting hay. As with the Foster quote above, practising the presence of God in our everyday activities will transform how we approach and enjoy those activities, but this is not a complete understanding of worship, or of worshipping in community.

Some post-charismatics have had their worship pendulum swing from the extreme of 'happy-clappy' to the other end of the spectrum, where worship includes anything *but* singing songs to God in a group setting. As with all reactions, time will temper this and draw people back to a balance, but it needs to be said that singing in worship is a natural, normal, Spirit-inspired response.

Is any one of you in trouble? He should pray. Is anyone happy? Let him sing songs of praise. (James 5:13)

Do not get drunk on wine, which leads to debauchery. Instead, be filled with the Spirit. Speak to one another in psalms, hymns and spiritual songs. Sing and make music in your heart to the Lord. . . (Ephesians 5:18–19)

> Let the word of Christ dwell in you richly as you teach and admonish one another with all wisdom, and as you sing psalms, hymns and spiritual songs with gratitude in your hearts to God. (Colossians 3:16)

Not to belabour the point, but the Old Testament, particularly the Psalms, is filled with examples, stories, and actual commands for worship in song to be a normal part of expression in the gathered community. Throughout the book of Revelation, singing is repeatedly shown to be a normal, natural reaction to the presence of God. Particularly in chapters 4 and 5, there is quite a cacophonous expression of worship going on 24/7 around God's throne.

And as people created in the image of God (or *eikons* as Scot McKnight has suggested), it should come as no surprise that God also sings. 'The Lord your God is with you, he is mighty to save. He will take great delight in you, he will quiet you with his love, he will rejoice over you with singing' (Zephaniah 3:17).

Without getting into an entire theology on the subject of worship, suffice it to say that worship in community that neglects or deliberately ignores singing and making music together is missing an important component.

What if worship looked more like the kitchen parties that were mentioned at the beginning of this section? What if there was space given to a variety of expressions of worship, but in the context of a community meal, which was an important part of the Corinthian church's practice – important enough that Paul wrote them a stinging rebuke for abusing it (1 Corinthians 11:17–34)?

Foster comments: 'The decision to set the mind on the higher things of life is an act of the will. That is why celebration is a

Discipline. It is not something that falls on our heads. It is the result of a consciously chosen way of thinking and living.'[16]

In light of the post-charismatic baggage that surrounds the whole area of worship and singing, celebration as a community can often be a risk-taking venture. Hence the need both for creating a safe place for this kind of risk-taking, and also for heeding Foster's reminder that community celebration is a conscious choice; what is needed is a community dynamic similar to the Celtic band's kitchen parties, but with an added element of worship that transcends this to become 'sacred space'.

We have long been advocates of a high model of participation in our worship gatherings. When we lived in Los Angeles my weekly visits to the Venice Beach Drum Circle only served to intensify my desire to see worship gatherings become more participatory and less spectator-oriented.

Since somewhere in the early 1990s we have used what we call 'Worship Jams' as part of our ministry. They're akin to the Worship Circle idea that people like Ben and Robin Pasley have pioneered (their *Enter The Worship Circle* albums are recorded in an acoustic jam format, and they freely give away music charts for groups to use). Basically, a worship jam is where there are multiple worship leaders, as many instruments as people can bring (and hopefully play), lots of food (brought by the participants), space for art and dance, and the understanding that there is no set programme once the jam gets under way.

It's always been a challenging and exciting time of learning to listen to each other and the Holy Spirit, and to make space for different people's gifts to be used. Because we had no set lists or 'whose turn to lead next', it truly was a growing exercise of learning how to relax, back off, and let the Spirit lead – although to be historically accurate, there were the occasional train wrecks along the way, but that's what 'learning' usually includes! We found that if we were willing to make the kind of space where mistakes weren't seen as devastating, then risks could be taken more easily.

At times, we've had five or six guitars, six or more djembes, a keyboard, bass guitar, a mandolin, a saxophone, lots of singing voices, a didgeridoo, some dancers, painters, and a six-foot-four, sixteen-stone reader of Scripture (when he reads, people listen!).

The reader of Scripture was named Logan. A Native American man who quickly became one of our closest friends in L.A., Logan came from a Church of Christ background, and had a profound love for reading the Bible. During our jams, Logan would stand up during a song, and all the musicians would quiet down somewhat, and Logan would simply read a passage from the Bible that he felt God wanted him to read. It was great to see the diversity that the Spirit had gifted people with.

On the night which will for ever be my favourite jam when we were in L.A., Logan asked me beforehand if he could be in charge of the jam (considering he doesn't sing or play an instrument, I wondered what he was up to), and I said, 'Sure, I trust you.'

What Logan did was simple, yet extremely profound. As people arrived at our house, food and instruments in hand, Logan greeted each person at the door and informed them that our living room was 'out of bounds' for anything but prayer, until the worship part of the jam began. People were free to hang out and party in the kitchen and other areas, but the living room (a converted two-car garage) was 'Sacred Space'. Logan had worship CDs playing in there, and only prayer was allowed.

People at first had looks of 'okay, dude, whatever. . .' on their faces, but then something very cool started happening. People began leaving the party, and actually entering the living room to pray. At one point, there were about a dozen people at a time in there, kneeling, sitting, squatting on the floor, praying quietly (the group's age demographic went from 14 to late-30s).

Once we finally opened the room for the jam to begin, we were treated to one of the most dynamic and Spirit-led times of worship we had yet enjoyed as a group – singing, playing, laughing, dancing, painting. . .

And Logan, standing up by the fireplace, reading from the Bible.

Celebration as a community. Sacred space.

Bringing it on home

> In 1980 I had a long, animated discussion about the charismatic renewal with David Watson. He was receiving reports that the charismatic renewal could be over, that some were even saying we were in a 'post-charismatic' era . . . Have we entered a post-charismatic era, or is the charismatic movement entering a new stage of its development?[17]

The above conversation between John Wimber and David Watson happened over a quarter of a century ago (note that Wimber's use of the term 'post-charismatic' is quite different from how I have employed the phrase here). Wimber was questioning whether the charismatic movement had somehow become irrelevant, but his conclusion is not far from the thesis of this writing: that the charismatic movement is in need of change, and a post-charismatic (as I have defined it) expression of the faith is both a necessary corrective and an exciting possibility.

Dennis Bennett wrote, in 1991, '(The church) must be charismatic. It must manifest the Gifts and Fruit of the Spirit, for they are the continuing signs that Jesus is alive and ready to bless people now.'[18] Whether one adopts the post-charismatic term as presented here, or chooses to retain the charismatic descriptor but with a re-imagining of what that looks like, or calls oneself nothing specific beyond 'apprentice of Jesus', Bennett's reminder that the fruit and gifts of the Spirit function as signs of Jesus' ongoing, personal involvement with us is of extreme importance.

And deep down, I am convinced that a post-charismatic praxis goes far beyond simply sorting through charismatic baggage and once again picking up a few familiar emphases and expressions. Even as this writing project progressed, I found myself more convinced than ever that we must have a post-charismatic understanding and praxis that is truly Spirit-led in the emerging church, or we will simply be building on our own efforts.

A.W. Tozer wrote, somewhat prophetically, 'Satan has opposed the doctrine of the Spirit-filled life about as bitterly as any doctrine there is. He has confused it, opposed it, and surrounded it with false notions and fears.'[19] Tragically, the sheer number of post-charismatics who have, by choice or neglect, walked away from anything remotely resembling 'Spirit-filled' (a loaded term all by itself) continues to testify that Tozer's assessment of Satan's opposition is still accurate.

And while there are quite a number of factors surrounding the post-charismatic exodus, as we have explored here, it would be naive to neglect mentioning the very real presence of an adversary who would like nothing better than for post-charismatics to reject or downplay the biblical and beneficial expression of the Spirit in our communities of faith. To allow ourselves to become post-charismatic *and post-Spirit* would be a victory for the enemy of our souls.

Interestingly, Dr John White had this to say about revival in general: 'From a safe distance of several hundred years or several thousand miles, revival clearly looks invigorating. What could be more glorious than a mighty work of God in our midst, renewing thousands and converting tens of thousands? But when we actually look at a revival, we find . . . sin and infighting and doctrinal error. Why does our expectation not match the reality? Why is revival sometimes so messy?'[20]

Post-charismatics are on the other end of these revivals – they are not offended by something new that the Spirit is doing, they are disillusioned with the problems that Dr White alludes to. The errors and excesses that have accompanied every revival are all too familiar to us. In short, it's messy. And at times, that messiness distracts and detracts from how the Spirit of God is genuinely working in people's lives.

But in consideration of the first half of Dr White's quote, is there anyone, identifying themselves as post-charismatic, who would not want to see a genuine move of the Spirit that resulted in renewal and the advancement of the kingdom of God? Would we be willing to revisit and attempt to address some of the messiness that Dr White mentions, if we thought there was a chance of seeing 'the radical middle' of Spirit and praxis?

For many of us, recognising that we are post-charismatic starts with a season of grieving. The disillusionment and, for some, the pain of what they have seen – and sometimes sup-ported, which adds guilt to the mix – is like a form of death. And grief doesn't resolve itself overnight.

In the late 1990s, I was one of the founding members of a small group that met every Monday night at the King's Head Pub in Winnipeg; we called ourselves the Dead Pastors' Society. There were two rules in our group:

1. Discussion of past experiences at former churches was acceptable, even encouraged, but only with the intent of detoxing and getting past the memories and pain; wallow-ing and whining wasn't the intent. Watching hockey on the big-screen TV was also valued.
2. In the short term, for most of us, there was no option but to allow the season of being burnt out to run its course, but we were committed to pursuing vibrancy in our walk with Jesus and with each other, however long that might take.

But in the first week of 1999, as I enjoyed lunch with a friend on my birthday, I realised that when it came right down to it, I and only I was responsible for the choice of whether or not I would pursue life in the Spirit. That didn't mean that I quit the Dead Pastors' Society, but it did mean, as the season of detox and grieving began to pass, that I discovered a new resolve to pursue the things of the Spirit – in a post-charismatic fashion.

J. Lee Grady was quoted in the prologue as saying, 'Burned out on hype and pulpit showmanship, weary of learning 95 ways to use spiritual gifts when they recognize more basic needs, these believers are in search of a deeper spirituality that emphasizes the fruit of the Spirit as much or more than the gifts.'[21] The balance of Spirit and praxis, however, means that we don't choose one over the other.

Among Pentecostal, charismatic, and Third Wave groups, another chapter of the Bible that is so over-familiar it has lost its sense of wonder and awe – even more than the love chapter of 1 Corinthians 13 – is the second chapter of Acts. As post-charismatics, I would like to challenge all of us to read this passage again with fresh eyes, and see if the Holy Spirit begins to stir something within us.

> They devoted themselves to the apostles' teaching and to the fellowship, to the breaking of bread and to prayer. Everyone was filled with awe, and many wonders and miraculous signs were done by the apostles. All the believers were together and had everything in common. Selling their possessions and goods, they gave to anyone as he had need. Every day they continued to meet together in the temple courts. They broke bread in their homes and ate together with glad and sincere hearts, praising God and enjoying the favour of all the people. And the Lord added to their number daily those who were being saved. (Acts 2:42–47)

Chrysalis: from post-charismatic to charismissional

Ever since this writing project first began, I have struggled with the term 'post-charismatic'; while it is certainly accurate as a description, it lacks the ability to point to a way forward, which was the whole reason for writing in the first place. It also had the added potential of being seen as too trendy, for if there is any prefix currently suffering from extreme over-exposure, it would be 'post'-anything.

Post-charismatic is not unlike the phrase 'detoxing from

church' – it's a descriptive label that people can relate to, but like the detox metaphor, it speaks more of where people are coming *from* than where they are headed. For a while, I employed the phrase 'post-charismatic, but not post-Spirit' in conversations about these issues, but still found myself looking for something more pithy.

I like the imagery of the chrysalis as a metaphor for the journey that post-charismatics find themselves on. In the cocoon stage, a caterpillar looks – in the outer expression – dead and withered. Yet a metamorphosis, a transformation, is taking place in a deep and hidden place.

And finally, the chrysalis stage ends as the transformed life emerges. And like the chrysalis, the exit from the post-charismatic cocoon is hard-fought; wholesale rejection of all things charismatic would be easier, yet there is something stirring in many post-charismatics that does not allow for this option. There is something that produces strength when the new expression of life is not easily attained, but is rather won through reflection, struggle and overcoming.

My own journey has included seasons of 'detoxing from church' as well as wrestling through the extremes and abuses in a movement that I loved, where the label 'post-charismatic' certainly applied to me as well. At present, I find myself content to live in the tension of attending a local charismatic church, enjoying friendship and fellowship with house/simple church gatherings, while being a full-time staff member with Youth With A Mission (YWAM) and navigating the postmodern waters of the emerging/missional church. And the number of post-charismatics I encounter in the emerging/missional church is, at times, staggering.

In conversations about finding a more positive, forward-looking phrase to describe the journey that post-charismatics find themselves on, a friend who blogs under the pseudonym Grace (http://kingdomgrace.wordpress.com/) suggested 'charismissional', which she defined as 'Spirit-led missional living'.

Grace's coupling of *charis* and *missional* immediately appealed to me; the phrase takes the incarnational missionary-to-our-own-culture impetus of 'missional' (see Rick Meig's www.FriendofMissional.org for a fuller exploration of missional), and highlights the important element of being Spirit-led and Spirit-empowered. Charismissional takes the best of the missional approach to life/ministry and grounds it in the vibrancy of life in the Spirit.

This creates a dynamic ethos of pursuing a practical incarnational lifestyle with being the kind of people who fit Jesus' description: 'The wind blows wherever it pleases. You hear its sound, but you cannot tell where it comes from or where it is going. So it is with everyone born of the Spirit' (John 3:8).

For those who have walked the path of becoming post-charismatic, and who have discovered a continuing and deep desire for the manifest presence of the Holy Spirit in their lives, may the chrysalis emerge into the ongoing renewal of becoming charismissional.

Many hundreds of years ago, the Lord commanded Moses to speak specific words of blessing on his behalf over the people of Israel. Over the centuries, this blessing has been quoted many times, in many cultures, and in many languages. It seems fitting to close this writing with that same blessing over those who are post-charismatic, but moving towards charismissional:

The LORD bless thee, and keep thee: the LORD make his face
shine upon thee, and be gracious unto thee: the LORD lift up
his countenance upon thee, and give thee peace.
(Numbers 6:24–26, KJV)

Notes

Prologue

1. Deere, Jack – *Surprised by the Power of the Spirit*, page 53.
2. Grady, J. Lee – *What Happened to the Fire?*, page 58.
3. Ibid., page 169.

History

1. Grady, J. Lee – *What Happened to the Fire?*, page 15.
2. Gonzalez, Justo – *A History of Christian Thought Volume 3: From the Protestant Reformation to the Twentieth Century*, page 313.
3. Christianity Today – *The Cleansing Wave*, page 3.
4. Synan, Vinson – *The Origins of the Pentecostal Movement*, page 2.
5. Christianity Today – *The Cleansing Wave*, page 3.
6. Synan, Vinson – *The Origins of the Pentecostal Movement*, page 3.
7. Storms, Sam – *Post-Reformation and Contemporary Developments in the Pentecostal and Charismatic Movements*, page 2.
8. Christianity Today – *The Cleansing Wave*, page 4.
9. Storms, Sam – *Post-Reformation and Contemporary Developments in the Pentecostal Movements*, page 4.
10. Ibid., page 4.
11. *The New International Dictionary of Pentecostal and Charismatic Movements*, page 727.
12. Storms, Sam – *Post-Reformation and Contemporary Developments in the Pentecostal and Charismatic Movements*, page 5.
13. Ibid., page 6.

14. Ibid., page 6.
15. *The New International Dictionary of Pentecostal and Charismatic Movements (Revised and Expanded Edition)* – page 787.
16. Ibid., page 787.
17. Ibid., page 479.
18. Synan, Vinson – *The Origins of the Pentecostal Movement*, page 8.
19. Bennett, Dennis – *God's Strength for this Generation*, page 2.
20. Storms, Sam – *Post-Reformation and Contemporary Developments in the Pentecostal and Charismatic Movements*, page 10.
21. Synan, Vinson – *The Origins of the Pentecostal Movement*, page 8.
22. *The New International Dictionary of Pentecostal and Charismatic Movements (Revised and Expanded Edition)*, page 1141.
23. Synan, Vinson – *The Origins of the Pentecostal Movement*, page 8.
24. Storms, Sam – *Post-Reformation and Contemporary Developments in the Pentecostal and Charismatic Movements*, page 12.
25. Jackson, Bill – *The Quest for the Radical Middle: A History of the Vineyard*, Vineyard International Publishing, 1999, (introduction).
26. Bennett, Dennis – *God's Strength for this Generation*, page 8.
27. Ibid., page 10.

Latter Rain

1. *Dictionary of Pentecostal and Charismatic Movements (Burgess, Stanley M., editor)*, page 831.
2. Storms, Sam – *Post-Reformation and Contemporary Developments in the Pentecostal and Charismatic Movements*, page 8.
3. *The New Dictionary of Pentecostal and Charismatic Movements*, page 831.
4. Ibid., page 830.
5. Storms, Sam – *Post-Reformation and Contemporary Developments in the Pentecostal and Charismatic Movements*, page 8.
6. *The New Dictionary of Pentecostal and Charismatic Movements*, page 832.

7. Jackson, Bill – *The Quest for the Radical Middle: A History of the Vineyard*, Vineyard International Publishing, 1999.

8. Branham, William – *The Laodicean Church Age* (43).

9. Branham, William – *Five Definitive Indications of the True Church of the Living God*, (106).

10. Branham, William – *The Thyatirean Church Age* (25).

11. Branham, William – *The Pergameum Church Age* (188).

12. Branham, William – *The Laodicean Church Age* (277).

13. Branham, William – *The Sardicean Church Age* (65).

14. Ibid., (101) Branham, William – *The Serpent Seed* (5–1).

15. Ibid., (7–1).

16. Branham, William – *The Laodicean Church Age* (49).

17. Ibid., (52).

18. Branham, William – *Condemnation by Representation* (5–2).

19. Branham, William – *The Laodicean Church Age* (47).

20. Branham, William – *Condemnation by Representation* (6–1).

21. Branham, William – *The Serpent Seed* (19–3).

22. Ibid., (21–3,5).

23. Ibid., (23–4).

24. Ibid., (23–8).

25. Ibid., (24–5).

26. Ibid., (26–5).

27. Ibid., (30–1).

28. Ibid., (35–4).

29. Ibid., (3–5).

30. Branham, William – *The Laodicean Church Age* (124).

31. Ibid., (143).

32. Ibid., (204).

33. Ibid., (261).

34. Ibid., (290).

35. Branham, William – *The Serpent Seed* (1–5).

36. Branham, William – *The Pergameum Church Age* (290–300).

37. Branham, William – *The Manifested Sons of God* (49).

38. Ibid., (35).

39. Ibid., (197).

40. Warnock, George – *The Feast of Tabernacles*, page 2.

41. *The New Dictionary of Pentecostal and Charismatic Movements*, page 831.

42. Warnock, George – *The Feast of Tabernacles*, page 10.

43. Ibid., page 9.

44. Ibid., page 57.

45. Ibid., page 102.

46. Ibid., page 3.

47. Ibid., page 17.

48. Ibid., page 39.

49. Ibid., page 37.

50. Ibid., page 62.

51. Ibid., page 100.

52. Ibid., page 96.

53. Ibid., page 63.

54. Ibid., page 90.

55. Ibid., page 47.

56. Ibid., page 38.

57. Ibid., page 85.

58. Ibid., page 32.

59. Ibid., page 69.

60. Ibid., page 41.

61. Ibid., page 42.

62. Ibid., page 94.

63. Ibid., page 99.

64. Ibid., pages 61–62.

65. Ibid., page 76.

66. Ibid., pages 61–62.

67. Ibid., page 101.

68. Ibid., page 62.

69. Warnock, George – *From Tent to Temple*, page 2.

70. Jackson, Bill – *The Quest for the Radical Middle: A History of the Vineyard*, page 186.

71. Warnock, George – *From Tent to Temple*, pages 6–7.

72. Ibid., page 8.

73. Ibid., page 20.

74. Jackson, Bill – *The Quest for the Radical Middle: A History of the Vineyard*, page 200.

75. Ibid., page 219.

76. Ibid., page 231.

77. Ibid., page 234.

78. Ibid., pages 239–240.

79. Ibid., page 187.

Prosperity and Healing

1. Grady, J. Lee – *What Happened to the Fire?*, page 132.

2. McIntyre, Joe – *Plagiarism of E.W. Kenyon by Kenneth E. Hagin?*.

3. Ibid.

4. *The New Dictionary of Pentecostal and Charismatic Movements*, page 992.

5. McIntyre, Joe – *An Open Letter to the Critics of E.W. Kenyon*.

6. *The New Dictionary of Pentecostal and Charismatic Movements*, page 819.

7. Ibid., page 687.

8. Ibid.

9. Ibid.

10. Kenyon, Essex William – *Claiming Our Rights*.

11. Hagin, Kenneth E. – *Possessing the Promise of Healing*, page 11.

12. Copeland, Kenneth – *The Laws of Prosperity*, page 90.

13. Copeland, Gloria – *God's Will is Prosperity*, page 5.

14. Hagin, Kenneth E. – *Knowing What Belongs to Us*, page 11.

15. Kenyon, Essex William – *Claiming Our Rights*.

16. *The New Dictionary of Pentecostal and Charismatic Movements*, page 993.

17. Ibid., page 993.
18. Assemblies of God Position Paper: *The Believer and Positive Confession.*
19. Copeland, Kenneth – *The Laws of Prosperity*, page 50.
20. Ibid., page 32.
21. Assemblies of God Position Paper: *The Believer and Positive Confession.*
22. Kenyon, Essex William – *What We Are In Christ.*
23. Kenyon, Essex William – *Underestimating Jesus.*
24. Hagin, Kenneth E. – *How Faith Comes*, page 10.
25. Copeland, Kenneth – *The Laws of Prosperity*, page 87.
26. Assemblies of God Position Paper: *The Believer and Positive Confession*, page 3.
27. Ibid., page 4.
28. Kenyon, Essex William – *Claiming Our Rights.*
29. Ibid.
30. Hagin, Kenneth E. – *How to Win your Unsaved Loved One, Part 2*, page 10.
31. Kenyon, Essex William – *What We Are In Christ.*
32. *The New Dictionary of Pentecostal and Charismatic Movements*, page 992.
33. Ibid., page 992.
34. Hagin, Kenneth E. – *Knowing What Belongs to Us.*
35. Assemblies of God Position Paper: *The Believer and Positive Confession*, page 9.
36. Kenyon, Essex William – *Jesus the Healer.*
37. Hagin, Kenneth E. – *Possessing the Promise of Healing*, page 10.
38. Ibid., page 10.
39. Copeland, Kenneth – *The Laws of Prosperity*, page 61.
40. Ibid., page. 32.
41. Kenyon, Essex William – *Jesus the Healer.*
42. Kenyon, Essex William – *What We are in Christ.*
43. Copeland, Gloria – *God's Will is Prosperity*, page 1.
44. Kenyon, Essex William – *What We are in Christ.*
45. Copeland, Kenneth – *The Laws of Prosperity*, page 9.

46. Hagin, Kenneth E. – *How to Win Your Loved Ones, Part 2*, page 11.

47. Copeland, Kenneth – *The Laws of Prosperity*, page 26.

48. Copeland, Gloria – *God's Will is Prosperity*, page 4.

49. Copeland, Kenneth – *The Laws of Prosperity*, page 43.

50. Assemblies of God Position Paper: *The Believer and Positive Confession*, page 2.

51. Kenyon, Essex William – *Claiming our Rights*.

52. Copeland, Kenneth – *The Laws of Prosperity*, page 88.

53. Ibid., page 44.

54. Hall, Franklin D. – *Atomic Power with God through Prayer and Fasting*, page 9.

55. Ibid., page 37.

56. Hagin, Kenneth E. – *How to Win your Loved Ones, Part 2*, page 11.

57. Hall, Franklin D. – *Atomic Power with God through Prayer and Fasting*, page 40.

58. Ibid., page 41.

59. Assemblies of God Position Paper: *The Believer and Positive Confession*, page 3.

60. Ibid., page 3.

61. Ibid., page 6.

62. Ibid., page 7.

63. Ibid.

64. Grady, J. Lee – *What Happened to the Fire?*, page 131.

65. Assemblies of God Position Paper: *The Believer and Positive Confession*, page 9.

66. Grady, J. Lee – *What Happened to the Fire?*, pages 131–132.

67. Hall, Franklin D. – *Atomic Power with God through Prayer and Fasting*, page 13.

68. *The New Dictionary of Pentecostal and Charismatic Movements*, page 993.

69. Hagin, Kenneth E. – *Possessing the Promise of Healing*, page 11.

Covering and Authority

1. *Where Are We Going?* – WA Van Leen, CCG Ministries; http://www.ccgm.org.au/Articles/ARTICLE-0098.htm.

2. Brother Maynard – *The Church Uncovered: A New Answer to the Question, 'Who is your covering?'*, page 2.

3. Grady, J. Lee – *What Happened to the Fire?*, page 146.

4. Ibid., page 148.

5. Mallone, George – *Furnace of Renewal: A Vision for the Church*, page 83.

6. Wikipedia – *Watchman Nee*.

7. Vinzant, Don – *The Discipling Dilemma*, page 128.

8. Nee, Watchman – *The Normal Christian Life*, page 95.

9. Ibid., page 100.

10. Ibid., page 107.

11. Nee Watchman – *Authority and Submission*, page 6.

12. Ibid., page 1.

13. Ibid., page 8.

14. Ibid., page 6.

15. Ibid., page 19.

16. Ibid., page 26.

17. Ibid., page 32.

18. Ibid., page 19.

19. Ibid., page 80.

20. Ibid., page 92.

21. Ibid.

22. Ibid., page 95.

23. Ibid., page 97.

24. Ibid., page 73.

25. Grady, J. Lee – *What Happened to the Fire?*, page 150.

26. Nee, Watchman – *Authority and Submission*, page 52.

27. Ibid., page 52.

28. Ibid., page 55.

29. Ibid., page 64.

30. Ibid., page 102.

31. Ibid.

32. Ibid., page 104.

33. Ibid., page 105.

34. Ibid., page 108.

35. Mallone, George – *Furnace of Renewal: A Vision for the Church*, page 85.

36. Grady, J. Lee – *What Happened to the Fire?*, page 141.

37. Moore, S. David – *The Shepherding Movement: Controversy and Charismatic Ecclesiology*, page 20.

38. Ibid., page 43.

39. Ibid.

40. Ibid., page 26.

41. Ibid., page 27.

42. Ibid., page 29.

43. Grady, J. Lee – *What Happened to the Fire?*, page 142.

44. Moore, S. David – *The Shepherding Movement: Controversy and Charismatic Ecclesiology*, page 180.

45. Ibid., page 41.

46. Ibid., page 42.

47. Ibid., page 48.

48. *The New Dictionary of Pentecostal and Charismatic Movements*, page 1060.

49. Moore, S. David – *The Shepherding Movement: Charismatic Controversy and Ecclesiology*, page 54.

50. Ibid., page 55.

51. Ibid.

52. Ibid., page 53.

53. Ibid., page 56.

54. Ibid.

55. Ibid., page 57.

56. Ibid., page 61.

57. Ibid., page 70.

58. Ibid., page 89.

59. Ibid., page 74.

60. Ibid., page 75.

61. *The New Dictionary of Pentecostal and Charismatic Movements*, page 1061.

62. Ibid.

63. Moore, S. David – *The Shepherding Movement: Charismatic Controversy and Ecclesiology*, page 95.

64. *The New Dictionary of Pentecostal and Charismatic Movements*, page 1061.

65. Moore, S. David – *The Shepherding Movement: Charismatic Controversy and Ecclesiology*, page 104.

66. Ibid., page 105.

67. Ibid.

68. Ibid., page 109.

69. Ibid., page 110.

70. Ibid., page 113.

71. Ibid., page 114.

72. Ibid., page 117.

73. Ibid., page 119.

74. Ibid., page 120.

75. Ibid., page 148.

76. Ibid., page 112.

77. Ibid., page 141.

78. Ibid., page 147.

79. Ibid., page 149.

80. Ibid., page 163.

81. Ibid., page 165.

82. *The New Dictionary of Pentecostal and Charismatic Movements*, page 1062.

83. Moore, S. David – *The Shepherding Movement: Charismatic Controversy and Ecclesiology*, page 166.

84. Ibid., page 168.

85. Ibid., page 169.

86. Ibid., page 170.

87. Ibid., page 172.

88. Ibid., page 177.

89. Ibid., page 178.

90. Ibid., page 174.

91. Ibid., page 175.

92. Ibid., page 173.

93. Ibid.

94. Grady, J. Lee – *What Happened to the Fire?*, page 143.

95. Ibid., page 150.

96. Moore, S. David – *The Shepherding Movement: Charismatic Controversy and Ecclesiology*, page 175.

97. Ibid., page 174.

98. Assemblies of God Position Paper: *The Discipling and Submission Movement (1976)*, page 1.

99. Ibid., page 2.

100. Mallone, George – *Furnace of Renewal: A Vision for the Church*, page 83.

101. Assemblies of God Position Paper: *The Discipling and Submission Movement*, page 2.

102. Ibid., page 2.

103. Moore, S. David – *The Shepherding Movement: Charismatic Controversy and Ecclesiology*, page 182.

104. Wagner, C. Peter – *Spheres of Influence*, chapter 2.

105. Ibid., chapter 2.

106. Ibid.

107. Ibid.

Five-fold Reconsidered

1. Viola, Frank – *Who Is Your Covering?*

2. Grady, J. Lee – *What Happened to the Fire?*, page 160.

3. Ibid., page 162.

4. Mallone, George – *Furnace of Renewal*, page 83.

5. Assemblies of God Position Paper: *The Discipleship and Submission Movement (1976)*, page 2.

6. Grudem, Wayne – *Systematic Theology*, page 551.

7. Grady, J. Lee – *What Happened to the Fire?*, page 160.

8. Ibid., page 161.

9. Hjalmarson, Len – *Five-Fold Ministry and the Birthing of New Movements*.

10. Brother Maynard – *Servant Leadership and the Five-Fold Ministries: Ephesians 4 Gifts Reconsidered*.

11. Assemblies of God Position Paper: *Apostles and Prophets (2001)*, page 5.

12. Grudem, Wayne – *Systematic Theology*, page 911.

13. Assemblies of God Position Paper: *Apostles and Prophets (2001)*, page 4.

14. Assemblies of God Position Paper: *The Discipleship and Submission Movement (1976)*, page 2.

15. Brother Maynard – *Servant Leadership and the Five-fold Ministries: Ephesians 4 Gifts Reconsidered*, page 4.

16. Ibid., page 5.

17. Assemblies of God Position Paper: *Apostles and Prophets (2001)*, page 6.

18. Ibid., page 9.

19. Ibid., page 11.

20. Bailey, Brad – *Our Ministry Statements* (Vineyard Christian Fellowship Westside).

21. Mallone, George – *Furnace of Renewal*, page 85.

People of Faith

1. Assemblies of God Position Paper: *The Believer and Positive Confession (1980)*, page 8.

2. Wimber, John – *Power Evangelism*, page 125.

3. Girard, Robert C. – *Brethren, Hang Loose (Or, What's Happening to My Church?)*, page 65.

4. Sherman, Amy L. – *Loving Our Neighbor's Welfare.*

5. Ibid.

6. Wimber, John, as quoted by Steve Beard – *Good News Magazine, 1998.*

7. Clark, Jason – *Over-Promising?*

8. Hjalmarson, Len – *Renewal: The Hype, the Hope, and the Reality.*

9. Beard, Steve – *Remember John Wimber.*

Spiritual Formation

1. Bernard of Clairvaux – *On Loving God.*

2. Brother Lawrence of the Resurrection – *The Practice of the Presence of God*, page 53.

3. St Bernard of Clairvaux – *On Loving God.*

4. Grudem, Wayne – *Systematic Theology* 1994, page 754.

5. Erickson, Millard – *Christian Theology*, page 968.

6. Wimber, John (with Springer, Kevin) – *The Dynamics of Spiritual Growth*, page 144.

7. Grudem, Wayne – *Systematic Theology*, page 748.

8. Hunter, Todd – *Spiritual Disciplines.*

9. Foster, Richard – *Celebration of Discipline*, page 17.

10. Grudem, Wayne – *Systematic Theology*, page 747.

11. Foster, Richard – *Celebration of Discipline*, page 17.

12. Ibid., page 19.

13. Grudem, Wayne – *Systematic Theology*, page 749.

14. Foster, Richard – *Celebration of Discipline*, page 34.

15. Wimber, John (with Springer, Kevin) – *Power Healing*, page 49.

16. Chevreau, Guy – *Catch the Fire*, page 14.

17. Campbell, Wesley – *Welcoming a Visitation of the Holy Spirit*, page 196.

Community of the Spirit

1. Stott, John R.W – *Christian Counter-Culture*, page 174.
2. Grudem, Wayne – *Systematic Theology* 1994, page 859.
3. Foster, Richard – *Celebration of Discipline* page 191.
4. Ibid., page 187.
5. Ibid., page 145.
6. Stott, John R.W. – *Christian Counter-Culture*, page 176.
7. Vinzant, Don – *The Discipling Dilemma*, page 124.
8. Grudem Wayne – *Systematic Theology*, page 859.
9. Stott, John R.W. – *Christian Counter-Culture*, page 180.
10. Wimber, John – *The Dynamics of Spiritual Growth*, page 158.
11. Grudem, Wayne – *Systematic Theology*, page 1029.
12. Mallone, George – *Those Controversial Gifts*, page 44.
13. Brother Maynard – *private email*.
14. Mallone, George – *Those Controversial Gifts*, page 38.
15. Foster, Richard – *Celebration of Discipline*, page 193.
16. Ibid., page 195.
17. Wimber, John – *Power Evangelism*, page 125.
18. Bennett, Dennis – *God's Strength for this Generation*, page 2.
19. Tozer, A.W. – *How to be Filled with the Holy Spirit*.
20. White, John – *When the Spirit Comes with Power*, page 35.
21. Grady, J. Lee – *What Happened to the Fire?*, page 58.

Bibliography

Assemblies of God website resources
  The Believer and Positive Confession
  http://ag.org/top/Beliefs/Position_Papers/pp_4183_confession.cfm
  The Discipling and Submission Movement
  http://ag.org/top/Beliefs/Position_Papers/pp_4174_discipleship.cfm
  Apostles and Prophets
  http://ag.org/top/Beliefs/Position_Papers/pp_4195_apostles_prophets.cfm
Bailey, Brad – *Our Ministry Statements* (Vineyard Christian Fellowship Westside) http://www.vcfwestside.org/doc-leadership.html
Beard, Steve – *Remember John Wimber*, Good News Magazine
  http://www.thunderstruck.org/archivevault/Wimber.htm
Bennett, Dennis – *God's Strength for this Generation*
  http://www.emotionallyfree.org/dennis-strength.htm
Branham, William Marion
  Serpent Seed
  http://www.williambranham.com/messages/The_Serpents_Seed_58_092
  8E.php
  Manifested Sons of God
  http://www.livingwordbroadcast.org/LWBWBTextfiles/gettf.php?textfile
  =60-0518.htm
  Pergameum Church
  http://www.livingwordbroadcast.org/LWBWBTextfiles/gettf.php?textfile
  =60-1207.htm
  Laodicean Church Age
  http://www.livingwordbroadcast.org/LWBWBTextfiles/gettf.php?textfile
  =60-1211E.htm

Thyatirean Church Age
http://www.livingwordbroadcast.org/LWBWBTextfiles/gettf.php?textfile
=60-1208.htm
Five Definitive Indications of the True Church of the Living God
http://www.livingwordbroadcast.org/LWBWBTextfiles/gettf.php?textfile
=60-0911E.htm
Sardicean Church Age
http://www.livingwordbroadcast.org/LWBWBTextfiles/gettf.php?textfile
=60-1209.htm
Condemnation by Representation
http://www.livingwordbroadcast.org/LWBWBTextfiles/gettf.php?textfile
=60-1113.htm
Brother Lawrence of the Resurrection – *Practicing the Presence of God*, Paulist Press, New York 1978
Brother Maynard – *The Church Uncovered: A New Answer to the Question 'Who is Your Covering?'*
http://www.subversiveinfluence.com/wordpress/?page_id=576
Servant Leadership and the Five-fold Ministries: Ephesians 4 Gifts Reconsidered http://www.subversiveinfluence.com/wordpress/?page_id=536
Campbell, Wesley – *Welcoming a Visitation of the Holy Spirit*, Creation House, Lake Mary 1996
Chevreau, Guy – *Catch the Fire*, HarperCollins 1994
Christianity Today – *The Cleansing Wave*,
http://www.christianitytoday.com/ch/2004/002/7.22.html
Clark, Jason – *Over-Promising?*
http://www.jasonclark.ws/2005/09/overpromising.html
Copeland, Kenneth – *The Laws of Prosperity*
http://kcm.org/download.php?id=1
Copeland, Gloria – *God's Will is Prosperity*
http://www.kcm.org/studycenter/finances/pdf/gods_will_prosperity.pdf
Deere, Jack – *Surprised by the Power of the Spirit*, Zondervan Grand Rapids and Kingsway Eastbourne 1993

Erickson, Millard – *Christian Theology*, Baker, Grand Rapids 1983

Foster, Richard – *Celebration of Discipline*, Harper San Francisco and Hodder & Stoughton London 1978, 1988, 1998

Girard, Robert C. – *Brethren Hang Loose (Or What's Happening to My Church?)*, Zondervan, Grand Rapids 1972

Gonzalez, Justo L. – *A History of Christian Thought, Vol. 3: From the Protestant Reformation to the Twentieth Century*, Abingdon Press, Nashville 1975

Grady, J. Lee – *What Happened to the Fire?*, Chosen Books (Baker), Grand Rapids 1994

Grudem, Wayne – *Systematic Theology*, IVP Leicester and Zondervan Grand Rapids 1994

Hagin, Kenneth E.
   Knowing What Belongs to Us, Word of Faith Magazine, February 2004
   Possessing the Promise of Healing, Word Faith Magazine, March 2004
   How Faith Comes, Word of Faith Magazine, May 2004
   How to Win Your Unsaved Loved One, Part 2, Word of Faith Magazine April 2005

Hall, Franklin D. – *Atomic Power with God through Prayer and Fasting* http://www.gloryofhiscross.org/fast.htm

Hjalmarson, Len
   Five-fold Ministry and the Birthing of New Movements http://www.nextreformation.com/html/leadership/five-fold.htm
   Renewal: The Hype, the Hope, and the Reality http://www.nextreformation.com/html/articles/renewal-hype.htm

Hunter, Todd – http://www.toddhunter.org

Jackson, Bill – *The Quest for the Radical Middle*, Vineyard International Publishing 1999

Kenyon, Essex William
   Claiming Our Rights (http://www.peterwade.com/articles/kenyon/claim.shtml)
   What We Are in Christ (http://www.peterwade.com/articles/kenyon/inchrken.shtml)

Underestimating Jesus
(http://www.peterwade.com/articles/kenyon/underest.shtml)
Jesus the Healer
(http://www.peterwade.com/articles/kenyon/kenyon03.shtml)

Mallone, George – *Furnace of Renewal: A Vision for the Church*, IVP Downers Grove and Kingsway Eastbourne 1981
Those Controversial Gifts, IVP, Downers Grove 1983

McIntyre, Joe
Was Kenyon Plagiarized? http://www.kenyons.org/faq.htm#Plagiarism
An Open Letter to the Critics of E. W. Kenyon http://www.kenyons.org/faq.htm

Moore, S. David – *The Shepherding Movement: Controversy and Charismatic Ecclesiology*, T. & T. Clark (Continuum), London and New York 2003

Nee, Watchman
The Normal Christian Life, Victory Press (Kingsway), Eastbourne 1961
http://www.ccel.org/ccel/nee/normal.html
Spiritual Authority, Christian Fellowship Publishers, Richmond 1972
(Original version '*Authority and Submission*' available online
http://www.peacemakers.net/unity/wnauthority&submission.htm)

The New International Dictionary of Pentecostal and Charismatic Movements (Burgess, Stanley M., editor), Zondervan, Grand Rapids 2002

Sherman, Amy – *Loving Our Neighbor's Welfare*, Assemblies of God Enrichment Journal, Spring 2004;
http://enrichmentjournal.ag.org/200402/200402_050_loveneigh.cfm

St Bernard of Clairvaux – *On Loving God*
http://www.ccel.org/ccel/bernard/loving_god.html

Storms, Sam – *Post-Reformation and Contemporary Developments in the Pentecostal and Charismatic Movements*;
http://www.enjoyinggodministries.com/article.asp?id=354

Stott, John R.W. – *Christian Counter-Culture*, IVP Leicester and Downers Grove 1978

Viola, Frank – *Who Is Your Covering?*, Present Testimony Ministries
http://www.ptmin.org, 2001

Vinson, Synan – *The Origins of the Pentecostal Movement*
  http://www.christian-faith.com/revival/pentecostal.html
Wagner, C. Peter – *Spheres of Authority*, Wagner Publications, 2002
Warnock, George
  Feast of Tabernacles http://www.kingdomlife.com/warnock-feast.htm
  From Tent to Temple
  http://www.templebuilders.com/index_tenttotemple_preface.php
  Where Are We Going? http://www.ccgm.au/articles/article-0098.htm
White, John – *When the Spirit Comes with Power*, IVP, Downers Grove 1988
Wikipedia: *Watchman Nee*, http://en.wikipedia.org/wiki/Watchman_Nee
Wimber, John
  Dynamics of Spiritual Growth, Hodder & Stoughton, London 1990
  Power Evangelism, Hodder & Stoughton, London 1985
  Power Healing, Hodder & Stoughton, London 1986